40 Innovative Programs In Early Childhood Education

Edited by

Berlie J. Fallon

Associate Dean for Graduate Studies, College of Education
Texas Tech University, Lubbock, Texas

Lear Siegler, Inc./Fearon Publishers
Belmont, California

Federally Funded Programs

Several of the school programs reported in this book received funding from federal sources. Materials reported concerning these programs do not necessarily reflect the position or policy of the funding agency, and no official endorsement by the funding agency should be inferred.

To all young children everywhere
  and to a special one
    who inspired these lines:

> In memory's lucid fount recall'd
> Thy childhood laughter, babbling trills,
> Pink ribbons, dolls and picture books,
> Soft silken tresses, lace and frills.

and to her little one, as yet unborn,

and to Winona, Laine and David,
  who gladden life's days.

"... and a little child shall lead them."
Isaiah 11:6

Contents

PROGRAMS FOR BILINGUAL CHILDREN

THE OPEN SCHOOL CONCEPT

LEARNING CLIMATE

DIFFERENTIATED STAFFING

USE OF PARAPROFESSIONALS AND VOLUNTEER AIDES

TEACHER PREPARATION

SECTION II. Resources Section

Preface

Early childhood education in the United States appears destined for as much development as any other single level of education during the decade of the seventies. This thrust, heightened initially by federally funded programs for disadvantaged children, has spread rapidly to involve America's young children in all strata of society. Most states have passed permissive legislation providing for public support of kindergarten programs, and prekindergarten programs flourish in many states. It is doubtful that either the critics or the rising cost of education will deter the increasing emphasis on the creation of improved educational opportunities that influence the mental, physical, and emotional development of young children.

This book contains detailed descriptions of early childhood education programs currently in operation in school systems throughout the United States. Two things will soon become evident to the reader—a strong practitioner orientation and a certain exuberance in the reporting styles of the contributing authors. Seemingly, the enthusiasm of the reporters is characteristic of those who have experienced the pleasure of noting gains in development on the part of children for whom, without the benefit of early childhood programs, there would have been little hope of maximizing educational potential.

The exemplary and innovative programs reported herein are submitted to readers not as models to be superimposed on their schools, but as stimulants of further experimentation and adaptation. Readers may find some programs with which they disagree. In the opinion of the compiler of this volume, such exposure is healthful, in that controversy sparks a more careful look at one's own favorite ideas and beliefs.

We hope this book may serve to benefit the young children of this country by pointing the way to worthwhile guidelines for program development. We believe that the following groups can profit by the use of this volume:

1. School systems seeking new ideas and approaches to improving their early childhood education programs
2. Students in college and university classes devoted to the training of personnel to serve as teachers and resource specialists in early childhood education
3. Teachers in early childhood education programs
4. Parents of children enrolled in early childhood education programs
5. Researchers and research organizations interested in the compilation and dissemination of research materials pertaining to early childhood education

The forty early childhood education practices described here are innovative in the sense that each represents new departures and approaches for the implementing school system. The schools providing descriptions of their programs were sufficiently enthusiastic to be willing to subject their efforts in early childhood education to scrutiny by a wide reading audience. Any school system that finds one or more worthwhile ideas in this book opens avenues for innovation within its own program.

This book contains two main sections. Section I, Innovative Programs in Early Childhood Education, offers descriptions of the forty programs by the contributing authors. Section II, Resources Section, includes an overview of the field of early childhood education and fourteen excerpts from materials provided by schools with exemplary programs.

The glossary, the Table of Descriptor Terms, is a carefully catalogued list of terms used by the school systems reporting their programs; each entry in the glossary is keyed with the program number(s) in which it appears, as a handy guide to the many useful and novel ideas and concepts contained in the book.

It is hoped that the organization of the book will enable the reader to focus on major areas of interest with a minimum of time and effort.

Berlie J. Fallon

Lubbock, Texas

Acknowledgments

Grateful appreciation is expressed to the school systems providing descriptions of their early childhood education programs for this book. A special measure of thanks is due those persons who prepared the descriptive materials for their schools. Without the help so willingly given by these specialists, the project could not have materialized. The resource materials in Section II were supplied by the individual school districts and printed with their permission. Colleagues at Texas Tech University, Indiana University, the University of Tennessee, and Florida State University provided helpful suggestions concerning the format and organization of the materials.

Gratitude is due Miss Mary Jean Bench for her patient and persistent effort in the typing of the manuscript.

Innovative Programs in Early Childhood Education

Overviews of Programs

1

Early Childhood Education in the Public Schools of the Nation's Capital

Alma M. Blackmon *Kindergarten Supervisor,*
Department of Elementary Supervision and Instruction,
District of Columbia Public Schools, Washington, D. C.

Description

Preprimary education in the public schools of Washington, D.C., has had a long and varied history. It began in 1898 with the establishment of a kindergarten department consisting of sixteen segregated kindergartens, eight for white children and eight for black children. Through the years the public school system has grown from a racially divided organization into one vast, integrated system, and the kindergarten department has grown in size from the original sixteen teachers of 1898 to more than 235 teachers. It now serves nearly 10,000 children. Of this number, 186 children are enrolled in two federally funded Follow Through programs.

One Follow Through program enrolls 101 kindergarten children who have experienced a year-long Head Start program. This is a community action program designed to teach reading, language, and arithmetic to disadvantaged five-year-old children from low socioeconomic neighborhoods. The program is based on the Engelmann-Becker approach to early childhood education, which originated at the University of Oregon. It

3

enables the children to respond readily to individualized teaching procedures utilizing maximum reinforcement and correction. The social, psychological, and medical needs of the children are stressed in order to prepare them for an ongoing learning process. The aims of the accompanying parent program are similar to the aims of the children's program.

The other Follow Through program organizes its eighty-five kindergarten children into multi-age groups called teams. Children four to seven years old are allowed to move at their own rates of development, regardless of their ages. The multi-age groupings permit four-year-olds who can work as six-year-olds to do so. In addition to these kindergartens, we have established a public school Montessori kindergarten in our city.

Preschool Programs

The Model School Division of the public schools established the Preschool Program in 1966. Funded by the U.S. Department of Health, Education, and Welfare, the program employs twenty-one teachers and enrolls 400 three- and four-year-old children in seven locations based on the principles of project Head Start. The general staff for each center consists of a coordinator, the teachers, the teacher assistants, a corps of volunteer workers, a cook, and a custodian. The staff is assisted by the Child Health Services of the Washington, D.C., Public Health Department, which arranges for health, dental, and hearing screening, schedules regular visits of doctors and nurses, and provides follow-up services and nutrition counseling. The Director of Social Services leads the pupil recruitment program, helps children keep their appointments for follow-up health services, obtains clothing for children in need, and directs parents to the community agencies that can take appropriate action in regard to their problems. The parent program that operates in each center is a valuable and integral feature of this comprehensive program. The entire program operates under the supervision of the Director of Preschools. Similar in support and organization is the Anacostia Preschool Program that enrolls 300 three- and four-year-olds under the administration of the Anacostia Community Project.

Introduction of the prekindergarten level for four-year-olds into the regular public schools has been of great significance. Inspired by our summer Head Start and Model School preschools, and in response to the recent public awakening to the importance of the early years in learning, the Washington public schools opened seventy-five portable prekindergarten classroom suites in the fall of 1968. Each prekindergarten is staffed by a teacher and a teacher aide who serves as an instructional assistant. Each instructional team may enroll from fifteen to twenty four-year-olds. With the emergence of prekindergarten as an accepted level in the elementary schools, principals who have had an extra teacher and appropriate classroom space have been permitted to open prekindergartens of eight children per session without a teacher aide.

The Prekindergarten Curriculum.   Our prekindergarten curriculum consists principally of firsthand experiences—sensory, exploratory, investigative, manipulative, and creative. It offers the children daily opportunities to form concepts from their own real life experiences. Then on the basis of things they know from personal experience, they will be able to understand oral accounts of related happenings and to grasp generalities. The prekindergarten provides this background of firsthand experiences in preparation for the learning that will come later from books.

Children in the prekindergarten pursue their firsthand experiences in the form of play—the heart of the prekindergarten curriculum. Because play is the young child's way of thinking about the things that he knows, his learning is accelerated when he is exposed to a wide variety of multi-sensory stimuli in a setting that allows him plenty of time for spontaneous, expressive play. At school, the prekindergarten child enters a carefully prepared environment that has been organized into well-defined learning zones equipped with multi-sensory toys and materials. Here the child begins to select his own learning sequences and embarks upon a personalized series of firsthand experiences through play in the doll corner, playhouse, blockbuilding center, library, science corner, water table, sandbox, music center, or at the workbench. He may decide to play for a while with manipulative construction toys or transportation toys, or he may choose to create with crayons, paints, clay, construction paper, scissors, or paste. He may decide to use the indoor large-muscle equipment or to observe the classroom pets. The child's choice is greatly respected, because the materials that he encounters in his exploration of the prekindergarten are placed there because each of them offers the child an opportunity to explore basic concepts that are related to some school subject that the child will one day pursue in a more formal fashion.

The prekindergarten teacher plays an important part in the learning process. Through her interest in the child's choices and through the explanations she offers, the teacher supplies the language for the child's discoveries. She brings his experiences within the realm of his understanding.

Through highly personal interaction with the class, both individually and in small groups, she helps the children relate their classroom experiences to things they already know, thus broadening their areas of knowledge. In a given period of self-selected activity, the teacher may become involved in the rudiments of science in sand and water play, the discovery of mathematical concepts in the various shapes and sizes of building blocks, the social recognition of adult family relationships in the playhouse, the realization that the tone bars on the xylophone range in steps from low to high, the joy of a child who can at last control his paint brush and make the same shape again and again, and the fascination of the children's rich oral language that occurs in all dramatic play situations. The prekindergarten teacher must meet the unique curriculum challenge of teaching any and all subjects simultaneously!

Class field trips also provide firsthand experiences. The prekindergartners take frequent trips through the neighborhood, because the neighborhood is itself a textbook for early learning. The teacher helps the children become more aware of things in the immediate neighborhood by supplying words for the things the children cannot name, by pointing out items of interest seen during the trips, and by pausing to permit the children to investigate thoroughly those things which engage their attention. When questions arise in classroom discussions, the children take field trips to find the answers. Explorations of the school grounds, safety walks through the city streets, nature walks in parks and the woods, and trips to fire stations, post offices, libraries, grocery stores, drug stores, department stores, shopping centers, bakeries, lumber yards, pet shops, farms, and the zoo offer practical answers to children's questions. Our teachers are also privileged to arrange for the children's attendance at appropriate special events, such as the National Symphony Orchestra Tiny Tots Concerts, the Department of Commerce Book Fair, the national Christmas displays at the White House Ellipse, the puppet shows sponsored by the Anacostia Museum and the National Theater, and the Flower Show at the National Guard Armory. Thus, full use is made of the community's resources.

As the teachers arrange these varied field trips, the children's five senses continue to gather all kinds of perceptual information. These percepts, when interpreted, form the base of the child's conceptual understanding of his world.

Informal Assessment of Prekindergartens. Although our prekindergartens have been in operation since 1968, there has been no systematic evaluation of their effectiveness. However, kindergarten teachers who enroll children with prekindergarten experience express their strong approval of the program when they assess these children's capabilities. It is interesting to note that early education serves to widen the range of abilities within a kindergarten when children of prekindergarten experience are compared with children who are entering a school setting for the first time.

Progression to the Kindergarten Level. The kindergartens of Washington, D.C., enroll a substantial number of children who have had previous school experience. Each September more than one-fifth of the entering children come from the public school prekindergartens. The total number of children coming from the city's Head Start programs is not known. We do know, however, that the prekindergartens and the Head Start programs are compensatory in purpose and that they have been established in target areas of the city so that the children there may have an opportunity to make up for their deficiencies in learning. In addition to these children, there are others who have attended day care centers and some who have attended private and cooperative nursery schools. Nevertheless, for the majority of our children, kindergarten is the first major step away from home. Regardless of his previous experience, the young kindergartner finds himself to be one of twenty-five to thirty-five peer children taught by one teacher. This high pupil-teacher ratio poses a challenge for children and teachers alike.

Although their environments and interest centers are similar, kindergartens differ from prekindergartens in many ways. The provision of first-hand experiences continues, and play is still recognized as the child's most dynamic learning method. For this reason the kindergarten day includes a long work-play period that aims at an objective not sought in the prekindergartens. From the random multiple exposures to toys and materials, characteristic of the prekindergarten level, the kindergarten child is gradually led to choose one activity to pursue throughout the work-play period. In order to help increase the length of his attention span, the child often receives motivational assistance in setting up problems that are sufficiently challenging to engage his attention for a longer time. Thus the child who works and plays with materials and toys familiar from his prekindergarten days will make more mature use of them now in ways that have a direct relationship to his ever-increasing experiences.

During other periods of the day, the children participate in curriculum experiences that help them organize the random information they have gathered. This relatively formal curriculum constitutes the major change from prekindergarten. Teachers select objectives that are increasingly instructional as they present fifteen-minute lessons in number readiness, social studies, and science in order to establish a solid background of conceptual information. These lessons involve pupil participation in firsthand experiences, direct experimentation with objects, and discussions about pictures and charts that enable the children to share the processes of learning with each other. The kindergartens also present an organized program in phonics to teach the children the beginning consonant sounds in our language. All of this takes place in half a day at school that includes music, rhythms, and storytelling; that alternates active and quiet periods, indoor and outdoor play; and that provides individualized experiences as well as small and large group interaction. The kindergartens, while advocating the children's right to grow in all ways at their own rates of speed, present a curriculum that aids achievement in both developmental and academic areas. Individualized instruction enables the staff to meet the needs of all the children, regardless of previous school experience.

Kindergarten Participation in the Reading Mobilization Year

In the summer of 1970, the Board of Education accepted a plan from the Metropolitan Applied Research Center, Inc., entitled *A Possible Reality: A Design for the Attainment of High Academic Achievement for the Students of the Public Elementary and Junior High Schools of Washington, D.C.* The Design, now called the Academic Achievement Project, contained those items its authors believed to be necessary for the attainment of academic excellence.

Among the items was the Sequential Inventory of Reading Skills that stated specific behavioral objectives for each grade level in the areas of (*a*) word perception, (*b*) comprehension and interpretation, (*c*) study-reading, and (*d*) mechanics of reading skills. A task force of kindergarten teachers met with the kindergarten supervisor to study the list of prereading skills and to design procedures and materials to develop these skills. The result of this work is a report entitled *A Systems Approach for the Development of Prereading Skills in the Kindergarten.*

The Kindergarten Task Force was challenged by several realizations:

1. That kindergarten children, having completed their initial period of sensory-motor development around age two, are still employing these means in their learning as they manipulate concrete objects and gather additional conceptual information.

2. That every kindergarten is equipped with materials, toys, and manipulative devices that, in the absence of a specifically designed readiness program, might be organized to develop most of the prereading skills.
3. That the behaviorally stated goals specified various performances expected of children rather than the recitation of information.
4. That individual differences among the children would affect their performance in terms of learning styles, speed and extent of comprehension, and depth of mastery.

The prereading skill of word perception was divided into subskills of auditory and visual perception. A pupil would be considered ready to read when he could:

1. Identify and discriminate sounds by tone, quality, and intensity
2. Listen with attention to rhymes, stories, and songs
3. Identify words that rhyme
4. Note likenesses and differences in words
5. Discriminate between the beginning sounds of spoken words
6. Discriminate between the final sounds of spoken words
7. Identify the middle sounds in spoken words
8. Hear syllables in spoken words
9. Recognize the plural forms of spoken words
10. Recognize shapes and pictures
11. Recognize differences in shapes and in pictures
12. Identify and match capital and lower case letters
13. Discriminate between letter forms and word forms

In comprehension and interpretation the child would be expected to:

1. Recall events in rhymes, poems, stories, and other literary forms
2. Demonstrate knowledge of the concept of a spoken sentence
3. Demonstrate that he understood the ideas in a spoken sentence by stating the ideas in his own words
4. Show his knowledge of the meanings of most words used by children his age
5. Supply the missing word in an oral context, using sense and word order as clues to meaning
6. Name the words that form a given compound word
7. Listen to poems and stories and relate the main ideas
8. Relate the details of poems and stories
9. Associate related ideas
10. Arrange pictures to show the sequence of a known story or rhyme
11. Hold a sequence of ideas in mind and relate events in the order of their occurrence
12. Make inferences from spoken ideas
13. Identify in a spoken sentence the word that does not belong
14. Demonstrate his knowledge of the difference between a series of unrelated words and a sentence
15. Use ideas to make a sentence

16. Identify in a story a sentence that does not belong
17. Answer questions
18. Draw conclusions in discussion situations
19. Associate spoken words with pictures
20. Interpret pictures
21. Recognize inflectional endings in spoken words, such as -s, -ed, and -ing

In study-reading skills the children were expected to show that they could follow simple oral directions. In the mechanics of reading they were to:

1. Demonstrate they understand that numerals, words, and a series of pictures are arranged from left to right
2. Demonstrate they understand that the beginning of a printed word is at its left

The Systems Approach.   A system is defined in educational circles as a collection of materials organized around the development of one specific goal or objective. Our systems approach consists of taking a prereading skill and restating it in terms of a more workable behavioral objective. In recognition of the young child's need for direct involvement and personal interaction with materials while learning, this approach places a heavy emphasis on small group instruction in vigorous twenty-minute lessons. By working with one-fourth of the class each day during the work-play period—the only time of day when the remainder of the class is purposefully engaged in independent activities of their own choice—the kindergarten teacher can accomplish an objective with her entire class in a given week. Records of pupil performance are made while the lessons are in progress, and children who did not achieve the goal are placed in an ad hoc group for reteaching on Friday.

A twenty-minute small group lesson consists of four steps:

1. Achieving the behavioral goal by interaction with sets of concrete objects placed on a table
2. Achieving the behavioral goal by interaction with manipulative pieces placed on a flannelboard
3. Achieving the behavioral goal by pointing to flat symbols on teacher-constructed charts or in teacher-constructed booklets
4. Achieving the behavioral goal by working independently at a task similar to that of the chart or booklet

The foregoing steps are carefully arranged in a sequence that permits the young learner to begin his perceptions with three-dimensional objects and to move gradually into work with movable two-dimensional symbols, then to immovable two-dimensional symbols, and finally to two-dimensional symbols on a work surface at reading distance from his eyes. It is also important to construct a system so designed that the child's behavior remains consistent through the four steps, although the materials change in type and in placement.

When the Kindergarten Task Force completed its design of the systems approach, the program was introduced to a wider circle of kindergarten teachers as a means of developing the prereading skills of the Academic Achievement Project in a manner compatible with the nature of the kindergartner as a learner. Through a series of demonstration lessons, workshops on reading readiness, classroom intervisitation, and supervisory visits to classrooms, the program spread to eight kindergartens.

Evaluation. Near the conclusion of the school year the participating teachers scheduled a series of area meetings for evaluation purposes. They brought their children's skills records so that they could report, skill by skill, the number of children who mastered each one and the number of children who failed to do so. Pupil mastery proved strong in the skills of shape and picture recognition, matching, visual similarities and differences according to colors, sizes, and shapes, identification of words that rhyme, discrimination of beginning sounds of words, left to right progression, and classification of like objects.

More difficult, but still achieved by the majority of children, were such skills as recalling events in stories and poems, arranging events in sequence, relating details of stories, discrimination between the final sounds of words, selecting the main idea, using another's ideas to make a sentence, making inferences from spoken ideas, recognition of letters of the alphabet, association of upper and lower case letters, discrimination between letter forms and word forms, association of ideas, and using sentences to answer questions.

Very difficult skills, missed by half or more than half of the children, were recognizing plurals of words, naming the words that form a compound word, and identifying the number of syllables in words.

The skill requiring children to follow simple oral directions received varying reports from teachers. Many indicated mastery, but a significant number reported their children's inability to follow directions for work-study.

On a printed questionnaire circulated during the evaluation workshop, teachers were asked if the systems approach had been effective. They all replied that it had been. When asked to what extent it had been effective, some replied as follows:

- The children grasp concepts quickly and clearly. They love to pick the objects up and touch them. They are eager to involve themselves in the group.

They seem to be more confident of what they can do. As a teacher, I have become more creative in finding different ways to present the skills to the children, and I know what each child in the class can do.

- The children are more interested, thus more attentive. I know my children better—academically as well as personally.
- The children have gained an independence that didn't seem to be there before. They are increasingly sure of themselves in the large group sessions.
- The children are quite eager to learn in this type of small group setting.
- I have found my children to be more receptive to my teaching. As a result, I am better able to assess each child's needs and to plan to meet those needs.
- I am now reaching the non-verbal child. I am more involved than ever in my work, for I am building the systems and am eager to find out how successful they are.
- It has given an old teacher a shot in the arm, and has forced me to pinpoint more specifically the sensory learnings that I had been taking for granted the children knew. Inarticulate children have become quite vocal.
- This approach has made my children more eager to talk in a group; made me more aware of individual problems; encouraged more peer help among children because the groups are flexible; made my teaching more sequential; and encouraged the children to reinforce their own learnings by periodically returning to use materials related to the various skills.

A Case Study

The systems approach was used at Blow-Pierce School. Blow-Pierce, according to Principal Frederick A. Smith, serves a neighborhood that has a mixture of low-income and very-low-income families. Most of the families live in one-bedroom flats in four-family dwellings. A few reside in rented houses, and still fewer are property owners. There is no public housing in the area. The families, though poor, seem to be families with pride. The kindergarten children appear happy and, for the most part, secure, having received the kind of parental care that preschoolers usually require. Mr. Smith reports that there were no substantial differences in the children who entered Blow-Pierce in September, 1970, when compared with the kindergarten entrants of September, 1969. Yet the Metropolitan Readiness Test results for the two groups of children were significantly different. For purposes of clarity, let us call the kindergartners of 1969–1970 Class A and the kindergartners of 1970–1971 Class B.

Class A had been taught the usual kindergarten program by two experienced kindergarten teachers. The following year, both teachers served as members of the Kindergarten Task Force and as demonstrators of the systems approach. Class B, therefore, experienced the systems approach in developing twenty of the prereading skills in addition to the usual kindergarten program.

In Washington the Metropolitan Readiness Test, Form A, is administered each September to first grade children. In September, 1970, Class A achieved a mean score of 41, Low Normal. It is not known what number of Class A children had entered first grade without kindergarten experience. We do know, however, that in Class B there were only four first graders tested who had not experienced the systems approach in the kindergartens at Blow-Pierce School. It would, therefore, be of interest to examine further the performance of the Class B children on the readiness test.

Of the seventy-four children tested, five received the letter rating A or Superior, meaning that the children were apparently very well prepared for first grade work. Twenty-two rated B or High Normal, indicating that these children had good prospects for success in first grade work. Thirty-four children scored C or Average, meaning that they were likely to succeed in first grade work if careful study was given to their specific strengths and weaknesses and instruction was planned accordingly. Eleven children tested D or Low Normal, indicating that they were likely to have difficulty in first grade work and that they were in need of more individualized help. Two children tested E or Low, meaning that these children would find first grade work extremely difficult under ordinary instructional conditions, and that they were in need of individual readiness work.

Because the kindergarten teachers had provided opportunities for building prereading skills by means of the systems approach, and because the Metropolitan Readiness Test was administered to determine the extent to which the children possessed such skills, it is interesting to mesh the two sets of skills to determine whether the systems skills contributed to the children's performance on the reading readiness subtests.

Subtest 1 on Word Meaning measures the child's store of verbal concepts and permits the child to indicate the breadth of his oral vocabulary. Using the systems approach, the children had associated spoken words with pictures, demonstrated that they knew the meanings of most words used by children their age, and classified animals, clothing, toys, food, furniture, and the like. On this subtest, seventeen children scored A, twenty-six scored B, sixteen scored C, fifteen scored D, and two scored E (the letter ratings having the same meanings as in the foregoing paragraph). The mean score on this subtest was 11 or B, which is High Normal.

Subtest 2 on Listening taps the child's knowledge of the world about him and his ability to comprehend oral sentences and paragraphs. Through the systems approach, the children had been given opportunities to interpret pictures, complete sentences, answer questions, make inferences, recall events in stories and poems, and demonstrate their concept of a spoken sentence. On this subtest, twenty-two children scored A, twenty-seven scored B, twenty scored C, three scored D, and two scored E. The mean score for Listening was 11 or B, which is High Normal.

Subtest 3 on Matching bears a close correlation to beginning reading because it calls upon the visual-perceptual skills needed for the discrimination of word forms. In their skills lessons, the children had recognized shapes and pictures, recognized differences in shapes and pictures, matched for similarities in objects and shapes, matched both upper and lower case letters, and discriminated between letter forms. On this subtest, three children scored A, twenty-one scored B, twenty-seven scored C, sixteen scored D, and five scored E. The mean score for this subtest was 8 or C, Average.

Subtest 4 on the Alphabet tests the children's ability to recognize letters of the alphabet. Through systems teaching the children had had opportunities to identify both upper and lower case letters and to associate upper case letters with their corresponding lower case letters. Their performance in school had indicated greater difficulties with letter identification than with any other prereading skill. On this subtest, five children scored A, fourteen scored B, thirty-two scored C, thirteen scored D, and nine scored E. The mean score was 9 or C, Average.

The mean scores of the reading subtests were ranked in descending order, and it appeared that the children responded better to the more difficult cognitive skills than to the skill of visual perception. The subtests were ordered as follows: (a) Listening, with a mean of 11, B, High Normal, (b) Word Meaning, with a mean of 11, B, High Normal, (c) Alphabet, with a mean of 9, C, Average, and (d) Matching, with a mean of 8, C, Average.

Adjustment to Beginning Reading. One might assume at this point that the teachers' use of the systems approach was a decisive factor in the level of readiness attained by the children of Class B. This assumption might be substantiated by an examination of the children's progress in the three first grade classrooms to which they were assigned, so the children's current reading levels were also studied. In the fourth month of the school year, twenty-one children were reading in Preprimer 2, thirty-seven in Preprimer 1, one was doing chart reading, and twelve were in reading readiness. Two of the children had been transferred to other schools.

An interview of the three first grade teachers was the next step in evaluating the effectiveness of the systems approach at Blow-Pierce. The teachers reported that they had been able to reduce the customary six-week readiness period to three weeks because the children gave indications of readiness to move on. Thus, for the first time in their experience, they had organized the initial preprimer reading groups in the fourth week of the school year.

By this time the Metropolitan Readiness Tests had been scored, and they showed that sixty-one of the children possessed various degrees of reading readiness. The teachers said that the children reflected the skills they had been taught in the kindergarten so well that the usual first grade readiness work seemed to be a review. Left-to-right progression was very well established, and the children showed power in visual discrimination, although they had scored less well on the subtest for this skill. The children's knowledge of letters of the alphabet was reliable in some cases and unreliable in others. The children were able to follow work-study directions in given skills, but the first grade teachers found it necessary to teach the paper-and-pencil skills needed for first grade seatwork. The attitudes of most of the children were positive. Maintaining the eagerness which they had brought to their kindergarten small groups for the systems approach, they read their preprimer stories with enjoyment.

The teachers were concerned about the twelve children who were still at the reading readiness level in the fourth month of the school year. They advised that these children were obviously not ready to read printed symbols and that they needed more work with concrete objects for the development of their perceptual abilities.

Supported by the analysis of the Metropolitan Readiness Test results, the children's first grade reading levels, and the opinions of their first grade teachers, we concluded that the use of the systems approach for the development of prereading skills in the kindergarten was responsible in large measure for Class B's attainment of a much higher level of readiness than had been reached by Class A the previous year.

Conclusion. While some other cities are now instituting their first public kindergartens, the established preprimary programs of the Washington, D.C., public schools are gaining experience and insights. Compensatory programs for disadvantaged three- and four-year-old children continue to be maintained. The prekindergarten is an established level of the elementary school, and expansion of this level is planned. The challenge of the prereading skills that are incorporated in the Academic Achievement Project is being faced in the kindergartens. The Graduate Division of the District of Columbia Teachers College supports the work by offering kindergarten teachers the opportunity to study the systems approach in a course entitled "Preparing the Young Child for Reading Instruction." As work with young children continues, the preprimary teachers respect more and more the adage that a good beginning has no end.

2

An Overview of the Kindergarten Program in the Memphis City Schools

Elizabeth Parker Martin   *Title I Kindergarten Resource Teacher, Memphis City Schools, Memphis, Tennessee*

Description

Kindergarten is a wonderful learning experience for children in the Memphis City Schools. Each day a flexible schedule is planned to meet the needs of five-year-olds. For many of them, it is the first step into a new world outside their home—a world where they can make new friends, learn to do many new things, and learn to live happily with others. The parents, the kindergarten teacher, the aide, and the school principal work together to make this step easier and more pleasant for the child.

The kindergarten teacher seeks to provide an environment where the child can continue to learn through doing. As each child interacts with his peers and with the instructional materials, the teacher observes his social, emotional, and intellectual development and guides him into challenging new learning experiences.

Our program is designed to:

1. Provide a balanced program of activity and rest
2. Develop the child's muscular coordination
3. Teach and strengthen the child's health habits
4. Teach the child how to use and take care of school materials and tools
5. Develop the child's ability to express his ideas
6. Teach the children how to listen to and enjoy stories and poems
7. Help the child develop self-control
8. Teach the child to follow directions

9. Help the child learn to assume responsibility
10. Develop the child's curiosity for learning
11. Teach the child to share and to live happily with others
12. Provide the child with many opportunities for oral expression
13. Offer the child many oppportunities to develop his vocabulary
14. Develop the child's number concepts

Learning Experiences. The main objective of our program is to make every day a good day for every kindergartner. The days in kindergarten should be enriched with experiences that help each child develop a good self-image, self-confidence, self-expression, and a curiosity for learning. These experiences should be continuous with the areas of instruction in the other elementary grades, including:

1. Science experiences, especially in the world of nature
2. Number experiences with concrete objects (counting), concepts of time and measurement (high-low and big-little)
3. Music, rhythms, and art
4. Activities promoting good health and physical stamina, rest, and relaxation
5. Language arts, emphasizing oral language development
6. Social studies, emphasizing home, family, school, and community relationships
7. Basic ingredients for thinking—sensory perceptions and real experiences with concrete objects

How These Learning Experiences Help Kindergartners. The kindergarten child needs time to work at his own pace and time to refine and extend the concepts he has of his world. Through play—by touching, acting, doing, seeing, hearing, tasting, and smelling—the child learns, explores, and tests his ideas.

These activities also help the child to:

1. Work in a group
2. Concentrate on one task at a time
3. Use and care for materials
4. Assume responsibility
5. Express ideas in complete thoughts
6. Listen to and follow directions
7. See relationships and make comparisons
8. Develop good work habits

Involvement of Parents. It is important that parents allow their kindergarten child to begin developing independence so he can assume responsibility for himself commensurate with his own growth pattern. Preparing a child for school is a responsibility of parents that begins at birth or even earlier. If a child is given love and security at home, and if he is in good health, physically and mentally, he is likely to be ready for kindergarten. For these reasons parents are encouraged to:

1. Be sure that the child has a regular bedtime and sleeps about ten hours each night
2. Teach him to bathe himself and to take care of his toilet needs
3. Teach him to dress himself and to take care of his own belongings
4. Teach him to hang up his clothes and to put his toys away
5. Be sure that he eats a good breakfast
6. Establish a regular pattern of meals
7. Allow the child enough time each morning to get ready for school, so he will arrive on time
8. Make sure he attends school every day that he is not ill
9. Send him to school clean and in a happy frame of mind
10. Teach him to respect the rights and property of others
11. Give him many opportunities to talk
12. Encourage him to call things by their right names

Relation of Kindergarten to the Regular School Program

1. The Library Services Division arranges a special Story Hour each week for the kindergarten classes.
2. The Department of Pupil Services provides teachers with consultation services on a learning readiness program. It also works with the children referred to it from the kindergarten project.
3. The School Food Service Division furnishes monthly menus in advance, enabling teachers to plan classroom eating activities before the introduction of new foods.
4. Kindergartners eat a well-balanced lunch at school.
5. A program designed by the Physical Education Department provides activities that help to develop the kindergartners' physical and motor skills.
6. Volunteer Services are provided when additional adult supervision or assistance is needed for field trips or special projects.

Staff. Our project includes forty-three kindergarten classes in poverty area schools. The program is staffed by forty-three teachers and forty-three aides, so a pupil-teacher ratio of twenty-five to one is maintained.

Criteria for Selection. The criteria for pupil selection are sent to principals and teachers of the participating schools prior to registration day. Principals and teachers make their selection according to the following requirements:

1. All pupils must be five years old by October 31 of the current school year.
2. Parents must present a health record and proof that their child has been im-

munized against diphtheria, measles, polio, smallpox, tetanus, rubella, and whooping cough.

3. As proof of age, a birth certificate must be presented during registration.

4. Eligibility is based on income. A child is eligible if the family's total annual income does not exceed $2,000.

Summary. Regular in-service meetings are scheduled to allow teachers and aides time to discuss matters pertinent to the success of the program. Evaluation of the program is a combined project of the Resource Teacher and the Division of Research.

Our main concern is that in an atmosphere of stability and security, a positive self-concept be fostered in each pupil in the kindergarten program. It is our belief that this goal can be reached by friendly teachers who have the support of concerned aides, parents, principals, and the entire community.

Programs for Disadvantaged Children

3

Head Start–Preschool

Wayne E. Emry   *Project Director, Poudre School District R-1, Fort Collins, Colorado*

Description

The Head Start–Preschool program in Poudre R-1 is unique because of the way in which the funds are being used. Head Start is funded by HEW and the preschool program is funded by Title I, ESEA. By combining these two grants, we can enroll almost twice as many children as under Head Start alone. In addition to all of the children qualified for Head Start, we can enroll those who do not meet the family income guidelines of the OEO, providing they live within the attendance areas of the Title I target schools. Our program began with sixty-four children funded by OEO and fifty children funded by Title I, a total of 114 underprivileged children.

In general, preschool education seems to be a constructive program for the underprivileged children of this age range. In fact, it has been more beneficial in our community than the earlier reports indicated. The children completing this program are not fearful of entering kindergarten. In addition, the parents have great interest in the educational welfare of their children and take an active part in school activities.

Purposes of the Program

1. To prepare underprivileged children for entrance into kindergarten
2. To create an effective educational experience for each child
3. To impress upon parents the importance of regular school attendance
4. To give serious attention and assistance to those children with physical and dental problems

Goals and Objectives

1. To provide experiences that will develop a positive self-concept in each child
2. To create an atmosphere that will stimulate a desire for learning
3. To enhance the physical development, the perceptual-motor development, and the well-being of each child enrolled in the program
4. To set up an environment that provides opportunities for each child to develop his cognitive and intellectual competence
5. To provide adequate models for language development and to encourage growth in linguistic skills

Selection Criteria

1. Needs of the individual child
2. Parental interest in the program
3. Qualification under OEO family income guidelines
4. Residence within Title I target school attendance areas
5. Fulfillment of the kindergarten age requirement (the child must be five years old by the following September 15th)

Planning the Program. Children in the program were grouped into seven classes located in four centers. One class met in a remodeled home where most of the children could walk to their classroom, one in an elementary school, another in a church, and four at the Mountain View Learning Center, which was formerly an elementary complex. The school district paid for transporting the children to the classrooms, and the project funds paid for their return home. Classes were held from 8:30 A.M. to 11:30 A.M., and the children ate a hot lunch at school before returning home. Each class had a teacher, a regular aide, and a volunteer aide. The teacher and her aides worked as a team throughout the program.

Beginning the Program. We had three half-day blocks of pre-service training sessions for the entire staff. The sessions were planned to emphasize child development. Consultants from the Colorado State Department of Education, the Office of Child Development, and Colorado State University, with selected staff members assisting, led these workshops.

The children were introduced into their classes a few at a time. Parents were invited to bring their children to the classroom on a specified day. Two or three parents were invited each day for the first week. By the end of the second week, the classes were complete. The teachers and aides used the Head Start Developmental Screening Test and Behavior Rating Scale as a basis for getting acquainted with each child and at least one of his parents.

A Parent Policy Committee was organized. The officers and two representatives from each class were elected by the parents of the children in the program.

General Procedures

The program involved the parents in many activities, such as field trips, volunteer work in the classrooms, and preparing the hot lunch. The teachers and aides visited in each of their children's homes. The aides were bilingual (Spanish and English), thus enabling English-speaking teachers to communicate without difficulty in Mexican-American homes where Spanish was spoken.

In-service training sessions were held once each month for all members of the staff, which included seven teachers, seven aides, two part-time aides, a parent-teacher coordinator, a half-time nurse, and the director.

The nurse scheduled the eligible children for physical examinations by the physician of their choice. All children had vision, speech, and hearing check-ups. Dental checks were made of the children in the program who were eligible for this service. Those needing medical and dental treatment received it at the expense of the program unless their parents volunteered to pay for it themselves. Many parents did so in appreciation of the program.

The parents' organization met once each month. It made the final selection of staff members, assisted the parent-teacher coordinator in scheduling volunteers, and planned various programs for general meetings. One of the highlights of their activities was a covered dish dinner for all the Head Start–Preschool families. They invited an outstanding speaker, who discussed "The Similarities and Differences of the Spanish-American and the Anglo-American Cultures." More than three hundred persons attended this dinner meeting.

Evaluation

At the request of the Poudre R-1 Director of Information and Research, an evaluation of the local Head Start–Preschool program was implemented by a Colorado State University research and evaluation team. Empirical evidence was sent to local, state, and national leaders, outlining the effectiveness of the program in an effort to insure their continued financial support.

It should be pointed out that I.Q. gains and the persistence of I.Q. gains have provided almost the entire basis for many previous Head Start evaluations. I.Q. gains are eye-catching and charged with emotion, but the true test of school experiences has included the performance of children in learning social, emotional, and physical behaviors, as well as intellectual skills. Possibly too much emphasis has been placed on the evaluation of general learning, measured by intelligence testing without emphasis on the evaluation of more specific objectives related to the classroom curriculum.

It was important to us that the evaluation reflect more closely our progress toward achievement of the program goals set by HEW and special goals set by our staff. We made the following assumptions about the child's development:

1. The preschool years are critical to the development of intellectual abilities, language skills, and conceptual skills.
2. The parents are the primary influence in the life of the preschool child.
3. The rate, quantity, and quality of his growth and development are unique for each child, regardless of his socioeconomic background.
4. Continuity between the child's home experiences and school experiences can be fostered through meaningful parent participation in the Head Start program.

Procedures.   The subjects of the evaluation were children from four to five years of age in the Fort Collins, Colorado, Head Start–Preschool program. An effort was made to test every child in each of the seven classes. In some cases this was impossible because of absenteeism, language differences, conflicts with field trips, late enrollments, and dropouts. The sample size, sixty-one children, reflected those children who were present for both pre- and post-tests on two instruments. Three control groups were compared with the Head Start–Preschool children. Two groups were primarily upper-middle-class children enrolled in excellent preschools. The third group was primarily lower-class children enrolled in a day care center.

First, we wanted to know how the Head Start–Preschool children compared with middle-class children, who presumably had more opportunities at home to develop their school readiness. Because the Head Start–Preschool was set up to remedy deficiencies, it was necessary to document the existence of developmental deficiencies in the lower-class children.

Second, it was important to demonstrate that these deficiencies could be ameliorated by the curriculum that our Head Start–Preschool teachers had planned. We wanted to know if the experiences in the Head Start–Preschool program increased the skills of the lower-class children or whether these differences in group scores could be attributed to other factors, such as maturation. The lower-class control group was observed at a welfare-operated day care center in Fort Collins. It served as a comparison group in assessing the effects of the two programs on lower-class children.

Test Results. Examination of the test data suggested that the two lower-class groups were comparable at the pre-test level and that the scores for both groups were different from those of the middle-class children. The children of the lower-class group were deficient in personal-social responsiveness when compared to the middle-class children, thus establishing the need for preschool experiences. Finally, the Head Start–Preschool children made greater than average gains, during the five-month interval between pre- and post-testing at our Head Start–Preschool. This gain was reflected in the increase of percentile scores computed with respect to age. Comparisons with the middle-class groups were difficult because the test ceiling was not high enough to accommodate the older and more advanced children.

Further examination of the data suggested that the lower-class children were deficient in associative vocabulary when compared to their middle-class peers. Here was further evidence of the developmental lag in lower-class children. The data suggested, too, that a planned program of instruction could improve the associative vocabulary of the Head Start–Preschool children. It was interesting to note that the only group increasing its percentile scores on middle-class norms was the Head Start–Preschool group.

The pre-tests showed a developmental lag of lower-class children in numerical concepts when they were compared with middle-class children. This finding further documented the need for preschool instruction. Analysis of the pre- and post-test difference in mean scores for these groups showed that the average gain in raw score was larger for the Head Start–Preschool group on middle-class norms, indicating that they reached average performance by the end of the program.

We found that the children in the lower-class group were deficient in the area of sensory activities when compared to the middle-class children. The Head Start–Preschool children made the largest average raw score and percentile gain of any group. Although it still scored lower than any other group, the lower-class group had reduced its developmental lag.

Summary. Both of the lower-class groups consistently scored lower than the middle-class group on all pre-tests, indicating that the lower-class children were deficient in these skills when compared to their middle-class peers. This documented developmental lag established the need for an instructional program.

The data indicated that the Head Start–Preschool children made the largest average raw-score and percentile gains of any group. Their gain was greater than could be accounted for solely by a six-month increase in age, indicating that the initial gap between the Head Start–Preschool group and the middle-class groups had been reduced. In contrast, the lower-class control group increased its percentile score on only one test.

The data on the Head Start–Preschool children indicated that preschool instruction can reduce the educational differences between lower- and middle-class children. The failure of the lower-class control group to make a gain sufficient to maintain the same percentile score from pre- to post-test suggested that unless appropriate intervention is planned, lower-class children will continue to fall further behind during their preschool years.

Recommendations. It was recommended that Poudre District R-1 continue to increase the length of the Head Start–Preschool program until it operates on a nine-month school year basis. The school administration, HEW, and Title I increased the length of the program from eight weeks to seven months for the school year 1970–71, and to eight-and-a-half months in 1971–72.

Although encouraging gains have been made by our children, they are still behind middle-class children in skills considered predictive of school success. It is therefore in the best interests of the community to extend and improve the Head Start–Preschool program.

The research team also recommended that the staff continue to identify priority goals for the program. Traditional nursery schools have usually been ineffective in reducing the developmental lag so characteristic of disadvantaged children. However, there is increasing evidence from all sides that more direct teaching methods can reduce many of these learning deficits. The evaluation of our current program underlined this possibility.

The researchers recommended that our staff continue working closely with the kindergarten teachers, first grade teachers, and auxiliary staff in identifying the skills that are most important to school progress.

They also recommended that all non-English-speaking children be enrolled in preschool programs regardless of eligibility requirements. The improvement in language ability of several non-English-speaking children during the 1970–71 project suggested that this was an excellent opportunity for them and that it should be available to other such children.

The evaluation team suggested that classes in kindergarten through the third grade should number no more than twenty-six children. The team felt that with a high quality and quantity of adult-pupil interaction, parent education and involvement, community cooperation, and reduced class size during the early grades, children will retain their initial head start in education. A constructive follow-through program can lead to mastery of academic and social skills, and, in the long run, be economical in terms of saving both human potential and program costs.

4

Preprimary Program

Margie Moffit   *Teacher-Coordinator, County Line Center,*
Preprimary Program, DeKalb County, Georgia

Description

DeKalb County's Preprimary Program for Disadvantaged Children has at its core a sound philosophy of developing learning activities that are individualized as far as practical to meet the needs of each child. This program's predecessor was a volunteer program for disadvantaged children. Its success encouraged school officials to lay the groundwork for the present federally funded program.

The county's program, enrolling approximately 400 five-year-olds, is housed in five former elementary schools located throughout the county, so that participants may be easily transported to the schools.

The program has been entitled *preprimary* rather than kindergarten in order that it may be expanded to include children even younger than kindergarten age. The term preprimary also implies a continuity with the primary level of education, making it an integral part of the county's continuous progress program. This progress is becoming a reality now that the preprimary staff works with the primary teachers and children in the follow-up aspects of the program.

The children are grouped into classes of twenty-five. Each class is staffed by one teacher certified in early childhood education and one assistant. During the first year of operation (1970–1971), each class also had a student teacher who worked with the children during his entire apprenticeship. There are sixteen classes in the DeKalb County program, and at each of the five centers one teacher has the added duties of coordinator.

Two of the centers are located in urban areas. These centers accommodate more than half of the children in the program. The other three centers, located in rural areas, have two or three classes. Hot lunches and snack trays are brought into the centers daily from nearby schools.

The preprimary program appears to be a pet project of the entire DeKalb County School System. The program has its own supervisor, and every department in the school system has been active in providing services for the children, including speech evaluation, hearing and vision examinations, and psychological testing.

Procedures

Because of the wide range of the children's needs, each teacher in the program has been given a great deal of freedom in setting up the curriculum and in designing the learning activities.

Not only are the children evaluated by the classroom staff as to intellectual, social-emotional, and physical development, but they are also evaluated on three standardized tests: (*1*) Slosson I.Q. Test, (*2*) Caldwell Preschool Inventory, and (*3*) Metropolitan Readiness Test. The Preschool Pittsburgh Academic Test is also used.

The Metropolitan Readiness Test is used as a post-test to compare children to national norms. The Pittsburgh Test, although not standardized, is a valuable prediagnostic tool and serves as an instructional aid as well.

The teachers and staff received weekly visits from Georgia State University professors who participated in in-service instruction in the classroom. These sessions included "theories into practice" lessons, video taping, and a great deal of reviewing previous research.

Many new educational methods are used, such as open classrooms, self-correcting learning materials, and direct teaching methods. No one method has been adopted, although all centers place a heavy emphasis on language and social development. All teachers agree that the young child is a physical learner, and, accordingly, they involve the children physically in most of their instruction. For example, when space concepts are taught, the child places himself beside, behind, or in a box. When learning number-numeral matching, each child has his own pile of objects to count and match.

Each classroom is well equipped with new child-centered furnishings and a wide range of learning materials. All the centers have record players, tape recorders, filmstrip projectors, overhead projectors, television sets, and 8mm cartridge-type projectors with twenty-five Disneyland nature films. The centers also have access to 16mm motion picture projectors. Books are borrowed from the public library.

Each room has a full-length, unbreakable mirror, and a family center with dress-up clothes. The teachers use either Wee Winkie Bear flannelboard materials or the Do-So kit as bibliotherapeutic aids in guiding social-emotional development. Although the centers are well equipped with purchased materials, a visitor will also see many teacher-made games in use. Funds are provided for each class to take at least five field trips, and more may be arranged.

The floor plans are similar to those of the British Infant School. However, activities here are usually more structured than the usual open classroom, and the rooms have a more orderly appearance. These preprimary children are often easily distracted, and though they need novelty in what they do, they also need clear guidelines.

There are learning centers around the rooms, and upon entering a classroom it is usually possible to tell what types of experiences the children are having. One small group may be playing a classification game, another group in the science corner may be checking out objects that float and sink, a few children may be playing in the family center or looking at books, or the entire class may be dancing or listening to a story.

The teachers group and regroup the children according to the learning experiences for which they are ready. If a child has mastered basic shapes he may move on to numeral recognition, number-numeral matching, or color recognition. If a child is able to distinguish initial letter sounds, rhyming word families, and has learned a few sight words, he may have time each day to work on reading with his teacher. Each child is encouraged to do what he can.

Teachers write daily lesson plans, and keep a record of what actually happens. Individual records are kept on each child. Some teachers record items daily, some weekly, and others keep a great deal of information about the children in their "personal computer." Teachers add information to the pre- and post-evaluation of the child, such as comments on his ability to adapt to life situations, the amount of mental imagery he indicates, the amount of determination he exhibits, and the amount of confidence he has or needs to develop.

Because more than half of the preprimary teachers in the DeKalb County program hold master's degrees in early childhood education, the teachers wrote their own in-service improvement program for 1971–1972. DeKalb County set up an in-service educational program for the assistant teachers with the hope that many of these paraprofessionals will become certified teachers.

Evaluation

Although Title I federal grant to fund this program was not approved until August, 1970, most of the teachers who initiated the program believed so strongly in it that they gave up other positions and waited to have the opportunity to serve in this program. These teachers work as a team, and their first concern is always for the children.

It is possible that the key to the success of this program is the quality of the teachers—the sincerity and sensitivity they show in caring for the children and the cooperation they have from school administrators and parents. Because of the racial balance in two of the centers, a group of parents gave impetus to a growth in understanding for the well-being of all children, without regard to their color or background.

The statistical analysis on pre- and post-Slosson I.Q. evaluation from one rural class made up of students from a predominantly black neighborhood appears on the next page.

Only thirteen students are listed because all others in the class either came in too late for the pre-evaluation or left before the post-evaluation. This particular group was selected only because of its availability.

Although it is recognized that this sample is too small to allow us to draw any firm conclusions, it is interesting to note that the children in this class who took both tests increased their I.Q.'s by an average of nearly twenty-two points, from 93.6 to 115.4, and that the only child who failed to show improvement was already at the highest level (158–150) in the class.

Because of the first year's success, all of the teachers work an eight-hour

Student	Pre-test Age	Sex	Pre-I.Q.	Post-I.Q.
A	5–7	F	75	115
B	5–4	F	75	102
C	5–5	F	75	110
D	5–4	M	78	102
E	4–11	F	78	100
F	5–9	F	78	112
G	4–11	M	83	119
H	5–9	M	87	94
I	4–10	M	95	106
J	5–7	M	97	109
K	5–2	M	115	140
L	5–0	M	123	141
M	5–4	F	158	150

day even though the children have a four-hour program. This schedule allows for a follow-up program in which teachers visit their former students and supplement their present educational program either by enrichment or by providing additional learning skills.

The good attitudes toward self, others, and academic tasks instilled by this program will benefit these children more than tests can ever show. Providing an educational background for the disadvantaged child is DeKalb County School System's goal. There seems to be an infectious spirit in DeKalb County. Almost everyone is trying to help.

5

Preschool Kindergarten Program

Edith B. Murray   *General Supervisor Preschool Programs, Cobb County Schools, Marietta, Georgia*

Description

Early in the 1968–69 school term, a committee of teachers, principals, and central office staff members was appointed to work on a proposal for kindergartens for disadvantaged students in Cobb County Schools. This proposal was to be financed by PL 89-10, Elementary and Secondary Education Act, Title I. Teachers on this committee were given released time for educational research and for planning the program.

The committee reported that it found evidence that the intellectual capacity of a child has already been determined by the age of five, and that poverty and the lack of environmental and intellectual stimulation go hand in hand. In view of these findings, the administration decided to use all of the system's Title I and Head Start funds for a Preschool Kindergarten Program.

Planning the Program. The kindergartens are located in six centers throughout the county. There are 140 children enrolled in the Title I project and forty children enrolled in the Head Start project. The children range in age from four-and-a-half to five years.

Program Objectives

1. To help diagnose and correct the maturational disorders prevalent among disadvantaged five-year-old children
2. To provide an environment in which children can develop appropriate learning and growth skills
3. To conduct an intensive school readiness program
4. To involve parents in educational activities

Staff. The staff includes a supervisor-director, a social worker, part-time psychologists, a full-time secretary, two clerical aides, nine classroom teachers, and nine teacher aides. The teachers and the teacher aides were given special training for the program through PL 90-35 EPDA, Title V. Continued in-service programs are provided.

Procedures. Eligible participants are identified from a survey taken during the spring of each year and from referrals by various social agencies throughout the county. This information is tabulated, then the most needy 180 children are visited by the social worker, teachers, and teacher aides. These home visits substantiate the eligibility of the children, acquaint the staff with the parents or guardians of the children, and provide an overview of the home and community.

Services. The Cobb County Health Department provides pediatric services for each center. All children receive a complete physical examination. Minor problems are treated and major ailments or defects are referred to specialists or appropriate institutions. Dental services are also provided. At dental clinics, the parents and children are taught how to brush and care for their teeth. Through a screening process, those children needing special dental care are referred to cooperating dentists.

The project social worker provides social services. She works with parents in the home, providing information and conducting special educational programs. The social worker also cooperates with the family caseworker and may recommend families for social services.

The project provides transportation services to all project participants through the regular school transportation department. Food services, which include a mid-morning snack and a balanced lunch, are also provided for all participants.

Curriculum Content

The Cobb County kindergarten curriculum deviates from the traditional kindergarten. Our curriculum encompasses the total environmental-developmental circumstances of the child. The following are some of the principles involved:

1. Each child participates in a learning curriculum characterized by:
   (a) A multi-sensory approach
   (b) Creation of problem-solving situations for development of the thinking processes
   (c) No artificial separation of learning content areas
   (d) Individual attention that helps fulfill each child's need for affection, thus promoting his success in school
   (e) The use of familiar speech, objects, pictures, and books to encourage the disadvantaged child to feel comfortable in the classroom
   (f) Conceptual development taught through systematic, guided, object exploration and manipulation, thus utilizing the natural exploratory tendencies of children
2. In the classroom, students are exposed to language symbols and have many opportunities to use them, including: listening, conversation, discussion, reporting, telling a story, dramatizing, language games, singing, and art activities.
3. Numerical concepts are developed through mathematical devices and games.
4. Emphasis is placed upon the skills and attitudes of working and playing with one another, and upon such social learnings as sharing, taking turns, respecting the rights of others, assuming responsibility, caring for personal and group property, showing consideration for others, and developing a wholesome self-image.
5. We help children achieve a better understanding of their environment through

experiments, field trips, visits from resource persons, and a collection of science books, pictures, and films.

The curriculum activities can be grouped into the following areas: cognitive understandings, quantitative concepts, language arts, creative activities, health and safety, social science, and science.

Materials. A wide variety of materials and aids are available in the classroom, including: housekeeping toys, trucks, cars, blocks, ropes, construction paper, newsprint, crayons, paint, paint brushes, puzzles, games, beads, measuring devices, safety signs, geometric forms and shapes, language developmental programs, indoor and outdoor play equipment, musical aids, science supplies, and other play apparatus. Each center has access to a 16mm projector, a film strip projector, a record player, an overhead projector, and a tape recorder.

The Daily Program. Teachers and aides work from 8:00 A.M. to 3:30 P.M. The children are in school from 8:30 A.M. to 1:00 P.M. The teacher and her aide use the time from 1:00 P.M. to 3:30 P.M. for lesson planning, parent conferences, or home visits. The day does not center rigidly around any one of the major learning areas. Teachers have the freedom to offer a well-balanced, integrated program based on an understanding of the children, their learning characteristics, needs, and interests.

Interest centers are provided in each classroom. These areas include: a general area for group activities, a housekeeping corner, a book center, and a play area. The remaining space is used for group instruction, group games, and other structured activities.

Because the children's early learning environments have been limited, instruction is facilitated by the use of concrete objects. Wooden blocks, for example, are used for building trains, or cardboard boxes are used for building bridges. The emphasis is not on the product but on the concept.

Heavy emphasis is placed on language development. The interest centers are used for dramatic play and for activities involving music, rhythms, and body movement. The teacher and her aide may work with individual children, small groups, or with the whole group. An adult is always present to give guidance and encouragement.

During the second semester, greater emphasis is placed on activities that will provide the skills needed in learning to read and to achieve cognitive and quantitative understandings. Attention is also given to other behaviors that may be expected of the children when they enter a formal school setting.

Pupil Evaluation

The Peabody Picture Vocabulary Test and the Slosson Intelligence Test are given to all students. The scores provide information for individual prescriptive teaching. Psychological evaluations are made of those children exhibiting unusual behavior responses in the classroom. This step is taken only after careful observation of the children by the teacher, teacher aide, and the psychologist. Parental consent is required before this kind of testing is done.

Toward the end of the kindergarten year; arrangements are made for the children to visit their future school. The children meet their future teacher and spend a part of the day visiting with first grade pupils. This visit usually extends through the lunch hour.

The kindergarten teachers prepare for the first grade teachers an evaluation of each child's readiness for beginning reading activities, his social development, and his emotional development. The child's interests, strengths, and weaknesses are also noted. Members of the kindergarten staff are available for consultation with the first grade teacher if special problems arise.

The evaluation techniques used during the year include faculty conferences, parent responses, and recommendations made by visiting specialists. The end-of-the-year assessment may include such things as a teacher and staff questionnaire, parent reviews, a check list, or a culminative narrative report. This information is used to determine changes that can be made to: (*1*) improve curriculum content and instructional methods, (*2*) provide additional materials and equipment, (*3*) provide additional services to children and families, or (*4*) improve administrative and supervisory practices.

6

A Preschool Program for Culturally Disadvantaged Children

Dorothy M. Platt   *Director, Preschool Program,*
West Haven Board of Education,
West Haven, Connecticut

Description

Since 1966 the city of West Haven has conducted a program for culturally disadvantaged students from preschool age through the middle school years. Initially the preschool program was organized as Operation Head Start and funded through the Office of Economic Opportunity for a six-week summer period only.

In 1967 funding was obtained under the Elementary and Secondary Education Act, Title I, and the State Act for Disadvantaged Children. The preschool children became a Core Group whose reading progress is to be followed through their elementary school years by the Reading and Communications Skills Center, also a Title I SADC project.

The 1970–71 school year saw the initiation of the preschool program on a full-year schedule in two centers for a total of four classes. The continuing six-week summer program included the full-year group and a few other children who met eligibility requirements but who had not had previous school experience.

Recruitment.   Contact with parents of potential, eligible enrollees in the project areas is made by mail, by telephone, and through home visits made by the teacher, nurse, or school community worker. Federal guidelines restrict the program to children who come from low-income families, to foster children, or to those whose families are receiving assistance under the Aid to Dependent Children program. Local regulations restrict the enrollees to children who would be entering a kindergarten program the next school year.

Transportation.   All children are brought to the centers by bus. An aide is usually assigned to ride the bus to supervise the children. Parents are encouraged to use the bus whenever they need transportation to the school. Parents at one center have volunteered to ride the bus as supervisors since a cut in funds precluded hiring an aide for this purpose.

36

Staff. The program is conducted at two centers, each with a morning and an afternoon session. That way, no group consists of more than fifteen children. Each class is directed by a teacher certified in early childhood education. An aide is assigned to each classroom. Volunteer aides also assist the teachers.

Activities. Flexibility and planning for the individual needs of children are stressed. Objectives include broadening the child's social adaptiveness, increasing his vocabulary and developing his visual-motor coordination. In broad terms the aim of the preschool program is to provide economically deprived children with a background comparable to that found in the homes of more affluent families, through cultural stimulation, socialization opportunities, and experiences which motivate a child to learn. Audio-visual materials and field trips supplement classroom activities designed to build academic skills.

Field trips include visits to the police station, the firehouse, the airport, the harbor, a bakery, a supermarket, the library, the beach, a local nature center, and children's productions at a summer theater.

Volunteers. A local women's club assists with medical screening procedures. Some parents accompany the children on field trips; other parents rotate times on a daily bus supervision schedule. Both parents and members of the community share their talents in music, art, storytelling, and puppetry with the children.

Home Visits. The teachers make home visits twice during the regular school year and once during the six-week summer program. These visits have a dual purpose: 1) the teacher gets acquainted with a child's environment, and 2) the family gets acquainted with the teacher as a person. During the visit, the aims of the program and the child's progress are discussed. Positive accomplishments and progress are emphasized and suggestions concerning the parent's contributions to the child's education are offered.

The school nurse also makes home visits when medical information needs to be shared. A school-community worker serves both the preschool program and the Reading and Communication Skills Center program, helping to keep the lines of communication open between home and school.

Medical and Dental Procedures. Vision and hearing tests are given to all children in the program. They are weighed and measured, screened by a speech therapist, and given a urinalysis and lab tests for lead poisoning, blood sugar, and hemoglobin. All findings outside the normal range are referred for additional evaluation or treatment either to the child's own doctor or to the parents' choice of available area doctors, clinics, or hospitals. A number of previously unrecognized problems have been diagnosed and, where indicated, treatment has been initiated. Problems uncovered have included visual deficiencies, anemia, lead poisoning traces, heart murmurs, caries, orthopedic abnormalities, epilepsy, and urinary tract abnormalities.

Parent Involvement. A parent advisory group meets regularly and is encouraged to play an active role in the program. All parents meet as a group at each center to discuss the program and have at least one more group meeting during the school year. Individual parent conferences and home visits are scheduled first in late fall and again in the spring. Parents also are free to drop in at dismissal time to discuss their child's progress or problems. A parent or responsible adult is present at medical screening procedures. Parents supervise the children on bus routes and accompany them on field trips.

Refreshments. Juice, crackers, and peanut butter are served as a daily mid-session snack. Occasionally, refreshments are made in the classroom—Jell-O, pudding, popcorn, or bread and butter. Funds for these snacks have come from several sources including local service organizations and the Board of Education. This activity not only provides sustenance but also serves as a learning experience related to nutrition, table manners, and good health practices.

Evaluation. For the summer programs, a school psychologist has designed a testing program to determine pre- and post-performances. The findings on vocabulary, visual motor development, and social maturity are used to individualize programs for the children. An outside agency that specializes in evaluating programs has designed a testing program to measure whether or not the objectives of the program are being met. Some of the major findings derived from the evaluation are discussed in the following section.

Behavior Observation Study

Purpose. The purpose of this study (prepared and conducted by John Bosnyak, school psychologist) was to measure certain behavior patterns in a preschool summer program for disadvantaged children. Patterns measured included the children's verbalizations, disruptiveness, ability to follow directions, distractability, and willingness to participate in independent and group activity. It was hoped that an overall picture could be obtained by the end of the study, indicating the group's likelihood of success in kindergarten.

Method. A simple tally sheet was used to count specific behaviors during classroom observations. The school psychologist was the only observer. Classes were observed in random order twice a day. Each observation lasted five minutes, so each room was observed daily for a total of ten minutes. The following behaviors were counted: spontaneous verbalizations by children, verbalizations elicited by the teacher, verbal disruptions by children, non-verbal disruptions by children, number of children unable to follow directions, children's responses to distractions, children unable or unwilling to work at an independent activity, and children unable or unwilling to participate in group activity.

Observations were not made on field trip days or days with lengthy special events. The observation days were those most like the routine days of kindergarten these children would have in the fall. Observations were made on twenty days throughout the six weeks of the program.

Results. The average number of verbalizations per child per day was tabulated; this was the most prevalent behavior during observations. The results indicate a slight upward trend in spontaneous verbalizations as the program progressed. Corresponding to this is a slight decrease in teacher-initiated verbalizations.

The number of disruptions per day was also tallied. Both verbal and non-verbal disruptions tended to decrease as the program progressed. During the first half of the twenty observation days, an average of 5.4 verbal disruptions was tallied; this number dropped to an average of 1.5 for the second half. The number of non-verbal disruptions followed the same pattern. An average of 4.9 non-verbal disruptions was counted during the first half of the study; the average dropped to 1.6 for the second half.

There was a marked drop in the number of children observed who were unable to follow directions. During the first three days of the program, thirty-eight instances of children unable to follow directions were counted. Only five instances were observed for the remaining seventeen days.

Inability or unwillingness to participate in either group or individual activity was not observed to be a persistent problem. Five children were unwilling to participate in a group activity on the first day of school. Only twelve such instances were observed for the remaining nineteen days. Through the entire program, only eight instances of children unable to work or play independently were observed.

Conclusions.   These preschool children seemed to adjust quickly to their summer program. They remained as spontaneous and verbal as four-year-olds should be and did not become dependent upon the teachers to elicit verbal responses from them. While maintaining their spontaneity, they were able to become less and less disruptive. They also became more attentive and less distractable. Group activity was cooperative and few of the children were unable or unwilling to participate in the daily activities.

The results of this study suggest strongly that this group of children will have a lot to offer in kindergarten. Its likelihood of success is high. It is hoped that the regular school program will continue to nourish the growth that was observed in the summer.

Evaluation

Purpose and Objectives.   The purpose of the evaluation was to determine whether or not the objectives of the program had been met. These objectives were:

1. To improve each child's social and behavioral adjustment to the classroom situation
2. To improve the students' readiness, reading, and math skills
3. To determine the teacher aide's role in the classroom
4. To determine whether program efforts to involve and interest parents in the summer program and to increase school-family communications have been effective

Method of Evaluation.   Objectives 1 and 2 were measured by using percentiles from the Pre-School Inventory, an instrument developed especially for Head Start programs and published by the Cooperative Testing Division of Educational Testing Service of Princeton, New Jersey. Baseline data consisted of pre-test results. Post-test results were obtained from tests administered at the conclusion of the school year for one group and at the conclusion of the summer program for another group.

Objective 3 was measured by means of an activity schedule for assistant teachers and teacher aides. The aides kept a record of the functions they performed in the program.

Objective 4 was measured by administering a brief questionnaire to parents at the conclusion of the summer program.

Table 1 Growth in Skills as Measured by Pre-School Inventory

| Subtest | Percentage of Students Scoring 50% or Above on Subtest | | | |
	Pre	Post	Average Change Over Six Months	N
Personal-Social	97%	100%	+ 3%	31
Associative Vocabulary	80	97	+17	31
Concept Activation:				
Numerical	55	80	+25	31
Concept Activation:				
Sensory	81	100	+19	31
Total Average	79.4%	86.5%	± 7.1%	31

Results

Growth in Readiness Skills. Table 1 presents the percentage of pre-school children scoring 50 percent or above on both pre- and post-tests for each subtest of the Pre-School Inventory. The table also shows the average percentage of change and the overall test results for the combined group of preschoolers.

Preschool students enrolled in the program showed improvement on all subtests and on the total score from the beginning to the end of the program. Greatest gains were noted on the Concept Activation: Numerical subtest, on which the students had the greatest frequency of low scores initially. Although lowest gains were made on the Personal-Social Subtest (average change of 3 percent), all of the students scored 50 percent or above on this subtest at the end of the program. Substantial gains, 19 percent and 17 percent respectively, were also noted on the Concept Activation: Sensory and the Associative Vocabulary subtests.

Interpretation. The parents indicated an extremely high level of satisfaction with the summer program among themselves and their children. The most impressive findings were that all of the parents felt that parent-teacher talks in the program made them interested in further communication with the school and that 97 percent felt that teachers gave them ideas for helping their children at home. These results suggest that the objective to involve and interest parents was met to a high degree in the summer program. Further substantiation of this point can be found in the teachers' journals of their home visits.

According to the teachers, these visits increased parent-school

Table 2 Parent Responses to Questions Concerning Summer Program (Preschool and Kindergarten)

Item	Number Responding and Percentage			
	Yes		No	
1. Satisfactory transportation	36	100%	0	0%
2. Satisfactory school hours	34	94%	2	6%
3. Child enjoyed program	Much		36	100%
	Some		0	0%
	Little		0	0%
4. Child learned from program	Much		34	94%
	Some		2	6%
	Little		0	0%
5. Opportunities program provided for	Better		28	78%
parent-teacher communication and	Same		8	22%
for learning about child and school	Less		0	0%
6. Teachers give ideas for helping child at home	35	97%	1	3%
7. Gained better understanding of child through program	34	100%	0	0%
8. Parent-teacher talks in program	Very interested		36	100%
promote interest in further talks	Fairly interested		0	0%
and visiting school	Less interested		0	0%
9. Understanding of child's actions	Better		24	67%
in class	Same		12	33%
	Less		0	0%
10. Child's attitude about going to sum-	More favorable		22	61%
mer school compared to attending	Same		14	39%
school during the year	Less favorable		0	0%

Frequencies and percentages are presented.   Percentages are based on a questionnaire sample of thirty-six students. Item 7 is based on thirty-four responses.

communication and encouraged parents to visit the school. More than half of the ninety-five parents attended the Open House, and ten to fifteen of them visited the classrooms as well.

Parent Response.   Table 2 shows the results of a survey of parental reactions to the program. The positive picture is encouraging.

Special Programs in the Subject Content Areas

7

A Highly Structured Academic Kindergarten Program

Nancy Hilburn   *Elementary Consultant, Council Bluffs Community Schools, Council Bluffs, Iowa*

Description

A good kindergarten must reflect the society it serves. A child's experiences in his first year of school have important influences on his future. It is important that the kindergarten experiences be planned so that each child develops a positive concept of himself as a learner. Kindergarten should be a place where a child can learn, does learn, and likes to learn.

With this philosophy in mind, the Council Bluffs Community Schools established a kindergarten to permit exploration, to encourage originality, and to invite children to try many kinds of activities. A flexible curriculum was devised, with a wide variety of offerings in the areas of prereading, language, mathematics, science, social studies, music, and art.

A kindergarten program should not be so formal that the joys of doing, seeing, feeling, and socializing are bypassed, yet it should be a challenge for all who need a challenge. It should be a springboard for learning and should whet the appetite for interesting explorations. It should be a place to live, work, and grow.

In working toward the goal of a balanced kindergarten program, we aim to provide opportunities for active and passive learning, noisy and quiet activities, and small and large group discussions with plenty of time for sharing plans and ideas through language. By providing an abundance of material, we attempt to offer many opportunities for children to perform according to their readiness and abilities. The use of special kits to develop visual and motor skills is an essential part of our program.

Much of the subject matter in kindergarten is explored verbally. Whether it is in the area of science, mathematics, prereading or social studies, the use of oral language and the five senses prevails.

Prereading is a program of instruction that stimulates the child's ability to use the language of the classroom and broaden his concepts besides providing practice in listening for sounds. Records, listening stations, and talking bulletin boards help point out the likenesses and differences of objects and pictures. Word cards, films, alphabet cards, and plastic objects are used to represent beginning sounds. For those who are ready, workbook exercises help reinforce these skills. Story charts, picture captions around the room, and other devices to stimulate an awareness of words and sounds are employed. Reading success is heavily dependent upon oral language skills. Children who speak well and listen well are likely to develop reading skills more rapidly, so we pay a great deal of attention to oral language development.

The science program encourages observation, classification, measurement, and manipulation through the use of special kits. Ours is not a textbook approach. We place the student in the active, dynamic role of investigator. Using the methods of a scientist, children learn through personal experience. The goal of this program is to awaken in the child a sense of the joy and excitement of scientific discovery.

Science exercises begin with the development of basic skills. Common objects are classified by function, color, form, movement, and environment. This part of the program is structured. Each exercise describes objectives in terms of observable and measurable performances, and the lessons progress from simple to complex. Each exercise builds on what the child has already learned and prepares him for subsequent exercises.

Mathematics concepts are developed through the use of many materials—blocks, beads, counting frames, sticks, puzzles, and felt objects. There are also worksheets for those who need further challenge. The children become aware of shapes, signs, and symbols. Our goal here is to develop an understanding of numbers. More than rote memorization of numerals is desired, so experiences are planned to help children develop concepts instead. Number work extends through songs, rhythmic counting activities, poems, stories, and games. Counting and an awareness of numbers appear in many kindergarten activities. Numbers become a part of life. In the kindergarten store, the playhouse, the train made of blocks and boxes, the bead frame, the discussion of the calendar, and the daily attendance, mathematics is involved in a meaningful way in real life situations. Kindergarten activities require many instances of counting. There are crayons to distribute, seeds to plant, cookies to eat, and cartons of milk to drink. Various mathematical concepts are used in reading the thermometer, using a scale, reaching for a book on a high shelf, placing blocks on a low shelf, selecting the biggest book and the smallest toy. Block games involve shapes from triangles to rectangles and the ability to refer to them by name. These skills are reinforced through the use of math worksheets.

Social studies provides a chance to share ideas about the people of the world—their occupations, feelings, moods, desires, hobbies, cultural likes and dislikes, and their similarities and differences. Social studies provides another avenue for sharing language. Large picture charts allow children to compare, infer, sympathize, and enjoy activities of diverse peoples around the world through class discussions.

Art and music are taught together. Available art materials include paint, crayons, clay, and sawdust, as well as a wealth of collage materials such as buttons, seeds, feathers, cloth, straw, and paper. Encouraging freedom of expression invites artistic activity, and the availability of suitable materials enables our kindergarten children to get the most out of creative activities.

Music and rhythms are areas in which enjoyment is the primary concern. They play a vital and influential role in the active kindergarten. Knowledge of high and low sounds, rhythmic interpretations, and music appreciation are all encouraged through records, tapes, instruments, and singing. We expose children to a variety of materials when they are ready, then let them progress at their own pace.

A good kindergarten should encourage every child to do his best, but should not pressure the child to move faster than he is able. It is extremely important that some time be allowed for free work-play. During this period, children have time to make up their minds, and time to change their minds; time to get involved, and time to put things away. Here, children enthusiastically choose their activities and their friends at the same time.

A kindergarten committee meets throughout the year to update supplies and curriculum, evaluate procedures, discuss anecdotal records, confer on conference procedures, compare registration processes, and talk about the general tone of the kindergarten atmosphere.

It is our feeling that learning activities must be directed if they are to prove satisfying to kindergarten children. Progress must be planned and constantly guided if children are to move ahead sequentially. Often, guidance is an individual matter because each child's needs are unique.

Because of the kindergartner's curiosity and eagerness for information, his desire for companionship, his readiness to reason, to think, and to grow in independence, the kindergarten is a setting in which a great deal of learning can take place.

Our goal is to help each child develop a positive feeling about himself, and to encourage him to develop self-discipline so that the desire to achieve comes more and more from within himself. We strive to provide the child with an environment that will lead to the best learning and living experiences possible, help him develop a strong sense of social responsibility, and make available to him teacher-pupil experiences that stimulate creative response and expression.

Evaluation

Program evaluation must be made in terms of the objectives toward which the teacher and children are working. Informal evaluation is continual. An evaluation procedure designed to measure growth considers both the individual child and how he is progressing in relation to the group. A standardized test measuring letter identification, auditory discrimination, and phoneme-grapheme correspondence is administered to each child upon his completion of each readiness level. Group evaluation is made before and after a work period in all areas. This helps children become aware of their own values so that they may build upon them. It is a very important part of their learning. Anecdotal records illustrating the progress of children in terms of intelligence, social, physical, and emotional growth are also kept.

The areas of social studies, science, reading readiness, music and rhythms, art, work habits, and social and emotional behavior are evaluated twice a year in a report card to parents. Satisfactory work is indicated by a check mark. If an area is not checked, it means improvement is needed. Space is provided for teacher comment and parent response. In addition to this growth report, two conferences, one in the fall and the other in the spring, are scheduled with each child's parents.

Cumulative record folders are kept for each child. Pupils are rated *Satis-*

factory, Needs Improving, or *Unsatisfactory* in reading readiness, social studies, mathematics, art, music, physical education, and science.

The Metropolitan Readiness Test was formerly given in kindergarten, although at present it is administered in the first grade. Even though some children do not take part in all areas of the readiness program, they, too, are placed in first grade where they receive extended prereading experiences. Each child works on a level at which he is comfortable and meets success. Teacher observations, general performance of the child, and screening tests help determine this level.

As long as a child is comfortable, happy, and free from pressure, yet challenged, kindergarten has contributed toward his first full year in school. His kindergarten experiences are bound to affect him in many ways throughout his life. Kindergarten is the most influential year in his education.

8

Movement Education in the Kindergarten

Eleanor Lewis Douthat   *Supervisor, Junior Primary First Year, Richmond Public Schools, Richmond, Virginia.*

Description

A commitment to early childhood education is inherent in the organization of the Richmond Public Schools. For approximately sixty-five years, we have provided kindergarten education for five-year-olds as an integral part of the total educational process. The program has enjoyed continuous support from the local school board, and has had significant overall impact.

After studying both our program and new developments elsewhere in early childhood education, we decided to emphasize movement education in the city schools. Because we believe that movement education holds potentially far-reaching benefits for young children, the Richmond Public

Schools have begun a program that is taking hold rapidly within the school system.

Emphasis on the Child as the Learner.   Ask any group of kindergarten teachers to say the word that first comes to mind in describing five-year-olds. Almost invariably, the answer will be *active*. As we seek better ways of teaching young children, we should capitalize on this knowledge of the nature of the child and use his physical movements to promote his total growth. Not only does the young child use body movement to communicate his feelings and needs, but movement is the means by which the child develops his nervous and muscular systems as well. It is helpful to picture the brain as a computer, and the eyes, hands, and feet working in harmony with it. The child must coordinate his eyes, hands, and feet with what he intends to do. This coordination of mind and body is essential to effective learning. Good kindergartens consider the whole child and direct their programs toward helping the child reach his full potential.

For years, educators have been aware that active bodily participation both fosters and reinforces learning. The Chinese recognized this in their proverb:

> I hear and I forget.
> I see and I remember.
> I do and I understand.

Today many specialists in early childhood education are focusing on creative movement as a means of involving the whole child in learning experiences.

The Nature of Movement Education.   Movement education is a new direction in the total education of the child. Based upon principles of learning, it employs the child's innate way of expressing himself. Education through movement stimulates thinking, helps children to understand their own feelings and those of others, breaks down communication barriers, and provides opportunities for creative expression. In motivating creative movement experiences, a teacher may use any meaningful experience, seasonal activity, or current event. For example, as children project themselves into a moon landing and identify with astronauts, they are deepening concepts and increasing communication skills while simultaneously developing bodily control. It is hard to imagine the extent of learning involved when a child puts on imaginary space boots and walks through the lunar atmosphere in which his body weight is one-sixth of his normal weight.

Movement education encompasses both the child's orientation in space and his relation in space to the objects and people around him. Through experiences in movement, concepts involving speed, weight, distance, height, and depth become meaningful. Movement experiences for the young child starts with body awareness. Through participation in games such as "raise your elbow—now your knee," the child learns to identify parts of the body. He begins to find out not only how his body moves, but the movement of which his body is capable. He discovers that he can move his body in many ways—fast, slow, heavy, and light. He begins to use basic movements, the same ones he will employ later in dance and sports.

The child who develops skill in the use of his body gains a feeling of well-being and accomplishment. As he develops body control, he grows in self-discipline and self-direction. He gains ease and grace of movement, and he experiences success in achieving goals that demand physical skill. Because of the individual nature of the program, each child has the opportunity to achieve success. Success in bodily movement enables him to meet new situations with confidence. The high correlation between a positive self-image and readiness for learning is well known to teachers. In summary, movement education promotes health and personal safety, physical growth and coordination, intellectual and social skills, and wholesome attitudes toward learning.

The Program Emerges.   In the fall of 1970, three learning centers were established in the Richmond schools as a part of a court-ordered plan to further integration. Children were bused to these centers on a regular basis. To Richmond educators, the centers represented a challenge. Here was an opportunity for them to provide outstanding educational experiences for the city's children. What happened was truly exciting! Dr. Gladys Andrew Fleming, who was developing a pilot project on children's dance in one of the Richmond schools, served as consultant for movement education in the learning centers. Instead of working directly with the children, she organized an in-service class for training the staffs of the learning centers, physical education teachers from throughout the public schools, and one key kindergarten teacher from each of the participating schools. This in-service class, "Movement As a Way of Learning," served as the nucleus for developing the program throughout the city. It was a class in which teachers were the students. They learned about movement education firsthand.

Activities initiated at the center were continued in the schools by the physical education instructors and the key kindergarten teachers. These teachers served as leaders in developing the program in their schools. As interest spread, workshops conducted by either Dr. Fleming or members of the physical education staff were held at various schools throughout the city. Two of the local television stations chose the movement education program as a noteworthy innovation in the Richmond school system and broadcast reports on it.

The introduction of movement education into the Richmond Public Schools was a cooperative effort of the general elementary supervisors and the physical education supervisor. Before the school year was over, a coordinator from the physical education staff had been granted one free day each week to further assist classroom teachers, on request, in implementing movement education programs. This step was of great importance because it served to endorse the program as well as to strengthen it.

One year after the program began, movement education was included in the orientation program for all new teachers. Following the regular preschool orientation, kindergarten teachers new to the system attended two additional workshops in movement education. The physical education coordinator was granted two unscheduled days each week to assist in movement education classes. In response to requests from the public schools, a local university now offers the course "Movement Education and Creative Rhythmic Movement." This opportunity for teacher training assures the continuation of interest in movement education and enables kindergarten teachers to increase their understanding and skill.

Curriculum

Movement education differs from a traditional physical education program in the following respects: (*1*) Movement education offers a problem-solving approach to learning. Once a problem situation has been introduced, children must work out a solution. The process involves exploration and discovery. A child must discover for himself what his body can do and how he can control it. (*2*) Content is drawn from curriculum. Movement experiences are most effective when correlated with all parts of the curriculum. Movement can be used to develop math and science concepts, to increase vocabulary and to deepen meanings, to stimulate creative writing, to encourage creative expression in music and art, to broaden understandings in social studies and current events, and to build respect for health and safety principles.

The following examples of movement tasks were developed by kindergarten teachers in the Richmond Public Schools.

Helping Children Assume Responsibility. The goal of this exercise is to assist children in taking responsibility for their movements in and around the school building.

Can you follow me? Can you do as I do?

1. Walk slowly	3. Skip
2. Run slowly	4. Take two steps, then stop

Follow Joseph to the water fountain.
Think about moving from here to the door.
Think about how you would like to move to get there. For example, you could run, jump, walk, or hop.
Think about the amount of space you will need so that you will not bump into anyone.
Find your space and perform your movements until you reach the wastebasket near the door.

Movement through Space

1. Run to a white, straight line.
2. Skip to a yellow circle.
3. Think of as many ways as you can to go around the circle.
4. Find someone wearing a color that you are wearing. Stand beside this person. He will be your partner.
5. Hop away from your partner.
6. Walk back to your partner.
7. Add one more person, and another, and another.
8. Keep adding people, hold hands, and keep moving toward your teacher.

Movement with Groups. Divide the class into five groups. Each group selects several tasks to perform. The teacher acts as leader for each group, making stick figure drawings to interpret movement words.

Group I	*Group II*	*Group III*
2 walks	2 hops	1 jump
4 jumps	4 walks	2 hops
5 bounces	6 jumps	3 walks
		4 jumps

Group IV	Group V
4 bounces	3 hops
4 walks	4 jumps
4 jumps	5 walks

Each group reads and performs its tasks. At the completion of its tasks, each group performs the next group's tasks and so on until they all return to the starting point. The teacher then asks each child to choose one basic movement and move to inner-space.

Movement for Concept Development

What is round?	is smooth?	is skinny?
is long?	is straight?	is slow?
is big?	has corners?	is rough?
is fat?	is short?	is crooked?
is fast?	is small?	

For each concept, the children name several objects, then answer the following questions with movements:

What does it look like? *(The child moves himself into the shape of the object.)*

How does it move? *(The child moves as he thinks the object would move.)*

How does it feel? *(The child responds to the way he thinks the object feels.)*

How can you make it move differently or look different? *(The child creates another action or pose.)*

Movement for Holidays

Christmas

Using music such as "Deck the Halls" or "Jingle Bells," children perform locomotor movements. When the music stops, everyone freezes into: Christmas tree decorations, candy canes, snowmen, Santa Claus, reindeer, or snowflakes.

Halloween

Let's be scarecrows! Stretch your arms out. Put your head up. Hold your body straight.

Pretend you are the scarecrow in a farmer's garden and the wind is blowing hard. Down goes your head. Plop—your arms go down. Woosh— your knees buckle. There is a hard gust of wind and over you go. Now you are nothing but sticks and rags. Close your eyes and relax.

Movement through Dramatic Play. Each child pretends to be a present—birthday or Christmas. Some presents are packed in round boxes, others are square, long, or tall. The teacher unwraps each package. Each child moves to show what present he is as other children try to guess.

Movement for the Alphabet: Santa's Magic Bag. Tape a large letter *S* to the floor with masking tape. As presents come out of Santa's pack, children name the ones that start with *S*. Afterwards, children walk along the taped *S*, putting one foot right after the other. "I am walking on the *S*. *S* is for Santa. Can you walk on the *S*?" The teacher asks: "Can you walk a different way on the *S*?"

Evaluation

The Children Grow. In discussing the young child's development and learning, Madeline Hunter, principal of Elementary Laboratory School, University of California, reports, "His motor behavior is the primary channel through which cognitive and affective behavior provides the observable evidence of learning."

Movement education centers around the child as learner. At present, the evaluation of this program rests upon teacher observation. One of the most gratifying results of the Richmond program has been the growth of individual teachers in their ability to observe children. Various kinds of records are kept on the children. In some instances, teachers have prepared a checklist of items such as: listens, follows directions, takes responsibility for self, is sensitive to others. Whatever the method of recording, the real value lies in the development of teachers' skills in observation.

The following observations were made by teachers of young children in the Richmond Public Schools:

"Children are enthusiastic. They show more spontaneity than before."

"Children are learning to follow directions."

"Children are growing in self-discipline."

"By involving all children, movement reduces the number of situations which require children to wait turns."

"Relationships have improved. Children are trying to help each other, and are showing more concern for each other now."

"Children are more aware of space. They have become sensitive to the rights of others during play, and when they are walking or standing in line."

"Children have to listen carefully when they are participating in movement, and their overall listening habits have improved as a result."

"Children are using many new words. There is amazing growth in vocabulary development."

"Children are demonstrating confidence in themselves."

"Children are acting out their problems and finding their own solutions."

"Children are seeing their teachers in a new role."

"Teachers are developing more initiative."

The following evidence illustrates the growth resulting from movement experiences. A group of young children who had participated in movement education during the previous two years was recently given swimming instruction at school. The instructor reported that during the first month of lessons, this group advanced more rapidly than any other group. (The control groups had had no experience in movement education.) The instructor noted: (1) the children followed directions readily, (2) they approached the new experience with eagerness and expressed enthusiasm rather than fear, and (3) by translating classroom movement skills to water, they easily learned to swim.

Teachers who have become involved in movement education have grown in enthusiasm, in sensitivity to children, and in their perceptions of children's creative development. Growth of teachers is contagious. They not only continue to improve, but often will set new goals for themselves.

As a result of the successes of the movement program in the Richmond Public Schools, some members of the physical education department have been called upon to take leadership roles in state meetings and conventions and others have been invited to demonstrate movement education at a national conference.

9

Oral Language Development in the Kindergarten

Julia P. Davis *Kindergarten Consultant, Mobile County Public Schools, Mobile, Alabama*

Description

Research substantiates the fact that a child must be able to communicate orally if he is to learn to read, and must have a good self-concept if he is to succeed. Many of our kindergarten and first grade children come from environments that do not provide adequate prereading experiences or satisfactory oral vocabularies. The language pattern of these youngsters is often nonstandard in nature. Even more critical is the poor concept they often have of themselves, and their lack of trust in others. The kindergarten curriculum emphasizes helping the child become aware of the many ways one can express thoughts and ideas. Kindergarten helps him become aware of himself as a person of worth, and helps him learn to trust adults who may be different from himself. The core of the program is play, exploration, discovery, and discussion. Strategies we employ to develop oral language skills, positive self-concepts, and trust are structured around the use of manipulative materials, interest centers, field trips, dramatizations, audiovisual materials, dramatic play, pets, commercial and teacher-made toys and games, and freedom for oral communication.

A curriculum designed to facilitate the acquisition of language is characterized by the following features:

1. Interest areas that are constantly being changed to arouse the curiosity and stimulating the inquiring minds of children, including housekeeping, science, art, music, math, library, and work centers
2. Movement and learning activities that aid in the development of psychomotor skills
3. A wide variety of manipulative materials
4. Audio-visual materials and equipment
5. Learning kits, such as DUSO, Winter Haven, Piaget, and Early Childhood Reading Readiness Programs
6. Commercial and teacher-made games and toys for auditory and visual perception and discrimination

55

Setting up the Program

Because the program was federally funded, we selected school locations that were readily accessible to a large number of participating children. One team began at Warren, a school that previously had been closed. Another team was assigned to rooms in a nearby elementary school. Later a third team was assigned to an elementary school a few miles away. Home base for all the federally funded kindergarten programs was at Warren.

The Warren staff consisted of one principal, one clerk, twenty-one teachers, twenty-one teacher aides, custodial personnel, a lunchroom manager and assistants, along with health, psychological, and visiting teacher services.

Beginning the Year. Two Early Childhood Education workshops were held before school opened, and each teacher was required to attend at least one. Many attended both. During September the teachers spent time studying, planning, and setting up their classrooms. Children began to enroll on a staggered basis early in October. Consultant services were secured from the local university, public school personnel, and various venders of supplies and equipment.

Testing. Each child took the Peabody Picture Vocabulary Test upon enrollment, and will take it again in the spring. The expected gain is 1.4 for each month the child is enrolled in the kindergarten.

Parent Involvement. We are in constant communication with the parents of our five-year-olds. The parents bring them in the morning and pick them up each afternoon. Both the principal and the child's teacher make a point of exchanging greetings and ideas with the parents, discussing the children, and making plans for visits, programs, field trips, bulletins, and lunch invitations. Parents are urged to visit class often and stay for lunch with the group. Teachers also arrange with parents for home visits.

Health Service. As a part of the local school system, the kindergarten has access to the same health services provided the other children in the district. These services include screening for vision, hearing, dental, and postural defects. School nurses make home visits when so requested by the teacher. Immunization programs are conducted by the local Health Clinic assisted by the Public School Nurses' Services. In cases where the parents are financially unable to provide corrective devices, aid is sought from local agencies. Both breakfast and lunch are served to the children at school.

After each meal, the children brush their teeth. After lunch, instead of being required to rest on mats, the children may engage in any type of activity that is quiet and restful.

Evaluation. Late in April or in May, each kindergarten child takes the Peabody Picture Vocabulary Test again. Along with the results of this formal test, informal testing scores, teacher observations, anecdotal records, and various checklists are kept on each child. These records are put in a file folder which we will forward later to the child's first grade teacher.

Curriculum

Our major objective is to provide an intensive readiness program for children identified as educationally deprived. We provide the child with a variety of experiences designed to develop his communication skills, muscle coordination, motor development, auditory and visual perception and discrimination, acceptable behavior patterns, wholesome attitudes, aesthetic feelings, creative expression, independent thinking, conceptualization, and problem solving abilities. Involved in these classroom techniques are several recognized approaches to learning as described by such authorities as Piaget, Montessori, Englemann-Bereiter, and proponents of the British Infant Schools.

We choose materials and procedures that foster growth, beginning at the child's present stage of development and carrying him as far as he is capable of going in a prescribed length of time. Materials we use include Winter Haven; DUSO—A Language Development Program; the Macmillan company's Bank Street Early Childhood Education; Lavatelli's Piaget Program: Early Childhood Curriculum; "I Can": A Movement and Readiness Program, Bulletin No. 670, Mobile County Public Schools; E. M. and R. Hardwood Teaching Aids; Distar, Englemann-Bereiter; Advantage; Getting a Head Start and Modern School Mathematics–Kindergarten, Houghton-Mifflin; D. L. M. perceptual skills materials; Guidelines to Readiness, Mobile County Public Schools; Language Experiences in Early Childhood; and ABC Dandy Dog's Early Reading Program.

Each teacher has classroom equipment that includes listening stations, record players, filmstrip projectors, overhead projectors, cassette recorders, and Study Mates (Graflex-Auto-Vance). Each teacher has access to television sets, 16mm projectors, copying machines, duplicator and mimeograph machines, and a laminating and dry mount press. To complete the interest centers, each teacher has an aquarium, terrarium, pet cages, housekeeping furniture, easels, flannel and magnetic boards, sand and water tables, and woodworking tables.

Field trips in and around the community, both on foot and by bus, are an integral part of the curriculum. We feel that through these experiences the children will, in the course of group discussions, begin to verbalize more effectively, thus enriching their oral vocabulary.

The teachers and aides work as guides to the program, rejecting the more traditional, rigidly structured role of a teacher. They could be characterized as overseers of a play-exploration program. Through experiences in science, social studies, math, language arts, art, music, and physical education in their broadest sense, the children become involved in exploring and questioning their kindergarten environment naturally—in the rooms, in the yard, and in the community—wherever their curiosity may take them.

Through practical application, they learn to use numbers. Through duties at school, they learn to take responsibility. By seeing, touching, tasting, hearing, and smelling they develop an awareness of their world. By exploring in the science center, in the play yard, on the field trip, they see, conceptualize, talk, and ask "why." Through records, books, and films, their world grows ever larger. Their vocabularies, their creative ideas, and their appreciation of the humanities expand. Through group interaction they learn to function in a cooperative way with regard and an understanding for the rights of others. But, perhaps most important of all, they are developing a wholesome attitude toward school and a willingness to trust others. They are developing inquisitive minds and an eagerness to learn.

Organization. Emphasis is on one-to-one teaching relationships. However, there are also large and small group experiences. The teacher-pupil ratio is not to exceed one to twenty.

Strategies. When the children enroll in the fall, the teacher and her aide spend a great deal of time getting to know as much as possible about each child. As information piles up, prescriptive strategies are developed to meet each child's needs as indicated by the accumulated data.

Materials and equipment are introduced slowly at first. As the children engage in free-choice role playing, the teachers observe them, noting stages of physical and emotional maturity, behavior patterns, language patterns, social interactions, cognitive development, vocabulary, and speech habits.

Information on each child is gathered on checklists. As new materials are introduced, we observe the reactions of each child. We note handedness, left-to-right, top-to-bottom and front-to-back progression, interest span, ability to concentrate, willingness to ask questions, and motivation. Early in the program, we found that motivation is a much more reliable determinant of interest span than the child's chronological age or his background. Some children from the most deprived situations may sit for thirty or forty minutes at one game, toy, or interest center. We observed children playing with a specific game or in the housekeeping center for even longer periods of time.

Helping the child to become aware of himself as a person and to be able to identify his body parts is the first structured phase of the curriculum. Materials and games are used to interest and motivate the children for each learning task. Surprisingly early, the children learn to recognize their printed names and the word *me*. They soon learn to recognize the names of their classmates, too.

Various activities are designed to teach the colors. Color Day is an exciting one for each child because all five senses are actively engaged on this special day. The records *Learning Basic Skills Through Music* have proved to be most effective in teaching colors and basic shapes. Winter-Haven basic materials are used for teaching geometric shapes. Other manipulative toys and games such as the chalkboard and templates serve as enrichment tools.

We always break broad skills and concepts into smaller parts to accommodate the child and his learning style. Our entire program is developmental, with each skill presented at its proper place on the continuum.

Art and music experiences involve both creativity and appreciation. We allow for children to experiment with all kinds of art media—fingerpainting, string painting, block printing, easel painting, cutting and pasting, papier mâché, paper sculpture, and crayons.

In addition to listening and singing, the children participate in interpretive rhythms and sounds and rhythm bands. Many music experiences involve listening to homemade music devices such as bottles, glasses of water, sand blocks, coffee can drums, and tambourines made from paper plates and bottle tops.

We have high expectations for this group of kindergartners. We believe a substantial improvement will be noted as these youngsters move into regular school experiences.

10

Kindergarten Language Development

Rosemary E. Ramsay   *Coordinator of Elementary Instruction,*
McAllen Independent School District, McAllen, Texas

Description

McAllen's kindergarten program, which is partially funded by Title I, is similar to many other federally funded programs. It follows national guidelines and policies implemented for enrolling the disadvantaged or language-handicapped child. In 1969 when this program began, it was entirely federally funded. Since that time, Texas law has provided for a gradual increase in funds for kindergarten, so program support is now being shifted to state and local sources. McAllen Independent School District has fifteen classes of five-year-old kindergarten children. The total enrollment of approximately 425 averages twenty-eight students to each teacher. Pupils in twelve of these classes meet state age requirements and are funded under the state minimum foundation program. The remaining classes, consisting of children whose ages are in the 5.0 and 5.1 year range, are funded under Title I. Over 95 percent of these children speak Spanish and have little knowledge of English.

Each teacher has a full-time paraprofessional aide. There is an in-service training program for both teachers and aides that centers on specific problems in language deficiencies, parental involvement, health services, and physical development of their students. We believe that the uniqueness of McAllen's program lies in the great emphasis we place on oral language development.

Because the students understand little if any English when they enroll, our teachers are either bilingual themselves or have a bilingual aide. In-service training makes teachers aware of instructional areas where the child needs extra help because of his unfamiliarity with English. Several English sounds are difficult for the Spanish speaker to reproduce simply because they do not exist in his language. English has twenty-four consonant phonemes and eleven vowel phonemes. Spanish has eighteen consonant phonemes and five vowel phonemes. For example, the following phonemes appear in English but not in Spanish: short *i*, *a*, *o*; hard *b*, *v*, *j*; and *th*.

Although many elements in their backgrounds are contributing factors, it seems that these children are unable to make average progress in school primarily because of their lack of facility with the English language. The primary goal of our kindergarten program, therefore, is the development of a basic oral English vocabulary and a mastery of the basic sentence patterns of the language. We emphasize the pattern drills and vocabulary used in reading readiness programs.

Teachers are given materials that develop readiness in all subjects, emphasizing correct pronunciation, intonation, and rhythm patterns. Every possible opportunity is utilized to provide further practice in English usage, whether it be at the child's lunch period or during a short field trip. All commercially produced materials must be adapted by teachers to fit our bilingual classrooms. The Peabody Language Development Kit, Level I, and the Rock Kit (Region I Curriculum Kit, H-200) are used as core material. The Peabody offers 430 full-color stimulus cards arranged in thirteen categories and a manual consisting of 180 lessons. Lesson plans include the use of puppets, plastic color chips, and a recorded tape of songs and stories, all supplied in the kit.

The key to the curriculum, essentially English as a second language, is to encourage repeated practice of sounds—without boredom. This is no small feat. Our teaching methods require the use of a wide variety of materials and audio visual equipment. Teachers have access to record players, Language Masters, Dukane filmstrip cassettes, rear screen projectors, tape recorders, overhead projectors, and materials to accompany these machines.

The tape recorder is probably the most frequently used tool. It enables a teacher to design specific drills in areas where her students need most help. Taping the student's responses enables both student and teacher to evaluate pupil progress. Tapes are also an effective means of improving enunciation, pronunciation, phrasing, and patterning.

The kindergarten program is structured around basic patterns, but not to the degree that all classes learn the same drills simultaneously. At the end of the year, all students will have experienced similar basic instruction. The use of creative dramatics, nursery rhymes, songs, finger plays, and poems provides a necessary vehicle for further language development.

Near mid-term when the children are ready, we introduce oral phonic drills, emphasizing not the letter name but the sound. Though some children learn letter names, the curriculum is not specifically designed to teach them. The objective of a lesson in teaching beginning sounds is to make the pupil aware of the consonant sound at the beginning of a word and to teach him how to distinguish it from other consonant sounds. Generally by the end of the school year, a child will know how to write his name, the numbers from one to ten, and often many letters of the alphabet as well. He will have mastered approximately thirty sentence pattern drills, and his basic oral vocabulary will number approximately 400 to 500 words.

McAllen kindergarten students are pre- and post-tested with the Peabody Picture Vocabulary Test. The average child doubles his pre-test score by the end of the school year. Many triple their original scores.

Because of overcrowded schools, the kindergarten children are presently transported by bus to and from their neighborhood schools to rented rooms in churches. Aides accompanying the children utilize this time to instill good learning habits. Teachers and aides eat the noon meal with the children. Establishing a daily routine is an integral part of our program. The child's attitude toward school begins in kindergarten. Teachers report that children show signs of being at ease in school by the end of three months. Every effort is made to provide a warm, healthful atmosphere so the children can share experiences while acquiring the use of the English language.

Parental involvement is a necessary part of any kindergarten program. Teachers visit each child's home at least twice a year. Aides serve as a link in establishing better communications between school and community. Frequently the aide, with the help of a teacher, is able to gain the trust of parents and change hostile parents into enthusiastic supporters of the school program by working with them informally.

Follow-up observations by neighborhood principals and first grade teachers indicate that McAllen's kindergarten program is effective in preparing the Spanish-speaking five-year-old for the elementary school curriculum.

11

Title I Prereading and Prenumber Skills Program

Harris E. Love *Director of Teacher Education and Instructional Innovations, Talladega City Schools, Talladega, Alabama*

Description

Title I guidelines encourage school systems to attack educational deprivation as early as possible. Results of tests administered to children preregistering in the spring revealed that 30 percent of them scored at least six school months below the standard reading readiness level. A disproportionate number of these children were from economically deprived families.

In an attempt to reach this group of children and prepare them for first grade, a preschool readiness program designed for the economically deprived was established at each of our elementary schools.

The children are organized into classes of fifteen to twenty-five students (average twenty-two) that meet daily for three hours. Each class is directed by a professional teacher and a half-time aide.

Although many of the activities are designed and improvised by teachers, our program is heavily dependent on the early childhood education materials published by McGraw-Hill. Some of the significant materials and their purposes are:

1. *Developing Learning Readiness* by Getman, *et al.* This is a unique visual-motor-tactile skills program that gives the children practice in general coordination, balance, eye-hand coordination, eye movements, form recognition, and visual memory.
2. *Stories for Listening: Learning Speech Sounds.* This record- and filmstrip-based program helps the child to listen attentively and creatively, to articulate more effectively and correctly, to speak more intelligently and fluently, and to improve general language abilities.
3. *Sullivan Associates Programmed Reading, Pre-Reading Sequence.* This program covers *a, i, o, h, p, t,* and *m* (twenty words).

Two additional materials utilized in a similar fashion are the *Hoffman Reader* and the *Talking Page*.

Evaluation throughout the year is made by informal observation. Some good indications of the success of the program are the students' outstanding attendance records and their excellent social adjustment.

12

Correlating Art With the Language Arts in the Kindergarten

Phyllis Gant *Kindergarten Teacher, Warren Elementary School, Marietta, Ohio*

Description

The first hour of our kindergarten program is scheduled as free activity time. The children move from center to center on their own. We have a large art center set up for them, though the children are never required to use it. Easel painting, cutting and pasting, clay modeling, and coloring with crayons are some of the activities available. We also use several other art media, such as finger painting, sponge painting, crayon resist, and collages. The easels and work tables are always set up before the children enter the room each morning. The children are not required to work on art activities, but may go directly to other centers—science, housekeeping, books, blocks, puzzles, or games.

When a child avoids the art center, it usually means that he lacks confidence in his work. A conference with the mother is usually all that is necessary for the child to become interested in the art media. Every child likes praise and compliments on his work. If we can encourage the mother to give him more attention and praise for his art work, the child usually becomes enthusiastic. All art work is displayed. We have a low bulletin board where children may display their own work if they wish.

In our kindergarten, art is used to encourage the child's growth. Growth is not something done to a child—it is something he does himself. The child is therefore left to select his own activities. Mainly, the teacher's role is to praise.

We do not use coloring books or mimeographed worksheets for children to color. In our opinion, these stifle creativity and do not stimulate the child's thinking.

Most of our children have used only crayons before they come to school and a few have had no experience whatsoever with art materials. Most of them therefore begin drawing or painting at the scribbling stage, advancing later to the shape stage and finally to the pictorial stage. We find that there are always a few that never advance beyond the scribbling stage during their year in kindergarten. They are the ones who usually become the slow learners in next year's first grade. We often recommend to the parents that these children stay in kindergarten another year, especially if they have a late birthday.

Language Arts.   Art is like reading for the preschool child. As he begins to draw and paint, he starts to name the objects he creates. They may be unrecognizable to the adult but quite real to the child. For this reason, an adult should always say to the child, "Tell me about your picture," and never ask "What is it?"

The more the child's pictures develop, the more detailed the stories about them will be. The experienced teacher can sense when a child is ready to have captions written under his picture. At this point, the printed word enters the child's world. Now the child becomes curious about words and letters. He begins asking his teacher to read the various words he sees around the room.

The most delightful time comes when the child picks up a book and realizes that he already knows some of the words on the first page. There is no way adequately to describe the light that is in the child's eyes and face as he shouts **"I** can read! I can read!" That is where it all starts—within the child.

Second Semester Activities.   When a child is ready to read, there is no end to the things he delights in doing. The following list describes some of the activities that children in our kindergarten have enjoyed:

1. Making a chart of pictures that rhyme, such as man-fan and rat-cat.
2. Making a kite tree with rhyming words. The child selects a word and the teacher writes it on his kite. The child's aim is to get as many words as he can to rhyme with the word on the kite. These words are attached along the kite string. The kites are pasted on a large sheet of chart paper, forming a tree.
3. Making cards for members of their family on birthdays and holidays.
4. Making lotto games from construction paper and pictures.
5. Dictating stories about their pictures into a tape recorder.
6. Cutting activities of all sorts. Discontinued wall paper sample books from stores are useful in stimulating the child's imagination. We use several of these books for cutting activities during the year, especially in the second semester after the child has developed good finger coordination.

In May a readiness test is administered. The results of this test, the child's attitude toward school, his ability to get along with his schoolmates, and general observations made by the teacher are submitted to his first grade teacher in a detailed, written report.

Summary

We consider the following items to be valid achievements of our special program for kindergarten children:

1. The program is individualized.
2. The children do not realize that they are learning. To them, everything is play—the natural means of growth.
3. The children are satisfying their natural curiosity, which in turn gives rise to more ideas and further increases their creativity.
4. The children are developing hand coordination.
5. The children's vocabulary is increasing, and the children are beginning to speak in complete sentences.
6. The children are learning to appreciate books.
7. The children are learning how to use many types of materials properly.
8. The children are developing the ability to organize and follow through on simple tasks.
9. The children are learning how to manage their emotions.
10. The children are experiencing classroom successes that will lead them to develop good self-concepts, the basis for emotional stability and social growth.

Programs for Bilingual Children

13

A Bilingual Approach to Early Childhood Education

Larry R. Shaw *Director, Bilingual Education Program, Intermediate School District 105, Yakima, Washington*

Description

The primary purpose of our bilingual kindergarten is to teach children basic educational concepts in both English and Spanish, thus providing the necessary foundation for their future success in school. Both languages are used for communication and instruction. In formal, individualized, and free play activities, the child has the opportunity to improve verbal expression and communication abilities in his native language while developing similar abilities in a second language.

The general goals of our bilingual program are:

To Increase Conceptual Development.   A child who does not understand the language spoken in the classroom cannot be expected to comprehend the basic concepts being taught. Our general aim is to teach concepts to this child in his native language while he is in the process of learning English.

To Increase Communication Skills.   The ability to communicate effectively is vitally important, regardless of the language in which we develop

67

this ability. In the bilingual program, the Spanish-speaking child benefits from a classroom atmosphere in which he is rewarded for verbalization and the development of communication skills in the language with which he is most comfortable. Increasing the child's skills in his dominant language helps to build his second language, which in this case is English.

To Transfer Learning From Spanish to English. A child needs to feel successful. If the child can learn concepts successfully in his native language, he will be more likely to learn the second language well later on. Comprehension of concepts and the ability to verbalize and communicate easily in his first language strengthen the child's ability to transfer learning to his second language. In essence, the English language becomes much more meaningful to him.

To Develop Bilingual-Bicultural Children. In our program, the Spanish-speaking child finds himself in an atmosphere where his language and culture are used and accepted as a part of the curriculum. He takes pride in his background. This child is able to take the best from both his native culture and from the new culture of which he now finds himself a part. He needs to understand and interact in both cultures because, in essence, he is a part of both. The English-speaking child benefits from this classroom, too, because he is exposed to the natural use of a second language and a second culture.

Bilingual Program Components

Instruction. The program centers around small groups and individualized instruction. The bilingual teacher and her two bilingual teaching assistants are trained to use bilingual methods and techniques in all phases of the curriculum. Each day, after the large group activities such as reviewing the calendar and singing songs, the children move into three or four small groups. The classroom is divided into several teaching and learning centers where the small groups receive instruction from the teacher, teaching assistants, or mechanical devices. Lessons usually last from twelve to fifteen minutes. The children move from center to center at the end of each lesson.

Half the subject matter in these small learning circles is taught in English and half in Spanish. For example, if polar adjectives are being taught in English to one group using one set of audio-visual materials, the same concepts are probably being taught in Spanish to another small group using other materials.

The following list describes the materials we use:

Michigan Oral Language Series (FLIC). These materials present a bilingual approach to the learning of basic concepts—classification, seriation, polar adjectives, opposites—that are essential to a child's future success in school. They also develop language usage both in English and in Spanish while teaching these concepts. The materials are designed to be used in Spanish and English small group learning circles, so that the use of one language reinforces the other. The FLIC materials are supplemented in the classroom and in the small group learning circles by materials from the Peabody Kit and the Kindergarten Keys.

Getting Ready to Read in English and *Preparadose para Leer* in Spanish (Houghton-Mifflin). Our teachers use these materials during the last five months of kindergarten to prepare the children for reading. Letter names and letter sounds are taught all year as a part of small group instruction, and the reading readiness program begins in January. The teachers also use *Phonics Program* and *Laminas Murales de Alfabetizacion* (Bremmer-Davis) to reinforce phonics in both languages.

Concepts in Science (Level K, Harcourt, Brace and World Series). These materials lend themselves readily to small group instruction. Any elementary science series might serve equally well, as long as it is used and taught bilingually.

Modern Mathematics (Level K, Houghton-Mifflin). Arithmetic is easy to teach bilingually because number concepts can be reinforced readily in either language. Any math series would probably serve the purpose, providing the children were learning the concepts in both languages.

Bilingual Social Studies and self-concept materials developed by the San Angelo, Texas, bilingual program. These lessons dealing with the individual, family, school, community, and country are developed in both English and Spanish.

Frostig materials. These are used for motor skills development. For the most part, this program is presented in small group activities, although it could become part of the large group physical education program.

Various songs, games, and dances that reflect both Anglo and Spanish cultures are taught in the large group setting. The children have time for resting and for free play activities throughout the kindergarten day. Class is held for three and three-quarters hours in one school and five and one-half hours in another school.

Staff Development.   Continuing assistance is provided for teachers and aides through in-service training. A two-week summer workshop, quarterly in-service workshops, and monthly classroom evaluation sessions give the teaching staff the opportunity to broaden and perfect their techniques of bilingual instruction. The two-week summer workshop directs itself to: ways of using various bilingual techniques and materials; the operation and use of audio-visual equipment and materials; the study of psychological and sociological needs of children; and the role of the teaching assistants. The quarterly sessions deal with implementing new procedures and improving the existing ones. Additional assistance is provided the teaching staff through bi-weekly and monthly evaluations.

Parent Community Involvement.   One of the bilingual program's basic obligations is to involve parents directly in the education of their children. This goal is accomplished through the use of informal education materials that encourage parents to help their children at home. Formal take-home materials that correspond with school subject matter are in the developmental stage and will be utilized in the future.

Community members and parents are encouraged to participate in school activities as members of the Community Advisory Committee. The parent participation program is coordinated by a part-time community aide who works with parents, teachers, and principals in making the classroom experience more meaningful to the children.

Management.   The program is a cooperative effort between Intermediate School District 105 and two local school districts. The Program Director and Program Evaluator work with each district superintendent and school principal to administer the program.

Evaluation

The evaluation plan for the program is a comprehensive one based on the concept of accountability. There are nine behavioral objectives for the instruction component, three for the staff development component, four in the parent involvement component, three in the materials acquisition component, and ten for the management component. All of these objectives are subject to measurement, data collection, and data analysis procedures designed to indicate progress.

A full-time Program Evaluator is on the staff to administer pre- and post-tests, and to collect and analyze data.

The McGraw-Hill CTB Test of Basic Experience (TOBE), level K, is used to measure achievement of objectives in the instructional component. The TOBE has four sub-tests covering language, mathematics, science, and social studies. The language sub-test is administered in English and in Spanish on separate occasions in an attempt to identify dominant language ability. The other sub-tests are administered in English and Spanish simultaneously.

The evaluator holds biweekly evaluation sessions with the staff of each classroom in order to ascertain to what extent the various materials are being used. In addition, a monthly check of classroom procedures is carried out by the Program Principal, Director, and Evaluator to ensure the use of proper bilingual procedures. Their reports comprise a record of the effectiveness of continuous staff training and become part of the project's overall documentation. Reports from pre- and in-service workshops document the staff development sessions and their value to participants. All aspects of the parent-community involvement component are thoroughly documented by personal observation, biweekly reports, and home visit checklists.

Materials acquisition is documented, then evaluated by a suitability checklist that states the criteria materials must meet. The project director and his staff maintain daily logs to measure attainment of the management and evaluation components.

The Project Evaluator collects and analyzes all these data, then submits interim and final evaluation reports indicating overall performance. In addition, an external educational auditor reviews the data gathered and analyzed by the evaluator and verifies or negates the evaluation reports.

Formal and informal evaluation data suggest that our bilingual kindergarten program is achieving its goals. Through this approach, the children are able to build the conceptual and social foundation they need for continued success in school and society.

14

A Bilingual Program for Migrant Children

Dwade King *Assistant Superintendent, McAllen Independent School District, McAllen, Texas*

Description

History. During the 1970–71 contract period, the Southwest Educational Development Laboratory completed the final phase of its three-year sequential program for three-, four-, and five-year-old migrant Mexican-American children. Funded by grants from the U.S. Office of Economic Opportunity and the U.S. Office of Child Development, this bilingual program was implemented at the Early Childhood Center in McAllen, Texas, home base for a large number of migrant families. The project had two basic purposes:

1. To design, pilot-test, and refine a program to provide children from the target population with the educational background essential to a successful first grade experience and to continued success throughout their school years.
2. To develop staff training procedures and materials for working with young migrant Mexican-American children and their parents.

Our program began in the fall of 1967 when the Laboratory, in cooperation with the U.S. Office of Economic Opportunity and the McAllen Independent School District, tested its Early Childhood Program with three- and four-year-old migrant children at the McAllen Early Childhood Center. By 1968, thirty three-year-olds and sixty four-year-olds were enrolled in the program. In 1969, with the additional support of the Office of Child Development and the Texas Education Agency, the Laboratory expanded the program to include thirty five-year-olds. During the 1970–71 school year, ninety children, comprising two classes of each of the three age groups, participated in the experimental program.

Program Emphasis. The Laboratory program focuses on the child's intellectual, physical, social, and emotional development. Emphasis is placed on teaching sensory-perceptual, cognitive, and language skills. To insure optimum conditions for learning in school as well as apart from the school setting, the program has three principal components—instructional materials, staff development, and parent-school-community involvement. These components comprise an early childhood program that meets the specific needs of the Mexican-American migrant child.

Rationale. Staff members of the U.S. Office of Economic Opportunity, the Office of Child Development, and the McAllen Independent School District well know the academic problems facing economically disadvantaged Mexican-American children. These problems are compounded when the children spend as much as half of each year following the seasonal harvests. Spanish is the native language for these children. Most speak little English when they start school, and many are unfamiliar with Spanish in the standard form. They are largely unfamiliar with the experiences, concepts, and values stressed by the traditional school system and the cultural base from which it stems. The combination of these factors results in a high dropout rate for first grade Mexican-American children. According to the 1960 Texas census, the median school years completed by persons over twenty-five years of age was 11.5 years for Anglos but only 6.1 years for the Spanish-surnamed.

Because first grade failure often indicates the likelihood of future school failure, the Laboratory has developed a program to alleviate the basic problems that children of the target population face when they first enter school. Bilingual language development is emphasized as concepts are taught first in Spanish, then in English. Activities are designed to provide classes with the experiences and knowledge common to children from more advantaged circumstances. The migrant children's own cultural background and experiences of travel add depth to this study. Curriculum components stress the importance of the Mexican-American culture as well as the Anglo culture, so each child develops pride in his own heritage.

Location. As the home base for many Mexican-American migrants, McAllen, Texas, is an appropriate site for testing an early childhood program for migrant children. It is located in the Rio Grande Valley in Hidalgo County, adjacent to the Mexican border. Because a large percentage of the residents are Mexican-American, the city's population is largely bilingual. Spanish is used as often as English in economic activities. McAllen is the hub of a large farming area. Principal industries are shipping and processing of the fruits and vegetables that are grown in the region.

Farm and field work provide the main source of income for the migrants. Most of them live below the poverty level in isolated areas called *barrios,* where they maintain a strong cultural identity and have little contact with the majority Anglo society.

Evaluation

Ninety children participated in our program in 1970–71. Two classes of fifteen pupils each enrolled in each of the three age groups. Evaluation was based on criterion-referenced tests given to experimental pupils at the beginning and end of the school year, and norm-referenced tests given to experimental classes and comparison groups of the same age, ethnic group, and socio-economic background who attended day care centers without planned instructional programs.

Test findings revealed that children in the Laboratory program met the criteria on the curriculum-referenced tests on all but a few of the twenty-five units. Experimental pupils scored higher than control pupils on tests of Spanish and English comprehension, general concepts, and non-verbal intelligence.

The Open School Concept

15

The Open Classroom and Individualized Education

Patricia Taber *Fairmount School, Mukilteo School District, Mukilteo, Washington*

Description

We are apparently entering an era of reduced financial support for education, one in which it is not realistic to plan expensive educational improvements. Therefore, it seems appropriate to describe here a teaching program that has already produced increased educational effectiveness for the same cost as previous programs, and that has the potential for further improvement. This program is an open-classroom kindergarten. The improvements in educational effectiveness seen here revolve around early detection of special needs—social, physical, emotional, and academic—of the individual child, and the prompt and effective provision of individualized education to meet these needs.

One of the major educational opportunities offered by kindergarten is that the attributes and abilities of children are still in the early stages of development. These abilities can often be recognized, and because they are in the process of being formed, it is not impossible to modify them. Looking at kindergarten in relation to the later grades, it could be suggested that kin-

75

dergarten is the place to educate the whole person in order to avoid the development of handicaps that would otherwise become increasingly difficult for the child and for society to deal with. Therefore, the particular aspect of kindergarten we would like to emphasize here is the early detection and prompt response to the needs of the individual child.

Many social, physical, and academic handicaps are relatively easily identified and dealt with by non-specialist teachers when the child is very young. The older the child is, however, the more difficult it becomes to remedy his handicaps, and hence, the more highly specialized the person attempting the remedy must be. The need for highly specialized people has a major drawback—there never seem to be enough of them to take care of the problems they are asked to solve. It is of utmost importance, then, to detect and remedy problems at a stage when they still can be handled by the classroom teacher or at small cost in specialist time.

Because our program is only in its second year, this report will deal sequentially with its development, its current functioning, and its future.

Development

Our kindergarten program was launched by staff who had no experience or training in open classroom teaching. Our background consisted only of the related books and articles we had read. At first we planned to give the children free choice of activities for the entire two-and-a-half hour daily period. The philosophy behind this plan was that the individual child will choose those activities most nearly suited to his present needs and capabilities. However, it took us only a few weeks to develop a more realistic approach to the open classroom. We retained the original concept of freedom of choice, but limited the time to about one hour of the two-and-a-half hour period. We had two reasons for this. First, when the children were given complete freedom, many of them spent a great deal of the time just wandering around the room. Others became wilder and wilder as time went on. Some would ask, "Teacher, what can I do?" We interpreted these actions to be signs that the majority of the children were lacking in self-direction. Clearly, our schedule needed *some* structure. Second, the teachers felt that many of the quieter children had little opportunity to express themselves verbally. We also felt that we were not becoming well acquainted with many of our children. We needed to meet in small groups to get to know them and to give them a chance to talk and carry out other activities under some guidance. So we divided the time, spending an hour and a half each day in structured activities. These activities were of four types:

1. *Individualized activities,* geared to the needs of specific children as observed by teachers. They included the following areas: enrichment, augmented academic, coordination, speech, dramatic play, art activities, and social adjustment.
2. *Small group activities* involving one-third of the kindergarten class with a teacher or aide. We read stories or poetry, discussed a film we had seen earlier in the day, talked about a special occasion, a current event, or a subject of general interest. We also had our Show and Tell sessions in small groups.
3. *Class activities* involving all the pupils at the same time. The entire class gathered each morning for singing and a discussion of the calendar and the weather. The group also exercised together in the gym, and they assembled once a week for a music class. Other whole-class activities included viewing films, listening to records, and watching TV programs.
4. *Reading and numbers readiness programs* in which we used workbooks. These programs began after Christmas. For reading, the class was divided into four ability groups.

Midway in the first year of this program we began to be aware of the educational opportunity that is the theme of this report—the role the teacher can play in early recognition of specific problems—academic, social, emotional, physical—and the development of individualized solutions for them.

Given the physical set-up of the open classroom, this goal is easily accomplished if the teachers have time to step back and observe the children at work and play. We found that children adjusted quickly to having several teachers and even several other adults moving freely about the room. Visitors included the speech therapist, counselor, psychologist, nurse, various specialists or administrative personnel, visiting parents, and parent volunteers. A teacher can make many observations about a child by watching him interact with his peers and with other adults. There is a great advantage in having three or more teachers, each with a somewhat different viewpoint, observe a child. The three can compare notes and then confer with parents or specialists. In this way, conferences become an effective tool for planning and implementing a successful year in kindergarten for each child.

To achieve our goals we had to mesh several important elements. Classes were large; each one averaged about 60 pupils, and had two regular teachers and one instructional aid. Parent volunteers assisted the staff, and other parents frequently visited the classroom.

Parent Volunteers

We began our classroom parent volunteer program in early November of the first year. We were still feeling our way then, and made a number of tentative efforts before our volunteer program began to take shape.

Parents. During the parent orientation session, we explained the program as we envisioned it. We asked for parent volunteers to: (1) contribute one or more hours a week to work in the classroom, (2) publish a kindergarten newsletter, (3) provide food for our weekly snack, (4) gather needed materials, (5) serve as chaperones on field trips, (6) share special hobbies or interests, and (7) contribute any ideas they thought worthwhile to our kindergarten program.

By the time we began to organize the parent volunteers, we had already spent a great deal of time trying to coordinate philosophies and methods and to develop a realistic approach to the open classroom. However, because we were not sure just how we wanted to use the parents, many of them felt uncomfortable at first. Some parents, we discovered, were only comfortable when given a specific activity to conduct with a specific group of children for a specific length of time. However, after they had become familiar with structured activities, several of them initiated activities based on their own, sometimes new ideas. So as the program grew, we began to consider parent volunteers to be something more than extra pairs of hands.

The volunteers were used in four ways:

1. A selected group of children was directed to a volunteer for work in a specific activity, based on the needs of the children as determined by the teachers. Learning colors, counting, and vocabulary development were often emphasized.
2. The volunteer selected an activity or game she wanted to supervise—balls, jump ropes, stitchery, or dominoes—and the children could choose to go to her during their free time.
3. The volunteer presented a project of her own—dramatic play, puppet show, or art activity. Sometimes the children were directed to her for that specific activity, sometimes they chose it, and sometimes she chose them.
4. Volunteers prepared materials to be used in the classroom by students and teachers, such as dittos for worksheets and bulletin board materials.

We tried to schedule three parents in the classroom each day in order to give the teachers time to observe, time to work with an individual or a group on a specific problem, or time to concentrate on enrichment or accelerated instruction. In practice, however, the parent volunteers have not freed the teachers as much as we had hoped. A large amount of time must be spent training and working with the parents themselves.

Nevertheless, the teachers and parents who worked consistently throughout the year considered the volunteer program to be successful because:

1. The parents saw their children in a different light by observing them interact with their peers and other adults.
2. A wide variety of activities was made available to the children.
3. The kindergarten newsletter, published weekly or semi-monthly, kept all parents informed of kindergarten activities.

The fact that our efforts to free teachers for an appreciable length of time for observation or individual work were not as successful as we had hoped was largely attributable to two factors:

1. The teachers did not feel free to ask the volunteers to supervise activities they did not enjoy. Many parents, for example, found working in the paint center too messy! Nor did the teachers feel free to ask the volunteers to do menial tasks, such as cleaning the gerbil cage or mopping up.
2. Most of the parents chose to supervise activities they enjoyed, and these were not necessarily activities that freed the teacher. Thus the teacher often found herself doing the housekeeping chores while the parents worked with the children.

At the end of the year, the teachers prepared a questionnaire for parents about our open-classroom kindergarten. Those parents who participated as classroom volunteers were almost unanimous in expressing a desire for more in-service training. It is clear from our experience that great improvements can be made in the selection, orientation, and use of parent volunteers.

Classrooms

During the first year we were housed in the school's special education complex. This arrangement was not completely satisfactory for us, and there were complaints from our neighbors about the noise. The rooms were completely carpeted—not a good arrangement for painting, carpentry, clay, pets, or the home center. Our paint center and sand box had to be set up in the hall. Heavy pieces of equipment, such as television sets and film projectors, had to be brought from the main building. The room was far from the gymnasium and far from the bus loading zone.

This year we are more fortunate. The school district arranged to remove a part of the wall between two large rooms, leaving a column in the center large enough for our desks to stand back to back. This divider also served to stem the flow of traffic from our activity centers at the north end of the room to the quieter areas at the south end. Under the windows we now have a large carpet where the children play with blocks and run trucks and cars. The carpet helps reduce the noise.

Color Coding.   We found last year that the open classroom may appear to the unpracticed eye as sheer chaos. However, we also found that it requires far more organization and creativity on the part of the teachers than the traditional classroom. The mechanics of handling large numbers of children for routine tasks such as taking attendance, lining up, boarding buses, or passing out papers can stagger the imagination. We have alleviated the problem of identification by color coding. We use six colors—red, blue, green, yellow, orange, and brown. Each child has a name tag, a 2-inch square of tagboard that has a hole punched in the top and is reinforced with tape. The child's name is written in his assigned color on this tag. Each morning the tags are spread out on a table. One by one, as they enter the room, the children find their tags and hang them on a board lined with cup hooks. Theoretically (but rarely in practice!) the tags remaining on the table belong to absentees. By the first of December nearly all our children were able to recognize their names.

Next we carry the color coding a step farther, and teach the child to print his name in his assigned color. Until he learns to print his own name, someone else prints it for him. His name is printed in his color on all take-home papers.

At first the children put their completed work by color groups on a convenient table. Recently, a cooperative parent built a small, open-faced file with six shelves for us. Each shelf is painted white, except for the front ledge, which is painted one of our six colors. Now the children put their papers in this file.

We have found this system quite convenient. We use it for classroom grouping, mixing the colors periodically. We use it for clean-up, saying, for example, "If your name is written in blue or yellow, will you go to the block center and put the blocks away?" And we use it for lining up for the playground, buses, or gym.

Teachers.   The first year we opened school with one full-time and one half-time teacher for 115 children. In October, another half-time teacher was added. In November, a teaching assistant joined us. In late October the

P.E. teacher began to schedule weekly periods in the gym for our kindergarten classes. The music specialist came once a week throughout the school year. During the last month of school he worked with a group of fifteen kindergartners who were selected from our class of sixty-five children by a teacher. These children learned the descants to three songs in four fifteen-minute sessions. Under the music teacher's direction they sang harmony with the remaining fifty children in class, a performance much enjoyed by all.

It is obvious that not every teacher is suited for work in an open classroom. Some find the apparent chaos unnerving. Others lack the ability to respond creatively to unanticipated opportunities. Even when the teachers are wholly in sympathy with the open classroom approach, there are bound to be differences of opinion about teaching methods. In order for the teachers to develop into a smoothly functioning team, they must have time for discussion and planning. In actual practice, we have found that there is very little time for this, because each teacher is fully occupied all day, every day, with class activities.

Evaluation

The teachers and the aide spend as many hours as possible discussing philosophies and methods of teaching. We have found that our idea of combining structured activities with free-time activities is working well.

It was interesting for us to compare the children's choice of free-time activities in our room at the beginning and the end of the year. At first, approximately three-fourths of the class preferred activity centers where they could find physical, imitative, and manipulative activities. By the end of the school year, three-fourths of the children had moved to other parts of the room where the activity centers provided materials for practice in reading readiness, number readiness, and vocabulary development. They also visited the listening center, or centers where small groups could work on developing a specific skill or participate in creative activities with paper, thread, paint, or scissors.

The four first grade teachers who are now teaching last year's kindergartners report that these children are much better at working independently than are first graders who came from traditional kindergartens. This indication of success is most encouraging.

In spite of the limited time for observation, we were able to recommend that twenty children be assigned to a transitional first grade class this year.

We felt these children would not necessarily profit from another year in kindergarten, nor were they ready for first grade. A few children seemed simply immature, but most needed a concentrated enrichment or remedial program, or had undiagnosed handicaps.

When the reading readiness tests were scored, the teacher of the transitional class reported that these children were indeed unready for a regular first grade curriculum. By holding the enrollment to twenty, and by hiring a full-time aide, the school has been able to provide these children with an individualized program. Because we identified these children in kindergarten as unprepared for first grade, we can allow them time to develop the social, emotional, physical, and academic maturity they need before they are placed in a competitive classroom situation.

Because it is desirable, but highly unlikely, that the student-teacher ratio will be reduced, we believe that the open classroom is a practical, efficient, yet personal way to teach larger numbers of children with the use of paraprofessionals and volunteers.

We believe that the freedom of an open classroom provides a healthy atmosphere in which the child can mature with respect to himself and to others. Here, the social aspects of school are expanded far beyond those of a traditional classroom.

An open classroom provides teachers with many more opportunities to observe students unobtrusively and in different situations, than does a traditional classroom. Also, it seems likely that the observations of several people will enable teachers to make more accurate conclusions than they would be able to make on the basis of a single observation. Above all, the open classroom team-teaching method will work only if all the members of the team are willing to work and change together in the interests of providing better learning experiences.

Summary. We have discovered that in our open classroom we have a reliable means of discovering children's problems—observation by several people in a natural setting over an extended period of time. We feel that we have had reasonable success in identifying specific problems. We also feel we have had reasonable success in helping children deal with their problems through the open classroom.

Although the results so far have been encouraging, we believe that there are several ways in which the program could be improved. The teachers need more time for planning conferences, as well as for observing individual children, developing programs of individualized education, and executing these programs. The teacher should not spend time on sub-professional activities such as cleaning or playground supervision. Parent volunteers can provide much of this sub-professional assistance. However, because volunteers can also take up more of the teacher's time than they free, only effective volunteers should be used. These are people who are competent, willing to meet classroom needs, and able to give a substantial amount of regularly scheduled time to the class. If supplemental funds were available, a modest wage could be paid to some of these parents.

Another means of improving teacher effectiveness is the use of mechanical teaching aids. Devices such as listening centers, filmstrips, and tape recorders can be operated by parent-volunteers, or sometimes even by children, to provide well-designed individual and group instruction. A modest investment in such aids pays worthwhile dividends in teacher effectiveness.

Finally, the response of the specialists of the school system—the physical education and music teachers, the speech and physical therapists, and the psychologist—could be used more effectively than at present. Kindergarten problems are incipient ones that often respond readily to specialized treatment. But there is an unfortunate tendency for specialists to ignore the problems of kindergarten children because they are fully employed in trying to correct the problems of older children—problems, we must suppose, that would have been easier to deal with, and hence much more economically treated, at an earlier age.

16

Open Education–Dansville Primary School Version

William E. Brown   *Principal, Coordinator of Instruction, Dansville Central School District, Dansville, New York*

Description

Dansville Primary School, serving kindergarten, first, and second grades, opened in 1968. This building serves all pupils in these three grades who attend the district's public schools. The primary school has served as a visitation center for interested educators, parents, and architects, as well as for high school and college students throughout New York, seven other states, and three foreign countries. Several summer and school-year workshops have been conducted here. Many of the nearly 2,000 visitors have been asked their reasons for selecting Dansville as a visitation site, and their responses can be grouped into two major categories: (1) plant, and (2) program.

The school is designed in clusters composed of five groupings of three, four, or five classrooms each. Two clusters (seven rooms) are devoted to kindergarten children, one cluster to first graders, another to second graders, and the other to a multi-age group of first and second graders. The design of the building has had great impact on the nature of our program. Carpeting covers nearly every floor in the building, including the hallways and cafeteria. Rooms are designed without classroom doors or permanent interior walls. This attempt to create an open atmosphere is significant in terms of its impact on the educational program.

"Open education," that new catch-all phrase that we so glibly toss around, can mean everything or nothing at the same time. At Dansville, a diversified program has emerged in the Primary School. The utilization and development of our staff has been its most significant outcome. When teachers are thrust together to form a team, they must be compatible as well as productive individuals. Our teams have developed into cohesive units with unique styles. No two teams operate alike, and no one model exists that seems to be superior to any of their styles.

While some teams operate comfortably with a high degree of pupil mobility, others work best in a more restricted environment. There is no evidence to support the hypothesis that pupil learning and mobility within a classroom are related. The important factor seems to be, as always, the way a teacher deals with each individual and with the group. The kinds of experiences that are planned with, for, and by the learner remain top priority. Individuality may be as important for teachers as it is for students.

What successes can we claim in the past four years?

1. We no longer care if movable walls are open or closed. They are now used, as intended, to meet specific needs.
2. We now operate at a higher level of efficiency, in terms of planning and preparation time, than we have in the past.
3. Pupil mobility and grouping patterns are no longer rigid, but seem to develop spontaneously.
4. A higher level of pupil readiness has been achieved than ever before These

students, on the whole, are better adjusted to their freedom than any previous group.

5. Teachers are beginning to feel that the learning environment in some clusters is better suited to the needs of individual children than that in other clusters, and they are recommending that some youngsters be transferred within the school.
6. Material selection and use is more discriminating than ever before. Teachers know the material better and have prepared more items for individual pupil use.

Evaluation

Are there areas of weakness? Absolutely.

1. We still want to grant more freedom than most children are ready or able to handle. How do we find the right balance?
2. We have not developed sophisticated methods of tracking or monitoring student behavior. Using our present resources, how can we best gather all the important information about our students?
3. How can we better communicate to parents what school is like for their children today?
4. How can we be sure that the conflicting views of accountability and humanism are dealt with successfully?
5. Can we successfully handle individualized learning, despite escalating class size and fewer resources?

There are many more successes and questions. A progress report, after all, cannot confirm success or failure. It can only outline the growth in our understanding and approach to the complex problem of educating children in the Dansville Primary School.

17

Open Classrooms for the Kindergarten

Mrs. J. Graham *Kindergarten Teacher, Huron Public Schools,
Huron, South Dakota*

Description

Faced with prospects for larger classes, yet determined to tap the potential learning ability of every young child in my kindergarten, I realized I needed to change my teaching methods. To me, the following priorities seemed to be most urgent:

1. Individual attention
2. Up-to-date skills and lessons
3. Enjoyment of the learning process
4. Interaction among pupils and between pupil and teacher
5. Individual responsibility and opportunities for exploration
6. Good use of our classroom environment

"Open structure" is a method of teaching described in the book *Exploring Open Structure* by Virgil M. Howes. The book is published by the University of California at Los Angeles. Using this book as a guide for change, I have addressed the above priorities.

To enhance my method I use materials such as filmstrips, listening stations, flannelboards, manipulative games, materials for eye and hand coordination, reading readiness materials, books, puzzles, tapes, records, letter-form boards, phonovisual consonant sounds and games, and materials from the American Association for the Advancement of Science.

In order to determine the individual needs of each child, I use the first week of each school year as a testing period. Each child comes to enroll at an appointed time, and we then test his motor skills, auditory and visual perception, verbal expression, and vocabulary. Although the scores are not conclusive evidence of ability, the information I gather helps me to start grouping the children.

When arranging our four or five interest centers, I consider the needs of each child and change the centers accordingly each day. Tables, corners of the room, movable book shelves, and bulletin boards are used to separate the areas.

The following activities are found among the interest centers: science, phonovisual materials (workbooks and games), Winter Haven materials (shapes), number work, readiness materials (workbooks, shapes, and other prereading skills), writing names (spelling can be taught later in the year), handwork (cutting, pasting, coloring), balance beam, books, puzzles, clay modeling, manipulative games, listening stations, and flannelboards.

While the children are moving from one interest center to another as they choose, the kindergarten teacher is free to work with individuals or small groups that she feels need special help. The option of teaching on a one-to-one basis or working with as many as seven pupils simultaneously assures flexible instruction.

The open classroom program will not be successful without the use of aides because one teacher cannot supervise all centers. It is best to assign one aide to check the work in two areas and to urge children who stay too long in one area to move to another area. If a school has no finances for aides, volunteer high school students may be available. We have also used sixth-graders and mothers to assist with interest centers.

The most important outcome is individual attention for each child. The slow child can have extra help while the above-average child works on advanced material. This method gives students the responsibility to choose an area in which to work, and then to get their work done. Interaction among the pupils allows the children to develop an understanding of values they can apply to everyday life. If given the proper guidance, children can use their open environment well.

It is not necessary to use the open structure each day. Often it is preferable to present new materials to a large group. The net result of the open classroom system, however, is more individual help for each child.

Learning Climate

18

The Proper Social and Emotional Climate for Kindergarten

Pat Rinegar   *Kindergarten Teacher, Gertrude Burns Elementary School, Newcastle, Wyoming*

Description

In teaching kindergarten, it is a pleasant surprise to discover the immense potentials and capacities of five-year-old children. In Newcastle, teaching methods and techniques are geared to developing these potentials and capacities as far as possible, while keeping tension at a minimum.

It is my philosophy that a happy, contented, and relaxed child will learn because he wants to learn. In my kindergarten classes, I strive to create a happy, contented, and relaxed atmosphere for children in their first experiences at school. Just like first impressions, first experiences, too, are lasting.

The climate in which one child can work and feel at ease is just a little different from that of the next child, yet both need to feel relaxed and at home in the classroom. To find out how I can best create this feeling in each student and the group as a whole, I observe:

1. Does he work well with the class? If not, why?
2. Does he talk too much or hardly at all? If so, why?

3. Do other children leave him out of activities or include him?
4. Do changes in school routine upset him?
5. Does he do as I ask without apparent feelings of resentment?
6. Can he respond to feelings of love and caring without withdrawing?

Then I diagnose on the basis of these observations. How can I make each student feel that he is an important part of my class? I try to minimize differences and limitations, and capitalize instead on each child's assets. Actually, a teacher can establish a good emotional and social climate best through her attitude toward the class. Kindergarten students are extremely sensitive to meanings of facial expression. A kindergarten student "sees it like it is" and a kindergarten teacher must "tell it like it is." The teacher can do this best by presenting sincere attitudes that establish a social-emotional climate suited to the development of five-year-olds.

Evaluation

I use both formal and informal methods of evaluation. The report card, issued twice a year at parent-teacher conferences, is my primary formal method of program evaluation. It is also a good checklist for myself on individual children and on the climate within the classroom. Informal evaluation techniques are used constantly in the classroom. One method of evaluating the social and emotional climate in the class is to observe students' behavior and use of interest areas during the free play time. Another technique I often use is to pose questions and observe responses. The questions might be, "Why do we have rules?" or "What does the word *share* mean?" Reactions to these and other questions help me to evaluate students informally. Frequent and careful evaluations involving constant observation of each child are essential to a productive classroom and a good social and emotional climate.

Differentiated Staffing

19

A Differentiated Staffing Program for the Kindergarten

Allen J. Klingenberg   *Director, Instruction and Curriculum K–12, Independent School District No. 197, West Saint Paul, Minnesota*

Description

Public and non-public educational agencies across the country are facing a financial crisis as they attempt to make necessary improvements in school programs. Increasing costs, largely as a result of salary increases over the past decade, have caused extensive concern among both educational leaders and the taxpaying public. Public school teachers' salaries have recently increased an average of 28 percent for the state of Minnesota as a whole, and over 29 percent within the Twin Cities Metropolitan Area, according to the Minnesota School Board Association. If non-public and public schools alike are to continue to occupy their key role in advancing the progress of our society, serious and immediate attention must be given to these goals: (1) alternative sources of revenue, and (2) alternative and more effective uses of resources already consumed.

In order to achieve the second goal, Independent School District 197, West St. Paul, Minnesota, initiated a number of differentiated staffing projects through a grant from the Minnesota Project on Differentiated

Staffing. The Kindergarten Differentiated Staffing Program was undertaken for the following purposes:

1. To demonstrate that the quality of education offered students can be maintained or improved using differentiated staffing.
2. To demonstrate through differentiated staffing patterns that more effective use can be made of present resources, thus minimizing cost increases.

During the 1970–71 school year, Independent School District 197 initiated a differentiated staffing program in one school with control groups in two other schools. The average enrollment in the project classes was 58.5, and the average enrollment in the control classes was 31.6. Both the control and project kindergarten groups attended school for two-and-one-half hours each day and were provided the same readiness programs in reading, language arts, science, mathematics, and social studies.

The control classes were taught by regular classroom teachers, but the project classes were taught by a team consisting of the team leader, teacher intern, and teacher's aide. (The job descriptions of these staff members appear in Appendices A, B, and C.) The control groups were taught in standard classrooms of 900 or more square feet. The project kindergartens occupied two such rooms, one of which was used for quiet learning activities and the other for more strenuous activities. The specific readiness programs used in both the control and project classes were mathematics and science (Minnesota MAST and Addison-Wesley Kindergarten Program), reading (Ginn Kits A & B and 360 Level One), and social studies (Laidlaw materials).

Three hypotheses were tested in the Kindergarten Differentiated Staffing Program:

1. Project kindergarten children will score as high as those in traditional classes on a selected standardized test.
2. Kindergarten children taught by a differentiated staff will have as positive an attitude toward school as those taught by the traditional method.
3. The differentiated staffing approach to kindergarten instruction will cost no more than the traditional methods of instruction.

Methodology. Student learning was operationally defined as the performance of the classes on the McGraw-Hill Tests of Basic Experiences (TOBE). The project kindergarten class and two control classes were given these tests in early fall. The two control classes were not given the pre-test, in order to control the effect of the test on the project. The general concepts, mathematics, and language subtests were administered individually by the classroom teacher or team leader over a one-week period. The results indicated that there was no significant difference between the project and control groups on the pre-test. Each subtest consisted of twenty items. All control and project classes were post-tested in the spring. The following table indicates the post-test scores of the project and control groups.

	General Concepts Sub-test	Language Sub-test	Mathematics Sub-test
Differentiated Staffed Class	23.9	24.9	24.1
Control Class (No Pre-test)	24.0	25.0	24.1
Control Class 2 (Pre-test)	24.7	23.4	23.3

A student *t* test was used to compare the differences between the control and project classes. No significant differences were found.

Project kindergarten students' attitudes toward school were measured by parental responses on a questionnaire at the spring parent-teacher conference. The parents' responses to items two and three are relevant to the testing of hypothesis two. Of the ninety-six parents attending the spring conference, ninety-two indicated that their child's comments about the differentiated staffing project were positive. Two parents indicated a negative attitude and two parents gave no response. Random comments included:

- It was rough the first month or so, but from then on he was very enthusiastic.
- Her attitude is generally favorable; she has not had many complaints.
- He likes the things he has done, the painting and the other projects.
- He likes school and is anxious to attend each day.
- She has been very excited, talks about everything she does every day. She wouldn't miss a day, looks forward to school.
- Her general reaction has been excellent.
- He liked school. I don't think that the size of the class bothered him.
- He likes school and the other children.
- John's attitude has been most enthusiastic. He sings the songs he learned and works on letter sounds.
- Excellent. She is very stimulated by the learning environment in kindergarten.

In response to the question, "What are your comments about the kindergarten program as you understand it this year?", seventy-two parents made favorable responses, twenty-one made critical responses and three gave no responses. Random comments included:

- I think the program is good because the children are grouped. When they have teacher aides with them, the children can have extra help and it is more interesting to the children for learning.

- Very good. I like the individual help the interns gave—it seemed to work well.
- The teacher did seem to know my child quite well. I was concerned about that with such a large group of children.
- I feel much more was accomplished. The large size of the group didn't seem to matter.
- I believe that by having three teachers, each child can be evaluated from three different points of view. What one won't see, the other one will. Therefore, the child can be evaluated better.
- I think it's *great*. The program seems to be bringing out the best in my child.
- I thought the readiness program was excellent. I have been pleased with the materials and the program.
- I think that the first part was wasted by letting children learn how to get along with one another, but in the second part, I feel they really learned a lot. I feel quite satisfied with it.
- I liked the way it was set up. The children are certainly given ample opportunity to enjoy all phases of the curriculum. Kindergarten preparedness for first grade has definitely been upgraded. The program should prove to be a real asset.
- I feel they did a good job, considering the number of children involved.
- In all fairness to teachers and pupils, classes should be smaller.
- My general opinion is that the class is definitely too large to give each child the attention and help he needs.
- The groups were large, and there was neither enough flexibility, nor sufficient awareness of individual differences.
- I would like to see the smaller classroom reinstated using one qualified teacher instead of several helpers.
- Having had another child in kindergarten a few years ago, I feel that this way of teaching is impersonal by comparison, especially the switching of teachers among the children.
- The class size is too large, and there is not enough individual attention. The student doesn't identify with one teacher.

A cost analysis of the project and control classes was carried out using the average salary of all kindergarten teachers in the district. The average staff cost per student unit in the control classes was $146.69, but the average staff cost in the project class was $133.97. The cost saving per student unit in the project class was $12.72.

Results.   The results indicate that there was no significant difference in student learning between the project class and control classes as measured by the McGraw-Hill Tests of Basic Experience. The parents' responses indicated that their children were overwhelmingly pleased by the project experience, although the parents had some concern about the number of children in the project group. The cost analysis indicates that the staff cost per student unit was less in the project class than in the traditional classes.

Appendix A

Job Description for Team Leaders

Primary Function. The team leader heads the teaching team.

Line of Authority. The team leader is directly responsible to the building principal for his overall function and responsibility. He has a professional responsibility to the other members of the team and must maintain their confidence in his leadership. He has a staff relationship with the department coordinator.

Areas of Delegated Responsibility

1. He is responsible for the team's performance.
2. He is responsible for giving specific guidance to probationary teachers, interns, and student teachers.
3. He is delegated a share of the personnel responsibility of his teaching team, and he assists in hiring new personnel.
4. He is delegated a share of the responsibility for the development of objectives and the design of the curricula to implement them.
5. He is responsible for giving final approval to teaching assignments within the team.
6. He acts as a liaison between the school and the colleges or universities providing student teachers and interns.
7. He acts as a liaison between the school and the community.

Assigned Duties

1. While he is a team leader, he will retain student contacts as part of the teaching team and will work individually with students.
2. He will act as chairman for the team planning sessions.
3. He will work closely with the building principal in facilitating the operation of the program. This includes the scheduling of facilities and equipment, the grouping of students, and the assigning of duties to members of the team.
4. He will work for the improvement of the teaching skills and the expertise of team members, and he will demonstrate practical methods of instruction.
5. He will encourage experimentation with new ideas and instructional techniques, and he will assess the results of such experimentation.
6. He will interpret the needs of the program and make recommendations through proper channels.
7. He will effect procedures within the team that focus on the specific needs of individual students.
8. He will exhibit instructional skills, organizational skills, and skills in group and interpersonal relationships that reflect his position of leadership.

9. He will perform all other related duties necessary to accomplish the objectives of the total school program.
10. A new team leader may be elected by the team under the supervision of the building principal.

Appendix B

Job Description for Intern Teachers

Primary Function.   The intern teacher in Independent School District 197 is expected to instruct students while further developing his professional skills.

Lines of Authority.   The intern teacher is directly responsible to the classroom teacher to whom he is assigned. All District 197 personnel policies applicable to the assigned classroom teacher are also applicable to the intern teacher (except the fringe benefits).

Areas of Delegated Responsibility.   The intern teacher assists the assigned classroom teacher in diagnosing, prescribing, implementing, and evaluating classroom procedures.

Assigned Duties

1. He will work with children in large groups, small groups, and individually as the classroom teacher directs.
2. He will assist the classroom teacher in arranging, conducting, and evaluating parent-teacher conferences.
3. He will assume responsibility for diagnosing, prescribing, implementing, and evaluating the learning program of at least one individual student and one small group of students under the supervision of the classroom teacher.
4. He will plan, implement, and evaluate a unit of instruction covering approximately two weeks' time under the supervision of the classroom teacher.
5. He will take complete charge of the class for one week, performing all the tasks regularly done by the classroom teacher. The intern may ask the classroom teacher to assist with small groups and with individualization of instruction.
6. Under the guidance of the classroom teacher, he will measure, evaluate, and report the progress of a group of students.

7. He will participate with the classroom teacher in that teacher's District Curriculum Committee work.
8. He will perform any and (at one time or another) all of the administrative duties regularly handled by the classroom teacher.
9. With the classroom teacher, he will be responsible for maintaining the discipline necessary for a proper learning environment. However, the more severe discipline problems should be referred to the classroom teacher or the building principal for disposition.
10. He will become familiar with all building and district policies, procedures, and special services.
11. Under the supervision of the classroom teacher, he will be willing to innovate and experiment with more effective ways of educating children.
12. He will attend faculty meetings and cooperate with the entire faculty in constructive discussion and on school projects.
13. He will attend professional meetings and in-service workshops.
14. He will supervise students as requested by the classroom teacher.
15. He will perform such other duties as might be assigned by the classroom teacher.

Appendix C

Job Description for Teacher Aides

Primary Function. The teacher aide in Independent School District 197 assists the classroom teacher in instructing students.

Line of Authority. The teacher aide is directly responsible to the regular classroom teacher to whom he is assigned. (All District 197 personnel policies applicable to the regular assigned classroom teacher are also applicable to the teacher aide, with the possible exception of fringe benefits.)

Area of Delegated Responsibility. The teacher aide will assist the assigned classrom teacher in diagnosing, prescribing, implementing, and evaluating classroom procedures in the instruction of children commensurate with his level of training and experience.

Assigned Duties

1. He will work with children in large groups, small groups, and individually as the classroom teacher directs.

2. He will assist the classroom teacher by preparing equipment, showing films and filmstrips, playing records, leading small groups in discussion, listening, simple rhythms, and exercises.

Other Duties

1. He may assist the assigned classroom teacher in instructing students.
2. He may individually instruct students in a classroom setting upon the assigned classroom teacher's prescription and direction.
3. He may handle routine discipline problems arising in a classroom setting.
4. He may plan lessons with the assigned classroom teacher and present suggestions for innovation and experimentation.
5. He may supervise children during milk, rest, creative play, arrival, and dismissal.
6. He may assist in the administration of diagnostic tests.
7. He may help in room care and maintenance.
8. He may assist in recording student progress.

Qualifications

1. He must have at least a high school diploma.
2. He must have experience working with young children and a demonstrated ability to handle, control, and work with children.
3. He must have demonstrated an ability to assume responsibility.
4. He must have demonstrated an ability to get along with adults.

Use of Paraprofessionals and Volunteer Aides

20

Instructional Support Teams for a Kindergarten Program

Susan C. Parker   *Kindergarten Consultant, Richland County School District Number One, Columbia, South Carolina*

Description

Public kindergartens represent a relatively new venture in South Carolina. They symbolize the promise of the future in this state. Their very newness creates a climate that is hospitable to creativity and innovation. It is our belief that the utilization of instructional support teams is proving to be one of the most desirable of these innovations.

The early childhood program in Richland County School District Number One includes twenty-five kindergarten classes. Twenty-one of these are completely sponsored by federal funds and four are sponsored jointly by the state and federal government. The latter group meets in double sessions. In all cases, a serious effort is made to assist the children in reaching their maximum potential in areas frequently considered non-academic (physical, social, and emotional), as well as in those traditionally viewed as academic.

Each classroom is staffed by a professionally qualified teacher and at least one teacher aide. Two teacher aides are assigned to the classes on double sessions. The curriculum is designed with the interests and needs of the children in mind. We are concerned that these kindergartners learn to function effectively in group settings, improve their facility in communication, grow toward their maximum physical maturity, and increase their ability to respond to situations with appropriate autonomy. We are concerned, too, that they learn to develop curiosity in the world about them, think critically, and express themselves with that flair of originality we usually identify with the term creativity.

Classroom design must be compatible with the educational goals. Our design, therefore, presumes the establishment of learning centers and the daily provision of extensive opportunities for activity that, though discretely supervised, is genuinely self-motivated and freely selected by the individual participants. Our inclination is to minimize large-group instruction, emphasizing instead individual and small-group learning experiences. It is in this kind of classroom setting that the instructional teams will operate.

In his definition of the value of a true teacher, James Garfield spoke in 1871 of close student-faculty relations that are again being emphasized today: "Give me a log hut, with only a simple bench, Mark Hopkins on one end and I on the other, and you may have all the buildings, apparatus and libraries without him."

There can be no viable substitute for an effective teacher. This is particularly true when non-cognitive goals are included among the educational objectives.

It is our belief, however, that a sound early childhood education program demands more than good classroom teachers and teacher aides, important as they are. The services of what we call instructional support teams are also required. According to our design, these support teams include both professionally trained specialists and non-professional volunteers. Both groups are essential.

Professionally Trained Specialists

Among the professionally trained persons comprising the instructional support team are the following: consultant, music specialist, physical education specialist, nurse, psychologist, social worker, speech pathologist, learning materials specialist, and graphic art specialist. In addition, the home liaison workers and the bus drivers, though not *professionally trained* in the strict usage of that term, should also be included among these members of the support team. Some members of these support teams serve other federally sponsored school projects, devoting only part of their time to the early childhood education program. The following descriptions outline the responsibilities of these specialists.

1. *Consultant.* The consultant is responsible for supervising and coordinating the entire kindergarten instructional program. It is the consultant's task to work with the teaching staff both in their classrooms and in in-service training sessions to help them improve their skills. It should not be supposed, however, that the consultant will personally offer all of the instructional content in these in-service training sessions. Our plans have included enrollment in courses at the University of South Carolina (offered free to teachers and teacher-aides), lectures by specialists in areas of specific interest to the members of the teaching staff, field trips to observe other kindergarten programs, and sessions conducted by the teachers themselves.

In addition to coordinating the in-service training opportunities, the consultant is responsible for coordinating the activities of the instructional support teams. Teachers, however, need not request support team assistance through the consultant as intermediary. On the contrary, each teacher has a list of the entire support team and is encouraged to contact any member of the team when he needs assistance.

2. *Music and Physical Education Specialists.* The music and physical education specialists serve full-time in the early childhood education program. Each schedules regular bi-weekly sessions in the kindergarten classes.

The services of these specialists are utilized in three ways. First, they provide important counsel and training to the teachers in the areas of music and physical education. Thus, they play an important part in the total in-service training process. For example, these specialists help teachers set up learning centers in their classrooms. Second, they periodically visit the appropriate learning centers to serve as resource persons for children who choose to visit that learning center while they are there. And finally, they work with individual children, with small groups, or—on rare occasions— with an entire classroom in an organized, systematic manner.

3. *Nurse.* The nurse is responsible for establishing, operating, and maintaining programs for visual screening and for audiometric testing. She is also responsible for follow-up services to secure needed corrections in both areas. Further, she assists with arrangements for physical or dental examinations when screening procedures indicate such a need. Finally, she

consults with parents in their homes or at school regarding the general health of their children.

4. *Psychologist.* Available on a part-time basis, the psychologist observes children who have been identified by teachers as evidencing problem behavior. He then provides direct assistance to the child, and he offers counsel to the teacher as she continues to work constructively with the child. Wherever indicated, appropriate psychological instruments will be employed for additional assessment and evaluation. Also, the psychologist will refer individual pupils to other professional persons or agencies when he believes such assistance to be profitable.

5. *Social Worker and Home Liaison Worker.* Although there are significant differences both in training and function between the social worker and the home liaison worker, they share certain concerns. Both are interested in the social environment, broadly conceived, within which the kindergarten pupils live. Perhaps it would be helpful to compare the relationship between these two persons with the relationship that exists between the teacher and the teacher-aide. The teacher and the social worker possess certain requisite professional training. Each is assisted by valuable co-workers who are not required to have the same level of professional competence—the teacher by the teacher-aide, the social worker by the home liaison worker.

We have long recognized that the "whole child" comes to school. He is not merely a "mind," he is a person. And his learning potential is significantly influenced by his out-of-school environment. In many cases, it is imperative that the teacher know certain things about this environment if desired progress is to be made. In many cases, too, the school must establish a positive relationship with significant persons in this larger social setting if the educational objectives conceived by the school are to have a reasonably good chance of being realized.

The teacher, who is primarily responsible for establishing this desirable relationship between home and school, is free to call upon these resource persons for help in cases that seem to require special attention. The social worker may also wish to refer some families to other agencies in the community.

6. *Speech Pathologist.* Improving the child's skill in communication is one of our major educational objectives. Therefore, we have included a speech pathologist on the instructional support team. Our speech pathologist screens all kindergartners as early in the year as possible in an effort to identify those individuals with acute speech problems. The specialist will

work with these pupils during subsequent months. Equally important, however, is the opportunity for the speech pathologist to help teachers become more alert to signs of serious trouble in communication and to learn how to help others master with greater competence the basic communication skills.

7. *Learning Materials Specialist and Graphic Artist.* Although each child will inevitably respond to the learning situation in his own way, the effectiveness of the teacher's input into the teaching-learning experience has a profound influence on the final outcome. The learning materials specialist and the graphic artist work directly with the teaching staff. It is their responsibility to assist teachers in selecting and preparing suitable teaching materials for classroom use.

8. *Bus Driver.* For more than half a century, progressive educators have insisted that first-hand experience must be at the very center of the kindergarten curriculum. It is much more meaningful to bring the little white mouse into the classroom for the children to see and touch than it is to talk about little white mice. In like manner, it is more meaningful to drive children out to the busy airport than just to tell them stories of air travel. The provision of first-hand experience is of signal importance to kindergartners. The bus driver plays a vital role in facilitating field trips, and it is highly appropriate that he, too, be included among the members of the instructional support team.

By way of summary, we can make two observations concerning the professional members of the support team. First, these persons, in addition to other aspects of their assignments, are responsible for providing in-service training for the teaching staff. Indeed, in many cases this may be their most significant function. Second, although the members of the support team more often work as individual specialists with the classroom teacher and her pupils, there are occasions when the team meets in a conference session in order to deal with a problem situation. The staff conference enables the group to share insights and to bring the perceptions and expertise of their several specialties to bear on a given problem.

Non-professional Volunteers

The utilization of volunteers varies from school to school in the district; there is no uniform pattern. Special needs or interests in a given community may give impetus to a volunteer program in one school quite unlike that in another.

Volunteer services fall into one of three categories: volunteer parent assistants, male college volunteers, and high school and college students engaged in laboratory experiences for academic credit.

1. *Volunteer Parent Assistants.* At the opening of the fall term, parents are invited to volunteer their services in their children's kindergarten classes. The invitation takes the form of a checklist. Parents are invited to consider sewing doll clothes, constructing or painting equipment, playing a musical instrument for the class, providing transportation for or accompanying the children on field trips, and caring for a class pet during holidays.

2. *Male College Volunteers.* For many of the kindergarten children, the world of school is largely a woman's world, with few males present in leadership roles. For some of the children, virtually all of their world—both in school and out—is largely made up of women. We recognize, therefore, the need for male identity models in the school. Some college men have accepted our invitation to spend a part of each week in a kindergarten classroom as a volunteer leader, and this venture is presently in process of expansion. We believe that it holds much promise.

3. *Laboratory Students.* Several high school and college instructors use our kindergarten classrooms as laboratories for their own classes. At the college level, the students are generally enrolled in education courses. Among the high school groups, at least one is a class in home economics. These students come to our kindergartens as participants, it should be noted, and not merely as observers. They learn by doing, and in their doing they make a solid contribution to the educational experience in the kindergarten classroom.

In our judgment, the inclusion of non-professional volunteers in the early childhood education program is of real importance. The contributions of these members of the instructional support team fall in two main areas. First, they enrich the educational program itself. Their participation increases the number of caring adults in the lives of the kindergartners. This contribution alone is of major significance. Some of the pupils urgently need an adult who has the time and interest just to sit down and to listen. And in some cases, of course, these adults bring talents and skills into the classroom—talents and skills that would be absent had they not come. Second, the involvement of people from outside the school in the educational process serves to strengthen the ties between school and community. The establishment of bridges of this sort will almost certainly prove invaluable.

Evaluation

Our adoption of the instructional support team approach is too recent a venture to allow for critical evaluation. At this writing, less than four months have elapsed since the program was inaugurated. Already plans are being made for a reasonably thorough evaluation. At this point, only the most tentative observations can be recorded.

The teachers generally seem to endorse the instructional support team approach strongly, and they are seeking increasing assistance both from members of the professional support teams and from volunteers. This growing willingness on the part of the teaching staff to utilize the services of the support team is encouraging.

There can be no question but that a significant number of kindergarten children have been helped by persons representing the professional support teams. Although statistics are not yet available, supportive anecdotal reports are plentiful.

Volunteers are now being used in each of the three ways cited earlier in this report, and their use is increasing. Parents are involved in the program in various ways, laboratory students visit the schools regularly, and in some cases (particularly the college groups) they actually join the teachers in planning curriculum and teaching, and a few male college volunteers attend sessions on schedule.

Much more needs to be done to involve the volunteers, and most of this work must be done at the local level by principals and teachers. Local interest and initiative appear to be developing. Thus, the volunteer phase of the support team approach should prove increasingly successful.

In summary, available evidence does not enable us to substantiate claims of success for the instructional support team approach at this time. The evidence in hand, however, does offer solid encouragement. We are inclined to believe that the present design is generally a sound one and that its continued implementation will prove most beneficial to the kindergarten children in our districts.

21

Use of Teacher Aides in the Kindergarten

Marshia Emry   *Piñion Elementary School, Los Alamos, New Mexico*

Description

The practice of employing teacher aides in the public schools seems to be increasing every year. They can be of great help to the teacher at minimum expense. Teacher aides can be used in many ways. In a school that has three or four kindergarten teachers, the aide might be used by all teachers to do clerical work, such as keeping records, checking papers, mimeographing, cutting paper for art projects, mixing paint, and arranging bulletin boards. She may also serve as an arts and crafts supervisor in a resource room where children from several classes meet to work during their free time.

In our school system, however, the elementary schools have only one or two kindergarten teachers for both morning and afternoon sessions. In this situation it is best to have an aide who is an all-around helper. How an aide is used, of course, depends upon the need. The teachers must decide first on their program and then on the talents they will look for in an aide.

Procedure

Aide Application Form. The only requirement for employment as an aide is a high school diploma. The application form asks for a small amount of personal information and for a list of special talents, such as arts and crafts or music. Aides are also asked to state the grade level they would prefer working with and to list previous work experience.

Choosing the Aide. It is the responsibility of the teachers who will be working with the aide to select her. The teachers should review all the applications and set up interviews with six or eight people. The personal interview is most important because the personality of the aide should be one the teachers feel they can live with. If possible, it would be helpful to observe the applicants actually working with children. For our particular program, we decided that we would prefer someone who could play the

106

piano, had some experience in arts and crafts, and had some experience with children.

Using the Aide. The following paragraphs describe a program in which two kindergarten teachers and an aide work with fifty children in a two-and-a-half hour team teaching situation.

Our two classrooms are connected by a kitchen-workroom that allows teachers and children to move between rooms without having to go outside. Each child has a home room, although he spends time each day working in both rooms.

In September, after working with the children for about three weeks, we divided the pupils from both classes into four groups ranging from most to least mature. There are twelve to thirteen children in each group. During those first three weeks, the aide had worked with the children in both rooms so that she would be familiar with all of them, and they with her.

At the beginning of the day, the children report to their home rooms for attendance and Show and Tell. Then the children meet in their respective groups. Two groups (twenty-five or twenty-six children) go to one room where the aide directs an art activity, music and rhythms, or outside games. The remaining two groups go to the other room where each teacher works with one group of twelve to fourteen children. This academic work period consists of reading, number, and handwriting readiness. The work period lasts twenty to twenty-five minutes, then the groups switch. The children who have been working with the teachers now work with the aide and vice-versa.

Recess follows this fifty-minute period, then the children return to their home rooms for rest, snack, story, music, and social studies. It is during this time that the aide either works with individual children or prepares for the next day's activities. Working with the children takes precedence over housekeeping chores.

The individual instruction is part of a visual perception program that is best presented in a quiet place with no distractions. The aide can take charge of the children who need this attention and can work with them on a one-to-one basis while the teacher proceeds with the rest of the class. Because of this close working relationship, it is necessary that the aide really like children and have good rapport with them.

The aide sits in on planning sessions and is kept informed about children who have special problems, physical or emotional. For this reason, it is imperative that the aide not repeat anything of a personal nature which takes place at school. She is told this at the time of the interview.

Evaluation

We are pleased with the progress the children are making. The most mature children are much farther along in reading and number readiness than are their peers in regular classrooms. All the children are getting more individual attention because the teachers are able to work with small groups and because the aide spends time in the visual perception program.

Another advantage of our program is that the children in one group do not know what the children in another group are doing. Hence, there is no comparing or feeling left out as sometimes happens in a contained classroom. We also feel that sharing the children between teachers helped us to help them. Sometimes hearing another person's point of view concerning a child sheds new light on a problem.

Some of the advantages listed above result from team teaching. However, the major advantage—more individual attention—is possible only because we have an aide.

Working With Parents

22

Working with Parents in Project Follow Through

Bessie Chumley   *Project Director, Indianapolis Public Schools, Indianapolis, Indiana*

Description

Project Follow Through is a research and development program designed to provide continuity of instruction for Head Start children from kindergarten through third grade. A basic tenet of the program is that parents have the right and the responsibility to become involved in the education of their children. Therefore, parents play an important role in the classroom. In Indianapolis, parent aides are hired on a rotational basis for eight weeks each and are trained by another parent prior to entering the class.

The parent trainer also has a child enrolled in the project. She must have worked both as a parent aide and a teacher aide before she can apply for the parent trainer position.

Special one-week training sessions are held for all new parent aides. A typical training session will consist of:

1. A general orientation film and discussion of the total program. The film shows a busy classroom in which each adult is involved—teacher,

teacher aide, and two parent aides—and all the materials, techniques, and equipment designed for use in the Follow Through classroom are being used.

2. Since parents are primarily responsible for handwriting instruction, special emphasis is placed on teaching this skill. Parents are taught letter formation, capitalization, tracing, and other techniques. They learn how to use primary pencils, paper, and chalkboards. Every object used by students in the classroom is used by the parents during their pre-service training.

3. Parent aides who are selected as tutors are given special training which may include selection and preparation of material. Prior to the training sessions, teachers discuss specific problems with the parent trainer and will, in most cases, suggest appropriate teaching materials and methods. In other cases, several types of teacher-made or other supplementary materials are available, and the parent aide selects the ones she feels she will be able to use most successfully.

4. A tutoring manual for parents (developed by the sponsor, University of Kansas) also is reviewed and discussed during the training session. This brief booklet provides basic instructions for helping parents tutor their children at home, as well as in the classroom.

5. Parents are taught how to fill out the data forms and progress records which are kept on each child.

6. Daily planning sessions are an important means of coordinating the total classroom environment. Ways in which parents can participate in these sessions are discussed. One way of assuring parent participation is to ask the aides to report on their handwriting or tutoring sessions, to relate any significant gains made during the day, and to discuss any specific problems encountered with materials or students.

7. Sample materials, supplies, and equipment used in each classroom are available to parent aides during the training session. During their spare time they familiarize themselves with these materials.

8. The training session and parent participation in it are evaluated by a checklist and a short quiz. Parents are also asked to make a written evaluation of the session.

9. Each new set of parent aides must successfully complete one week of training and be able to train another set of parent aides during the final two weeks of their eight-week employment.

Follow-up on the initial training session is provided by the parent trainer as she makes weekly classroom visits to provide help and support to parents in the classroom. Weekly and biweekly in-service workshops provide additional training for parent aides.

The requirement of frequent attention and reinforcement for each individual child is difficult, if not impossible, for one teacher to meet if she must deal alone with an entire class of thirty or more children. In order to provide the necessary amount of individual attention, Follow Through classrooms are staffed by four adults. The lead teacher heads the team and generally takes responsibility for the reading instruction. The full-time teacher aide, a parent, usually takes responsibility for the math groups, and the two parent aides concentrate on handwriting, spelling, and individual tutoring. This team arrangement insures that every child receives the amount of personal attention and reinforcement necessary for him to learn at his maximum rate.

Summary

A program of parent participation is one of the key factors in the success of our Follow Through program. With proper training, the parents have become valued instructors in the classroom. Parents who have worked in the classroom are also extending the benefits of this program into the home situation. After firsthand experience in the classroom, parents are able to join professional teachers as partners in the education of their children.

Parents are employed in the classroom in a series of positions which lead to career opportunities. During the year, a parent serves for eight weeks in the classroom as a parent aide. This relatively short work period enables a large number of parents to have direct contact with the Follow Through program. At the next level, some parent aides are employed for an entire semester. Finally, some of those who have been semester aides are employed as fulltime teacher aides. The result of this sequence is a new kind of unity between school, home, and community, new opportunities for parents, and a new potential for individualized classroom instruction.

23

Ferguson-Florissant Home/School Program for Four-year-olds

Doris M. Stumps *Assistant Superintendent for Elementary Education, Ferguson-Florissant School District, St. Louis County, Missouri*

Description

The impact of a child's early experiences on both his ability to learn and to relate to others, is well documented. Beller, Bereiter and Engelmann, Goldstein, Gray and Kalus, Weikart *et al.*, and others have reported that preschool education results in (*a*) higher scores on tests of mental ability, (*b*) improved language usage and mathematical understanding, and (*c*) enhanced overall school adjustment. Both Gordon and Gray report that longitudinal intervention programs involving parents have shown maximum impact on the educationally disadvantaged child. In addition, most reports indicate that such programs foster a favorable attitude toward preschool programs on the part of parents.

The Ferguson-Florissant Home/School Program for four-year-olds is designed for all district four-year-olds and their parents, although environmentally disadvantaged children are the primary target group. *Environmental disadvantage* is defined here as that complex of environmental factors which makes it difficult, if not impossible, for a child to succeed in the school setting as it exists. Although the incidence of such disadvantage is highest among lower socioeconomic groups, it can be found to some extent in all segments of society.

The Home/School Program is based on the assumption that the child, the parents, and the school must be involved jointly in attacking the problem of educational disadvantage. The program has the following goals.

The child will: (1) develop a feeling of higher self-esteem as a result of experiencing success through appropriate instruction, (2) have a strong sense of identity with his parents because he is helped by them and observes them helping other children in the Saturday School, and (3) receive support at home for his work in school.

The parents will: (1) be more aware of the effects of the home environment on their child's development; (2) improve their ability to motivate and

112

teach their child, and (3) believe the schools want to, and can, attend to their child's individual needs.

The school will: (1) develop diagnostic instruments and learning activities designed to meet individual needs, (2) develop and successfully communicate to parents a description of those environmental factors that are most conducive to maximizing learning potential, and (3) develop an input system so that learning activities of the preschool program can constantly be changed as a result of parental and evaluative feedback.

Procedure

Program Planning. Initiation of a new preschool program should be preceded by (*a*) an extensive survey of the literature on early learning, (*b*) consultation with specialists in early childhood education, (*c*) a thorough assessment of local needs, and (*d*) study and observation of model programs with components that satisfy those needs. Groups represented in designing the program include the board of education, the superintendent's staff, elementary school principals and curriculum personnel, and kindergarten and primary teachers. Personnel from local related programs such as Head Start, Day Care, Education and Home Economics Departments of colleges and universities, as well as Health and Welfare agencies are also utilized.

Community Participation. Parents and other community members should be directly involved in program planning, operation, and evaluation. A Parent Advisory Council can be formed well in advance of the program's initiation. The Council, representing a cross-section of socioeconomic and occupational levels, can assist in assessing parent and community perception of the specific needs in preschool education, as well as in the identification of potential pupils. Direct communication of concerns and recommendations from area residents is solicited in order to continually refine program operation. The Council can make judgments from a community point of view on decisions regarding time schedules, parent training procedures, and information dissemination. Council members can interpret the program to community groups through slides and tape presentations or demonstrations.

Other methods of communicating with community members include: (*a*) a *Bulletin for Parents of Preschool Children* which is sent bimonthly to families with children up to five years of age, (*b*) Parenting Skill Sessions conducted by the Home/School staff and specialists in areas such as child guidance and physical skill development, (c) distribution to parents and other preschool educators of weekly Home Activity Packets, (d) press releases, and (e) observation and participation in Saturday Schools by the staff of other early education programs, by preschool teacher trainees, and by high school student aides.

Parent Contact.   Each child in the district who reaches age four on or before September 30 of the current year may enroll. Parents of potential pupils are contacted by a door-to-door canvass using current census information and responses to local press releases, or by announcements distributed by school children to families known to have four-year-olds.

Before the program begins, parents of prospective students attend an orientation session. The Saturday School and the Home/School program are described, and parental responsibilities are explained. These responsibilities include periodic participation as a parent-teacher in Saturday School, observation and participation in the home teaching session, and completion of the follow-up lessons assigned by the Home/School teacher. In general, the parents are concerned and willing to cooperate with the school when the plans are within the realm of their capabilities.

At the orientation meeting, parents complete a child performance checklist, *My Preschool Child.* The checklist includes approximately fifty specific behaviors in the areas of Personal and Social Development, Language and Concept Development, Physical Skill Development, and Interests and Experiences. Parents are asked to indicate the frequency with which they observe their child performing the task or displaying the behaviors listed.

Pupil Diagnosis.   Following the parent meetings, each prospective student receives an initial diagnosis. The diagnosis is based on a visual and hearing screening, a measure of intellectual functioning, a measure of receptive and expressive language, a measure of self-esteem, parent ratings, and a behavior checklist completed by the teacher. An analysis of the test results helps establish the extent of the need for the preschool program services, and gives initial direction in choosing appropriate learning experiences from the district's *Early Childhood Curriculum Guide Series,* and other resources such as *Intellectual Growth in Young Children* (Isaacs, 1966), and *Intervention with Mothers and Young Children: The Focal Endeavor of a Research and Training Program* (Gray, 1968).

In addition to the general assessment, procedures are available for the identification of learning problems due specifically to emotional disturbance, learning disabilities, physical handicaps, or underachievement. Problems so identified are referred to specialists for further evaluation and treatment.

Staff Training. Staff members in this program are experienced teachers of young children. They are employed half-time. They may need to be trained or retrained to teach to performance objectives determined to be appropriate through pupil diagnosis. Staff competencies that are required include writing and sequencing instructional objectives, designing learning experiences, diagnosing pupil needs, placing pupils along the continuum of objectives, and conducting small group and individualized lessons. In addition, staff members must be able to work as partners with parents, drawing upon potential parent contributions, as well as serving as a model teacher for them. These skills are developed through single objective training workshops, practical experiences with children, video tape analysis of teaching behavior, staff seminars on specific types of student problems, and curriculum writing sessions.

Saturday School. The Saturday program is planned to foster personal and social growth as well as intellectual development. Small group and individualized instruction is given in language development, math and science concepts, perceptual skills, physical skills, and the creative arts. The environment is structured for interaction by the child with other students, adults, and materials in a variety of problem solving situations.

Saturday sessions are held weekly for two-and-one-half hours. All program enrollees attend. Each teacher, assisted by parent-teachers, is responsible for a morning and an afternoon class of approximately twenty to twenty-five students each. Children work in groups of six to eight.

Saturday School is held in district kindergartens that are appropriate in terms of (*a*) accessibility to the target population, (*b*) space to accommodate a large group of children, as well as several small groups engaged simultaneously in a variety of activities, and (*c*) availability of materials and equipment which can remain in the facilities until the next Saturday session. There is space, too, for parents and other visitors who may wish to observe for a period of time before participating.

Learning Centers are set up. Each is designed around one theme and is supplied accordingly with a vast array of materials. There are centers for activities in mathematics, reading, science, cardboard carpentry, dramatics, listening, gross motor development, music making, and art production. Both the central theme and the materials change periodically.

The furnishings of the Centers are flexible. Each accommodates self-initiated independent investigation by several children, as well as groups of five or six learners and an adult engaged in a more directed learning experience. A round table, or several flat-topped desks moved together, fit most teacher-assisted lessons. Small desks, large cushions or hassocks, a couch, and floor stretch-out space may be used for independent or team activities. Hallways and unused rooms accommodate motor skill exercises and dramatics.

Training Parent Teachers. Parents are welcome to observe the teaching process several times before participating. They are also allowed to work with whatever part of the program is most familiar to them. Fathers as well as mothers volunteer. Before the start of the classes each Saturday, the Home/School teacher briefs each parent on his assignment, written out on a reference card. The Home/School teachers usually take major responsibility for mathematics and language instruction, while the parents work in other areas.

Additional parent training takes place during the Home Visit lessons, when the parent observes the interaction of his child and the instructor. The lesson that he is asked to conduct later in the week follows the same general procedures as the one he observed at home. Occasionally, it is suggested that a group of parents arrange to hold the follow-up activities in one home. A parent who has been particularly effective is asked to direct the lesson, thus providing a model for other parents.

Home Visits.   Home visits, an important outreach program component, are scheduled according to need. Some children in the Home/School Program may receive only one home visit, while those in the primary target group may be visited weekly. When any student needs a considerable amount of practice in the skill taught in Saturday School, home visits are scheduled. By the time such visits are made, the parent is acquainted with the Home/School teacher and is not usually threatened at the prospect.

Home visits usually last from thirty to forty-five minutes. They begin with some informal conversation and discussion of how the previous assignment was carried out. This review is followed by the new lesson, game, or other activity led by the instructor. The parents and younger siblings join in as appropriate. The teacher then leaves directions with the parents for a follow-up lesson.

Home Activity Packets and Lending Library. Home activity packets of ideas developed by the staff that make use of materials found around the home are given to parents each week. Periodically, learning activities developed by parents themselves are distributed to other parents through the home activity packets. The packets may also suggest sites and arrangements for field trips, for block group viewing of "Sesame Street," or for instructional group games and free play. Books, educational games, or other instructional materials are left in the home to assist the parent in his teaching during the week. The children are allowed to select items from among these to further develop the skills they are working on in the Saturday session.

Coordination with Regular School Program. Home/School teachers are invited to meet often with kindergarten and primary teachers of the school serving the area in which they work. Information regarding home visit procedures as well as knowledge of the child's learning needs is transmitted to the school staff. The Home/School teacher also spends some time working with the kindergarten program.

Ideally, the kindergarten staff has already established an individualized, small group instructional program based on diagnosed pupil needs. The regular kindergarten diagnosis will now be enhanced by the preschool battery, the Home/School teacher's recorded observations, and a parent evaluation form completed at kindergarten entrance. This information will provide for appropriate initial placement and will insure continuity in learning until additional data are obtained from the kindergarten diagnosis. In addition, kindergarten teachers receive in-service training on motivational and instructional techniques for working with the environmentally disadvantaged children, as well as those with other handicaps.

In the spring, prekindergarten children and their parents are invited in small groups to visit the classrooms they will attend that fall. The children participate in the program, and parents observe or assist as needed. The teacher then holds a question and answer session with the parents. Parents also complete the prekindergarten evaluation form, *Introducing My Child*.

Kindergarten and primary teachers have an open invitation to participate in Saturday School. They may also arrange to accompany the Home/School teacher on a visit to the homes of some of their future pupils.

Evaluation

Data indicate that early intervention is effective. Of the four-year-olds considered to be poor risks for school success, a substantial number made normal or greater progress in the eight-month Home/School Program.

Home/School Program Results

Test	N Making 8 or more month. growth
Peabody Picture Vocabulary	104
Merrill Preschool Language	122
Berry Test	94
Program N = 150	

Scores from one school in particular further support the effects of preventive intervention. On the Screening Test for Academic Readiness, administered in September 1970 at Central School, 76.5 percent of the kindergarten children, none of whom had the Home/School Program, fell below the 50th percentile on the district norms. When the test was administered in September, 1971, to kindergarten children, 60 percent of whom had attended the Home/School Program for four-year-olds, 62.6 percent of the population fell below the 50th percentile.

Although analysis of the data is not yet complete, the documented progress made by students, as well as the enthusiastic response of parents and children, has led to the development of a proposal and the subsequent funding for the Parent-Child Early Education Program (Title III, ESEA) with a longitudinal evaluation design. This program is based on the Home/School model, with an expanded component for handicapped children. It is now being implemented in all the Ferguson-Florissant schools.

Special Adaptations

24

An Experimental All-day Kindergarten Program

Katherine Henshaw *Primary Consultant, Sioux City Community Schools, Sioux City, Iowa*

Description

Current research, suggesting that young children can profit from early academic stimulation, has led to a reappraisal of what constitutes appropriate kindergarten education for Sioux City five- and six-year-olds. To achieve a stronger curriculum, we decided to extend the half-day program to a full-day. The additional time would allow us to provide sequential instruction in mathematics and reading without sacrificing individualized program activities and experiences. It was hypothesized that extending the kindergarten program from a half-day to a full-day program, with the consequent earlier identification and correction of visual, auditory, and motor deficiencies in the young child, could eliminate the need for additional readiness experiences in first grade.

A Title I B grant, secured under the Elementary and Secondary Education Act, afforded us the opportunity to conduct an innovative, experimental all-day kindergarten program for the school year 1971–72. Three Title I schools were selected for the experimental program and paired with three Title I control schools. In all, 150 children are involved in the experimental and control phases of the project.

Assessment Program.   The school psychologists and classroom teachers are conducting an extensive assessment program. A scale of social, emotional, intellectual, and motor skills was designed for use as one of the pretest instruments. This phase of evaluation was completed by the teacher. The Preschool Attainment Record, A.B.C. Inventory, Development Gestalt Test of School Readiness, and the Peabody Picture Vocabulary Test were administered in September by the psychologists. The same instruments and the Metropolitan Readiness Test are administered in May to measure student progress.

Statistical analysis will confirm or reject predicted outcomes of an all-day program. It is expected that the project will be extended for another two-year period. A longitudinal study will compare future achievement of students in the control and experimental groups.

Curriculum

The general kindergarten program is geared toward small groups and individuals, keeping whole group activities at a minimum. Because no one method of instruction is suitable for all children, the techniques and materials we use are varied and flexible. The same basic equipment is provided for all kindergartens in the system.

Half-day Kindergarten Program.   A typical kindergarten day includes the routine opening activities of roll call, pledge of allegience, marking the calendar and weather chart, followed by a work session. Interest centers include a housekeeping area, blocks and toys, art table, library corner, games, woodworking area, listening station, and a manipulation center consisting of alphabet letters and other flannel board materials, puzzles, clay, lego, cubes and cube design cards, peg boards and design cards, parquetry, bead stringing, and puppets. The physical education session comes next. It involves rhythm and movement exercises, games, stunts, folk dances, ball skills, rope skills, balance beam skills, and parallel bar skills. After a brief rest period, the half-day session concludes with music and literature activities. Field trips and the use of resource people assure firsthand environmental and social experiences.

Intellectual abilities are increased through the activities of the daily program. We present prereading and premathematics skills through a game approach with small groups or individuals. Reading readiness, alphabet, and kindergarten mathematics workbooks are available for teachers wishing to use them with selected children.

Experimental All-Day Program. The intent of the experimental all-day kindergarten program is to enrich, broaden, and build upon the existing half-day curriculum. In addition, planned, sequential instruction in beginning reading and mathematics is included. The skills influencing success in beginning reading and mathematics have been identified on the Prereading Inventory Check List and the Mathematics Readiness Inventory Check List. These checklists are shown here in their entirety.

Instructional activities and learning center activities in reading and mathematics are designed to fit the needs of students. Some children will complete the entire skills program, and others will master only a few skills.

Materials available for reading and mathematics activities include commercial reading readiness and mathematics workbooks, picture sets, flannelboard and magnetic letters, pictures and objects, Language Kits A and B, reading readiness filmstrips, Sight and Sounds Discovery Sets, consonant pictures, Kindergraph Kit, puppets, pegboards and design cards, cubes and design cards, games (Lotto, Picture Domino, Winnie the Pooh, Candyland, Chutes and Ladders, Spot the Set), literature and social studies films and filmstrips, book and record sets, plastic counting objects, First Talking Alphabet–Part I, alphabet sorting trays, alphabet fit-a-space, jumbo dominoes, numeral jig-saws, geometric shapes, and alphabet flashcards. Instructional activities and suggestions for teacher-constructed manipulative games appear in two locally-written curriculum guides: *A Curriculum Handbook for Teachers of Primary Readiness* and *A Curriculum Guide for Teachers of Kindergarten.*

The teachers are encouraged to write student-dictated sentences, experience charts, labels, captions, and news each day. Parent aides and upper grade volunteers can also be used to read to the children and to write their dictation.

Assessment of Skill Mastery. Ongoing evaluation through teacher observation and informal testing with manipulative materials determines the degree of skill mastery achieved by students. Each student's progress in mathematics and reading is charted on the check list inventories at various intervals throughout the year.

In-service. An ongoing in-service program for the experimental program teachers and principals is being conducted by the primary grade consultant. The consulting psychologist has also been involved with both experimental and control teachers for in-service training in test administration. Activities and experiences are described and demonstrated at the in-service meetings. Consultant demonstrations in the classroom provide additional support to the program.

Mathematics Readiness Inventory Check List

Name _____   *Year* _____

Skill _____   *Date Mastered the Skill* _____

Counts by rote through 30

Recognizes numerals and number words 0–10

Recognizes sets 0–10

Associates numerals 1–10 with the corresponding set

Understands ordinate: first to tenth

Compares two sets by one-to-one matching

Recognizes and names geometric shapes

Describes geometric shapes

Recites address and telephone number

Knows birthdate

Locates dates on the calendar

Recites the days of the week

Recites the names of the months

Identifies measuring instruments: ruler   yardstick   scale   clock

Arranges objects in order by: size   length   height
    Can explain why

Arranges objects in reverse order
    Can explain why

Needs Further Experience   *Little or No Understanding*

_____   _____

_____   _____

_____   _____

_____   _____

_____   _____

Prereading Inventory Check List

Name _____   *Year* _____

Skill _____   *Date Mastered the Skill* _____

Visual Perception and Discrimination
    Can copy patterns, designs, alphabet, words, and numerals
    Can match patterns, designs, words, alphabet
    Can classify objects according to size, shape, color, texture, and object
    Can detect likenesses and differences in objects, shapes, numerals, and letters
    Can identify objects, colors, alphabet, numerals, and sight words
    Can identify the letters of the alphabet in mixed order

Auditory Perception and Discrimination
    Can identify environmental sounds
    Can identify rhyme in verse and song
    Can identify consonant sounds
    Can identify pitch, intensity, and rhythm in sound
    Can follow oral directions with a minimum of assistance
    Can recall and recite poetry, stories, and songs
    Can listen to others without interrupting

Motor Skills
    Mastered most walking beam skills
    Mastered most balance board skills
    Mastered even rhythms: walk   run   hop   jump
    Mastered uneven rhythms: gallop   skip   slide
    Mastered ball skills: throw   catch   bounce

Coordinated Eye-Hand Movements
    Can use the scissors with ease
    Can work puzzles, parquetry, and peg boards
    Can stay within the lines when coloring and painting
    Can copy and write the letters of the alphabet

Language Skills
    Can express himself verbally
    Can recall and recite stories, songs, poems
    Can tell a story in sequence using pictures, objects, and experiences
    Can use a large vocabulary including contemporary terms

Has Good Thinking Skills
    Can tell main idea
    Can make inferences
    Can classify and generalize
    Can recognize and interpret emotions

Needs Further Experience   *Little or No Understanding*

_____   _____
_____   _____
_____   _____
_____   _____
_____   _____

Suggested Schedule for the All-day Kindergarten

Approximate Time	Activity	Student Involvement

9:05 A.M.	Opening activities
	    Lunch count
	    Pledge of allegiance
	    Roll call
	    Calendar and weather chart
		Total group

9:30	Planning session Preparations for the day	Total group
9:45	Emphasis for the day	Total group

	Select from one area:
	    Science
	    Social studies
	    Mathematics
	    Human relationships
		Small group (Small group activity concurrent with planned, independent activities)

10:15	Music
	    Singing games
	    Singing
	    Rhythm band
	    Records
		Total group

10:45	Activity centers
	    Self-selected activity at various centers
	    Teacher instruction center activity (remedial, corrective, and enrichment)
	    Art projects
		Individual, small group, total group

11:45	Lunch preparation	Total group
12:00	Lunch	Total group
12:30	Clean-up and restroom	Total group
	12:30–1:30 P.M. Teacher's free time	
	12:30–1:30 P.M. Class under direction of a paraprofessional	
12:45	Rest	Total group
1:30	Directed physical education	Total group
	Intensive directed activities (30 minutes)	Small group, individual

2:15	Language arts
	    Reading readiness*
	    Poetry and finger plays*
	    Story*
	    Literature filmstrips*
	    Dramatization*
		Small group (concurrent with independent work)
		Total group

3:15	Conversation and free play Individual conferences	Individual (concurrent with small free-play groups using large toys, slide, playhouse, blocks)
3:30	Evaluation and a look at tomorrow	Total group
3:45	Dismissal	

*30 minutes

Summary

Comment on the all-day program is favorable. Teachers have said that they feel less pressure to get everything worked into the day's schedule. They are finding it possible to pursue more long-term projects which do not have to be disassembled each day in preparation for the next group's arrival. More time has meant opportunities for many field trips to points of interest in the community. The teachers agree that the children in the all-day program appear more relaxed, friendly, and able to meet people outside the classroom, when compared to past groups who attended only half-day sessions. Additional time has been scheduled for students to initiate and pursue individual, self-selected activities. The all-day program has made it possible for the teachers to converse frequently with individuals and to provide remedial and enrichment activities on a one-to-one basis.

Parents have reacted favorably to the all-day program, stating that many of their children want to attend school all day. This reaction was expected, because parents of the three experimental schools were given the option of enrolling their child in the all-day program or the half-day program. Although teachers have noticed fatigue in some children attending the full-day session, parents have not felt this to be a problem.

Development of an all-day kindergarten curriculum for Sioux City youngters was based on the premise of beginning instruction at the child's present level of development, and providing informal and formal activities and experiences which lead him to the mastery of a continuum of cognitive, motor, and social skills. Overall success or failure of the all-day program versus the half-day program must await statistical analysis. The follow-up study, to be conducted over a two- or three-year period, should provide further insight regarding the value of the full-day kindergarten program.

25

The Use of Structured Tutoring Techniques in Teaching Low-Achieving Six-year-olds to Read

Grant V. Harrison   *Brigham Young University,*
Vern Brimley   *Provo School District, Provo, Utah*

Description

Teaching children to read is fast becoming top priority in many school districts as the federal government's emphasis on reading programs stimulates new interest in this perennial problem. All too often, when large amounts of Federal monies are made available to solve a particular educational problem, the proposed solutions are financially out of reach for most school districts. Consequently, they are rarely ever used.

The prime objective of this study was to devise a highly individualized beginning reading program for low-achieving six-year-olds that any school district could afford.

Previous research has demonstrated the effectiveness of *structured tutoring* using student tutors to help low-achieving primary grade children master basic math concepts. Structured tutoring utilizes principles of learning which have been identified primarily with programmed instruction. The tutorial procedures are carefully prescribed. They conform to the basic principles of programmed instruction, but allow for maximum sensitivity to the individual learning characteristics of the individual child. Structured tutoring has proved to be a form of individualized instruction, providing a degree of flexibility that has previously been possible only through computer scheduling. Two features of structured tutoring make it far superior to previous forms of individualized instruction. First, teachers can both require and monitor oral responses. Second, the cost of implementing a structured tutoring program in a school is nominal after initial development.

Reading, more than any other subject, requires individualization if low-achieving students are to succeed. However, unless the programs are reasonably priced, it is doubtful that reading instruction for low-achieving students will be individualized.

126

Procedures

In order to control for major variables, the study was conducted during the summer when the children were not attending school. We were thus assured that the children were not receiving any formal reading instruction other than in conjunction with the study.

Three schools in the Provo School District (Provost, Rock Canyon, and Wasatch Schools) identified prospective first graders who were considered low-achievers based on their performance in kindergarten and on various tests. These children were then given an individual criterion-referenced test to determine whether or not the child could do the following: (1) name designated letters of the alphabet, (2) read designated sight words, (3) produce the sounds of designated letters and digraphs, (4) read designated words that could be read phonetically, and (5) decode nonsense words composed from designated sounds.

The criterion-referenced pre-test established the following: (1) seven children could name designated letters, (2) three children could read designated sight words, (3) none of the children could produce the sounds of designated letters and digraphs, (4) none of the children could read the phonetic words, and (5) none of the children could decode the nonsense words.

Lists of upper-grade elementary students who wanted to be tutors were obtained from each school. From these lists one tutor was selected at random for each six-year-old student. One aide was hired and trained to supervise the reading program in each school. Their responsibilities included training student tutors to teach the following five items: names of letters, sight words, sounds of letters and digraphs, sound blends, and how to decode words. The aides were trained to: (1) use validated structured tutoring techniques commensurate with each instructional role, (2) arrange the schedule for the children being tutored, (3) make prescriptions for the individual children, (4) record each tutoring activity, (5) test individual children for skill mastery, (6) maintain individual profile sheets for each child being tutored, and (7) monitor the student tutors to assure that they were following the prescribed tutorial procedures.

The initial instruction each child received was specific to his needs as indicated by his performance on the diagnostic pre-test. The instruction of each child was systematically monitored to insure that he was not allowed to move from one segment of the program to the next until he had mastered the preceding segment of instruction. Individual profiles were maintained on each child, showing the child's performance on the pre-test and the date he achieved specific criteria. In addition, the supervisors maintained a daily log on each child, describing the material covered and commenting on the child's performance.

Each tutor was trained to work with a child on a specific prescription until he felt the child had mastered it. The tutor then reported to his supervisor, and the supervisor checked the child. If the child demonstrated mastery of the prescription, the supervisor gave the student tutor another prescription to teach. Each time he achieved a criterion, the child placed a star on his profile sheet. As further reward, the student tutors were trained to send notes home to the parents of the child, saying that the child had learned a particular letter sound and praising his work. The children were tutored for fifteen to twenty minutes a day, five days a week, for six weeks.

At the conclusion of the study, each child was given a criteria-referenced test that measured his mastery of the five objectives. Pre- and post-test scores, learning gains, attendance, and a summary of criterion achievement for each school were utilized in the analysis process.

Discussion

The use of student tutors in a structured beginning reading program for low-achieving six-year-olds seems feasible based on the results of this study. At the end of the program, all thirty-three children could name designated letters and read designated sight words. Twenty-eight of the children could produce the sounds of designated letters and digraphs. Nineteen could read designated phonetic words, and fourteen could read five out of eight nonsense words. The students' ability to read phonetic and nonsense words is most significant because several of the students did not receive instruction on blending and decoding. A large majority of the students who received individualized help with blending and decoding came very close to criterion or achieved criterion on the final two objectives. When these results are viewed in terms of whether or not the students received the various prescriptions, the results support the basic premises that were being investigated.

The potential of this approach for individualizing reading instruction is underlined by the fact that of the thirty-three children that ranked in the lower one-third of their kindergarten class in terms of achievement and reading readiness, only five were so ranked by their first-grade teachers.

Another significant point can be made by comparing the achievement of students at Rock Canyon with that of students at the other two schools. The entering skills of the children at Rock Canyon were considerably higher than those at the other two schools, yet the final achievement of these children was lower. We discovered that the aide at Rock Canyon had been involved in another tutorial project previously and had formed some definite opinions about tutoring—opinions that were not commensurate with structured tutoring. Consequently, she did not follow the prescribed program nearly as closely as did the other two aides.

Tutoring at all three schools was monitored throughout the summer in an effort to assure that the prescribed program was being followed. Although no specific data were collected along these lines, it is apparent that students achieved in direct proportion to the degree the program followed the prescribed format.

26

Multiage Grouping in Early Childhood Education

Kenneth Hensell   *Project Director, Principal of Belle Benchley School, San Diego City Schools, San Diego, California*

Description

"Thank you for letting me have more time at school!" was a four-year-old boy's response to the news that his teacher had just lengthened the school day by twenty minutes. Now the prekindergartners were in school as long as the kindergartners.

This boy is one of thirty children in a class of ten prekindergartners, ten kindergartners, and ten first graders. The class is one of nineteen in San Diego City Schools funded through a three-year ESEA Title III grant to test the idea of multiage grouping with emphasis on individualized learning and continuous progress.

The hypotheses of the experiment are as follows:

1. After three years in the program, those who entered as four-year-olds will exceed first graders in control classes by eight months on standardized reading and mathematics tests.
2. Five- and six-year-olds will have more positive attitudes toward school and will have made greater social growth than their counterparts in control kindergarten and first grade classes.
3. Four- and five-year-old experimental students will show measured readiness for reading and mathematics.
4. The experimental teachers will increase their abilities to individualize instruction by ten percent each year.

Development of the Project.   In the spring of 1970, the early childhood consultant for our district was talking with the teacher of a combined class of kindergartners and first graders. She suggested that the teacher might want to try a class of kindergartners and first and second graders next year. Instead, the teacher suggested trying a grouping of prekindergartners, kindergartners, and first graders. The principal approved the project, and before school was out in June, district approval had also been granted. No money was available to finance the preschoolers. Fortunately, however, the school remained low on the staffing formula that year and accommodated eight prekindergartners without overloading any teacher.

The chief reason for choosing multiage grouping was to help both children and adults break out of the constraints of grade level thinking. We realize that each child is a unique individual, but we have not traditionally organized our schools in keeping with this knowledge. Even our graded textbooks deny individual differences. In a class composed of children from two grades, the teacher can still teach the curricula of both grades. When a third grade level is added, however, the task becomes so difficult that the teacher gives up trying to separate the children by grade. Instead, she treats the children as individuals, and allows them to learn as individuals.

Children, their parents, the teacher, administrators, and visitors were so pleased with the original program that a group was called together in November, 1970, by the special projects office to write a proposal for an ESEA Title III grant to extend the scope of the pilot project. Parents, teachers, administrators, and a consultant worked diligently and met the application deadline. By June 1971, we were assured of funding.

Provision was made to include one class in a private, nonprofit school. Because of the short lead time, it was not possible for such a school to reorganize, so none participated. With more advance planning, it is quite certain that a private school will participate in the future.

Staff Development. In order to prepare nineteen teachers for their new assignments, we scheduled a summer workshop. A group of thirty children was solicited from the Benchley School community to attend a six-week summer session taught by the teacher who had just completed the first year with the pilot class.

During the second through fifth weeks, the early childhood consultant conducted a workshop for the teachers at the summer school site. The teachers discussed theories, examined various curriculum materials and equipment, and participated in the learning experiences with the children attending summer school. They listened to the philosophy of the pilot teacher and learned her strategies. Each teacher tried out her own ideas, too, and decided what materials and equipment to purchase with her allotted $600.

The nineteen teachers held monthly meetings after school in their classrooms on a rotating basis. Occasionally, an outside resource person presented new ideas. Usually there was time for each teacher to share one of her own innovative practices.

The teacher who had taught the pilot class and the summer school class became District Resource Teacher for the project. Her function was to assist the nineteen teachers in any way they might request. She was the glue that held the experiment together. She took the class of each teacher for a day in order that each one might visit other project classes. She provided reassurance and solutions when things weren't going just as the teachers thought they should.

Each teacher trained her own instructional aides—either college students or people hired from the community—as well as students, parents, and other adult volunteers. This system was preferable to group training because both school neighborhoods and teaching styles were widely diverse.

Teachers were enthusiastic about their new roles. Many said they would never want to go back to teaching a straight grade in the traditional manner. Two teachers indicated that this was the first time they had been able to be themselves in the classroom. One teacher who came to a project school in order to teach the multiage class admitted she had difficulty adjusting to the new approach. After the problem time was past, I asked how she was doing. She replied that she never thought teaching could be so much fun. The secret, she said, was "letting go." The nineteen teachers in the project reflected a wide range of experience. Four were in their second year of teaching. One was near retirement. Not all teachers were eager for the assignment. In a few cases they were asked by the principal to take a class.

The key to the success of this multiage, individualized learning, continuous progress experiment was the attitude of the teacher. And the attitudes could change, as the teachers themselves proved.

How the Program Operates.   Each teacher was encouraged by her principal and by the project support staff to conduct the class in her own style, just as each teacher accepted the diverse learning styles of her pupils. All teachers were striving for an open classroom.

The school day started for each child the minute he arrived. He might enter the classroom and choose what he wished to do from the vast array of materials. The teacher greeted each child as an individual rather than as part of a line of girls or boys who queued up outside the room when the bell rang. For the first part of the day, up to one hour after school officially started, the children continued to choose what they wished to do. Gone was the puritan ethic which dictated that they must do what the teacher wanted before they could do what they wanted. Teachers reported that behavior problems were not developing as they had in the more conventional classrooms of their previous experience. Children moved about the room freely. They talked with one another, and they helped one another. Some concentrated on their own reading or math, seemingly unaware of the din of purposeful noise that filled the classroom. Adults were available to help the teacher—her instructional aide, a parent or grandparent volunteer, sometimes a child from an upper grade, high school students, even a visitor.

A Typical Day.   Sometime during the morning, classes held the routine opening exercises. One teacher scheduled them just before the four- and five-year-olds left at noontime. This activity included the flag salute, a patriotic song, weather report, news items, and discussion of current events. Some teachers conducted this part themselves, and some asked the children to conduct the activity, taking turns. Usually, following the initial choice period, there was a work time when the teachers, aides, and volunteers helped a group of children with reading or readiness activities.

Time was also scheduled for social studies, science, music, writing, and physical education. Some activities were designed for the whole class, others for small groups or individuals. As a result of these arrangements, the role of the teacher changed. She no longer was the teacher as director.

She was now the organizer, the helper, the coordinator of services that many other people had to offer.

Fathers often came to help. In one class I spoke with a young father who was working in the grocery store with a group of children. He said that his wife was ill and unable to come to school that day, so he had come as her substitute. Later in the morning he took a group of children to the cafeteria for a reading period. Another father visited this child's class one day and was so enthusiastic about what he saw that he told the teacher, "I'm coming here every month on my day off. I've got to get home early so my wife can come, too." He did.

Reporting Progress to Parents. In addition to at least three meetings with parents of children in the multiage program, teachers also held conferences with the parents of each individual child. Most teachers preferred the conference to a printed report form for first grade children. Fortunately, the prekindergarten portion of the program is so new that no one has had time yet to devise a reporting form for it.

Letters from Parents

At the beginning of the year, each teacher held separate meetings with the parents of each age group. The chief concern of parents of first graders was whether their children would get the same work as children in a regular first grade class. The teachers assured them they would. Then, as parents visited the classrooms and talked with their children at home, they discovered that the children were not only learning as much as students in a regular room, but that they were learning more. The following excerpts are taken from letters written by parents of first grade children:

- My child used to come home tired, but now he comes bouncing in full of pep.
- The opportunity to help the prekindergartners has greatly enhanced his self-esteem and improved his attitude towards school. Each day now he looks forward to going to school.
- Multilevel grouping is, in my opinion, one of the greatest innovations brought to our school. My daughter, Keri, is a first grade student in the program. She enjoys the freedom of movement around the room, the flexibility, the responsibilities of "teaching" the preschoolers. She is proud of the fact that she can move into a second grade math book now after finishing her first grade book. She is proud of her reading accomplishments. In short, she feels comfortable in the room; it is natural. There are learning experiences all around, and nothing seems forced.
- Perhaps the most impressive side effect of the program is the involvement of

parents and community. The carry-over between the home and school is beneficial to all members of the family. Better than anything, though, has been Brad's changed attitude toward school and learning.

We feel the concept of individual progress and the emphasis on both freedom and responsibility suits Brad's personality (and that of most children, I'm sure) in particular. The lack of restrictions on moving around seems to me especially conducive to learning.

- I praise this program, having seen the results with our child: (1) A happier, more at ease child. (2) A child who has not lost a sense of competition but gained a better understanding of herself as an individual. (3) A child who has been able—and eager—to do work above her grade level. She is ready for it whether the school is or not! (4) A child who is more at home with a wider age group than before. I have only one reservation: what is going to happen to our child if she has to return to the traditional system and fill a niche and role that she has already abandoned?

Parents of kindergarten children wrote these comments in their letters:

- I am a firm believer in children's civil rights. It is extremely important to me how my children are talked to and treated by other adults. I am opposed to children being controlled and suppressed by adults arbitrarily exercising power and authority. Because of these beliefs I have especially appreciated the attitude of my son's teachers towards children and their method of dealing with them. They listen to the children, and they also talk to them in ways that do not put them down and damage their self-esteem.

- This program also seems to have eliminated authoritarian methods. The children are allowed to assume more responsibility for their own behavior as well as for the behavior of others. The teachers trust the children to be responsible and self-disciplined, and the lack of discipline problems in the classroom would seem to justify that trust. The main rules that I have seen enforced are (1) no one has the right to interfere with another's learning, and (2) no one has the right to physically harm another.

I also appreciate the absence of the use of rewards and punishments as incentives to learn. I feel such a system invariably results in some students "winning" and many others "losing." This is a program that gives children more freedom to learn on their own and at their own pace. They experience success and a sense of accomplishment. It offers more opportunity for individualized instruction and it encourages the children to act as teachers for one another.

My own son has benefited greatly from his experiences in this multiage class. He is developing self-reliance, self-motivation, and most importantly in my opinion, self-acceptance.

I believe this new educational program can improve our schools. I welcome it and encourage our administrators to continue trying out and testing its effects.

The following excerpts are taken from letters from prekindergartners' parents:

- I was fortunate to have a child born five days after the kindergarten entrance cutoff date, otherwise she might not have had a chance to be in such a fantastic program so young. I hope my children can be in multiage classes through first, second, third, and fourth grades.
- He is not afraid to try new things. If he has difficulty, he will say, "I haven't learned to do it yet," instead of, "I can't." Parent involvement has helped us.
- He is so excited about all he has learned. Instead of coming home exhausted, as I thought he might, he comes home elated. This is a real credit to you and the relaxed learning atmosphere you have created.
- Who would believe a four-year-old and a six-year-old discussing Lincoln and the Civil War? Who would believe a four-year-old spending time each day reading to his two-year-old sister? Who would believe a first-grader balancing his mother's checkbook? We would—after seeing them in our own family in the last few months. Both boys are excited about school and hate to miss. They count the days until vacation is over. When asked to name the worst part of school, the first-grader could think of nothing, and the four-year-old said the worst part was trying to decide what to do first. For our children, school is exciting and learning is fun.

27

Developing a Guide for Early Childhood Education

E. Alma Flagg   *Assistant Superintendent, Curriculum Services, Newark Public Schools, Newark, New Jersey*

Description

A concern for the education of preschool children has been present among the staff of the Newark Public Schools for many years. Perhaps its earliest expression was the establishment of a prekindergarten class at Cleveland Elementary School in 1964 with the support of the Victoria Foundation. Since that time, the Board of Education has set a policy for providing prekindergarten facilities in all new primary schools.

In accordance with the policy enunciated by the Board of Education, the Department of Curriculum Services committed itself to developing an instructional guide for early childhood education, embracing a two-year span because prekindergarten material was needed for the new level, and there was a great need for additional kindergarten material. The department decided that teachers should be familiar with children of both levels— their characteristics and needs, the experiences and materials conducive to their sound development, and the need for continuity in their living-learning process.

With all these things in mind, a committee that included prekindergarten and kindergarten teachers, Head Start and Follow Through personnel, and the Director of Elementary Education was formed to write the guide.

Procedure

The Early Childhood Education Committee held a series of meetings aimed at understanding the nature and needs of four- and five-year-old children, the content through which they could best learn about themselves and their world, and the learning experiences which would have both present meaning and future value. They concerned themselves with physical and mental health, and with the family because of its vital role—social, economic, ethnic, and moral—in the life of the child. The young child, they realized, must not be regarded as an empty pitcher or a blank page. He comes to school with a culture, a heritage, and a wide variety of experiences.

The committee members developed goals and delineated areas of instruction. They consulted parents, aides, and other teachers in addition to observing the children with whom they worked daily. In a sense, all the city's teachers of young children were involved in developing the curriculum guide.

When the committee had produced a tentative document, it was distributed to teachers throughout the system for comment and criticism. The teachers who reviewed the work were professional and practical in their criticisms and in their suggestions. Their comments were carefully read, discussed, and acted upon. The additions, modifications, and refinements in the guide reflected the thinking of teachers all over the city.

Results

The document *Early Childhood Education: A Guide for the Prekindergarten and Kindergarten Years* was adopted by the Newark Board of Education on September 30, 1971. It treats these topics: Goals, Learning

Environment, Self-Image, Evaluation and Record Keeping, Language Arts, Mathematics, Science, Social Living, Arts and Crafts, Music, Health and Safety, Motor Coordination, Auxiliary Personnel, Parent Involvement, and Multi-Media. The mention of specific subject areas is not meant to suggest compartmentalization, for we recognize the importance of integrated learning. However, the teacher as leader needs to know the specific goals that she hopes to achieve while she manages an interesting living-learning situation. The guide contains suggested schedules, sample lessons, vocabulary, and an evaluation sheet which is useful in observing and understanding pupils.

When any new curriculum guide is distributed in Newark, there is an orientation process for those who will use it. The planners, writers, and appropriate administrators are involved in this process. We hope this encourages its wise and effective use.

It is still too soon to judge the usefulness of the Early Childhood Guide. It is certain to be followed by a supplement or a handbook to provide additional material teachers need. Parents, too, are becoming more and more involved. The development of community schools in Newark points toward greater cooperation among parents, teachers, pupils, institutions, and agencies for the better education of our youth.

28
A Flexible Planning System for the Kindergarten

Patty Withrow   *Primary Specialist, Norfolk City Schools, Norfolk, Virginia*

Description

There is no dispute over the need for effective planning in any successful school program. There often is a problem, however, in defining the ingredients of meaningful planning. Teachers in the Kindergarten Program of Norfolk City Schools have designed a new approach to daily classroom planning, as well as redesigning the curriculum guide currently in the process of development. Some of the difficulties teachers encountered in planning the daily kindergarten program included:

1. Planning the school day for the most effective use of time
2. Adapting the variety of activities to specific learning needs
3. Devising a planning format which would be followed and understood readily by paraprofessionals, volunteers, substitute teachers, and classroom observers, as well as by the classroom teacher
4. Planning a system that would be flexible and easily adapted to those unanticipated teachable moments
5. Creating a system which would reduce the amount of valuable time teachers spend writing plans for frequently repeated activities

The School Day. Planning for effective utilization of time within the school day presents challenges for both full-day and part-day programs. In Norfolk, one recent school year proved to be especially challenging. The school day was lengthened to six hours and fifteen minutes and, for the first time, a part-day program of three hours was planned for schools lacking space adequate to accommodate additional full-day classes. In reality, the part-day program presented greater problems because all Kindergarten Demonstration Classes had been full-day programs previously.

Every teacher of young children can appreciate scheduling which permits her pupils to achieve confidence through anticipation of routine activities within the day. However, pupils and teachers alike need opportunities for a change of pace. What teacher has not suffered the frustrations of trying to follow her schedule while her pupils follow one of their own? It doesn't take long for the perceptive teacher to realize that hers is the one to change.

The optimum schedule allows time for assessing the needs of individual pupils. Some pupils may function best on a schedule that alternates relatively short periods of activity with short periods of rest. Others may handle with ease much longer periods of activity before needing rest. There may even be some who manage to remain quite active throughout the program. Pupils vary greatly in the length of time they need to complete an activity with a sense of satisfaction, but the joy of completion is diminished if they must wait until the next day for that satisfaction. A good teacher is aware of the need for flexibility, but all too often this need is not her first priority.

Suggested outlines of daily schedules are provided here to assist the teacher in solving some of these problems while devising the schedule which will be most appropriate for her classroom situation. The outlines will further assist her in varying daily activities to meet the changing needs of pupils. Utilizing large blocks of time allows for greater flexibility within the program. Here is one suggested schedule for the three-hour program and one for the full-day program.

Estimated Time (Minutes)	Activity
Three Hour Schedule	
15	Arrival, browsing activities, daily routines
90	Learning center activities
30	Outdoor activities
15	Story time (varied media)
15	Music activities
15	Planning for following day Dismissal
Six Hour Schedule	
20	Arrival, browsing activities, daily routines
150	Learning center activities
45	Preparing for lunch; lunch
30	Rest, quiet activities
40	Outdoor activities
20	Story time (varied media)
20	Music activities
20	Surprise time
15	Planning for following day Dismissal

Learning center activities include dramatic play, blocks, puzzles, manipulative materials, sand play, water play, games, books, art media, and informal experiences in language, science, math, and social studies. Surprise time provides for a special activity to end each exciting day of learning at school. Effective planning requires the selection of specific activities for each day.

Flexible Planning System

The Flexible Planning System evolved as our most effective solution to the difficulties we encountered. The system has proven to be most compatible to a child-centered approach to daily planning, and our teachers have responded to it with ever-increasing enthusiasm.

The basic materials include a teacher-made planning chart, an ample supply of 4″ × 6″ index cards and a plan book. The planning chart may be made from posterboard and has six to ten pockets. Teachers have found eight pockets to be adequate for most programs. Each pocket represents one time block of the daily program and is labeled accordingly. In essence, the planning chart becomes the outline of the daily schedule.

Planning cards are written for all activities. Each card states the objective of the specific activity, the materials needed by the teacher or the pupils, and gives a brief description of the activity. The cards are then placed in the various time pockets on the planning chart in the anticipated sequence of activities. At the end of the day, the teacher files the cards for future use. Now and then, she may make appropriate evaluation remarks on the card. Within a relatively short period of time, a large number of planning cards can be accumulated.

The planning chart and cards cannot replace the need for the teacher's plan book. They serve rather as an extension of the plan book. The need for long-range planning still exists, as does the need for maintaining a record of learning experiences. The plan book becomes the vehicle through which these needs are met. Few, if any, plan books truly meet the needs for adequate daily plans in activity-centered programs. Planning cards provide the opportunity to expand plans beyond an outline, and yet the cards alone cannot provide the needed overview of the continuing program.

Advantages

Teachers and administrators alike have been tremendously satisfied with the ways in which this simple idea has solved several problems. The process of relating activities to specific objectives has assisted teachers in maintaining a conscious awareness of pupil needs and abilities. Activities may be varied with ease to meet individual pupil needs. The young child needs to utilize his new knowledge in a variety of situations before it truly becomes a part of him. Additionally, an individual activity may relate to several objectives. Through the use of planning cards, the teacher is better able to plan appropriate activities for both small group and individualized instruction. Principals, who often lack an adequate background in early childhood education, have found the system especially valuable in increasing their understanding of the kindergarten curriculum.

The kindergarten classes in Norfolk are fortunate to have the full-time services of teacher aides. Finding adequate time for cooperative planning, however, is an ever-present problem. Lack of cooperative planning leads to frustration on the part of both teacher and aide. The format of the flexible planning system has become a successful element in increased utilization of the services of paraprofessionals and volunteers. Any assistant in the classroom may readily refer to the planning chart and set out the needed materials for scheduled activities. The planning cards further provide the assistant with the information necessary to guide pupils in their learning experiences. Volunteers who are not in the classroom on a regular basis are able to be of immediate assistance.

Parents and others visiting the classroom are able to perceive readily the values of observed activities. Most important, the format allows teachers and visitors to remove the card from the chart and use it as they work with pupils. As one teacher said, "I can have my lesson plan right at my finger-tips without having to carry around a bulky notebook."

As the teacher builds her file of planning cards, she also builds flexibility into her program. As those teachable moments occur, or that unanticipated opportunity presents itself, she may quickly locate in her file a variety of appropriate and related activities. When the planned activity does not interest pupils—and this situation does occur—the file can quickly yield other activities which are more appealing. Another advantage frequently cited by our teachers is the convenience the file offers for recording ideas and activities for future use. How often do we find an idea that we cannot use at that moment, but hope to remember when we need it? Perhaps it is important to remind ourselves that any planning is only as flexible as the teacher is willing to make it. The Flexible Planning System can encourage and aid flexibility only for the willing teacher.

The ease and speed with which our teachers can plan the day's activities are conducive to more complete daily plans. Writing detailed daily lesson plans consumes much of the teacher's valuable time. Because of the need for frequent repetition of many activities, planning becomes less than exciting. Through the use of planning cards, however, time may be spent planning additional activities and preparing materials rather than writing repetitious plans. As each teacher expands her file of cards, she has a wealth of resources at her fingertips.

The kindergarten teachers work cooperatively in expanding their planning files. Each teacher regularly contributes several of her most effective activity plans to the monthly newsletter. Using the format of the 4″ × 6″ planning card, each printed activity can be cut out, pasted on a card, and incorporated into the daily plan. This exchange of ideas provides a constant infusion of curriculum resources.

As behavioral objectives are developed, the system becomes even more valuable. At the suggestion of the teachers, the Kindergarten Curriculum Guide will be developed in a format consistent with that of the planning cards. It is anticipated that the guide will become the basis of the teacher's planning file, rather than remain a resource referred to only occasionally. All of our kindergarten teachers are involved in the development of the guide. They have much to offer in assuring that it will be meaningful to themselves as well as to future teachers.

The Flexible Planning System was originally introduced to kindergarten teachers as an experimental approach to planning, to be evaluated on a voluntary basis. The initial response was so enthusiastic that every teacher began using planning cards immediately. A meaningful approach to planning has resulted in a more meaningful learning experience for both teachers and pupils.

Prekindergarten Programs

29

Kindergarten Pre-entrance Screening

Gerald W. Ellis   *Assistant Superintendent, Glenview Public Schools, Community Consolidated District Number 34, Glenview, Illinois*

Description

More than 80 percent of the children entering the Glenview Public Schools' kindergartens each fall will have experienced some form of prekindergarten education. Some of the children will bring to the kindergarten two or three years of formal readiness experiences. The old concept of the kindergarten as a transitional center between the home and formal education is no longer valid. Legitimate nursery school experiences, the increased sophistication of children through the mass media, our national high rate of mobility, and our changing views about the readiness of children have led us to believe that the kindergarten experience must be redesigned to better accommodate a new kind of child—a child who is larger, stronger, healthier, and better prepared to enter school than ever before.

Kindergarten teachers in the Glenview Public Schools have been concerned about meeting this new kind of child with programs appropriate to his needs. Recently, they have been addressing themselves to planning a pre-entrance screening program that will provide teachers with valuable information necessary for them to carry out their obligations. Pre-entrance screening in May, preceding actual admission the following September, is designed to:

1. Give each teacher a considerable amount of advance data on the readiness of the child to perform at predictable levels in the fall
2. Provide parents with a list of suggested activities to help children gain the readiness they need
3. Alert professional supporting staff members (speech clinicians, nurses, social workers, learning development teachers) to potential problems
4. Give teachers an opportunity to secure necessary instructional materials and to make teaching plans that accommodate the unique needs of individual children.

Developing the Program

Planning. In developing a kindergarten education program that is contemporary, it is essential that it stand upon the strengths operating in the current program. One of the greatest strengths available to us is broad-based community support for prekindergarten and nursery school education. Attempts by a school district to create a program compatible with experiences children bring to kindergarten from their earlier training elicit an enthusiastic response from parents. The success of any pre-entrance screening is contingent upon parental support.

A round-up of incoming kindergarten children is held in each school near the end of May. The round-up requires participation of both the child and one or both of his parents. Prior to the date of the round-up, parents receive a packet including a cover letter and some information forms. They are advised that both parent and child are to attend on the appointed day and that each kindergarten candidate will receive vision, hearing, speech, and general development screening. Parents are assured that screening is not designed to exclude anyone, but rather to help teachers, children, and parents prepare for entering the kindergarten program in the fall. Both the parents and the children are invited to visit and explore the kindergarten room during the roundup. Previously, parents simply dropped into the school office on a designated day and filled out enrollment forms.

Included in the packet are several forms which parents are asked to complete before the round-up date. The first form is a physician's report. Illinois requires all entering kindergartners to submit a doctor's statement of physical condition and proof of birth date. The second form in the package is an enrollment data sheet that asks for emergency data and information about the family which might be helpful. Family data requested include such items as: languages spoken in the home besides English, occupation and place of employment of the father and the mother, and the child's position in relation to his siblings. The third form in the packet is an extensive pupil information form to be completed by the parents. It asks for information concerning the child's earliest experiences, any post-natal problems, any problems with parental or familial relations that would be helpful in understanding the child, the frequency with which he has moved, and the types of instructional experiences he may have had. The form asks parents to identify the types of motivation the child best responds to and types of motivational devices that probably ought to be avoided. Parents are asked to identify any symptoms of physical discomfort or malfunction such as squinting or stuttering. The form further asks the parent for a sociological assessment of the child, especially in terms of his ability to function independently and with others. Although the list of questions seems long, each item is designed to provide teachers with valuable information to be used in constructing sound instructional experience for the child.

On the day of the kindergarten round-up, the children arrive at school on a staggered basis, by appointment, so that the numbers of children proceeding through the screening process neither cause the child and his parents any unnecessary delays nor overburden the staff and volunteers conducting the screening activity. The Director of Pupil Personnel Services assigns district nurses, speech clinicians, the staff psychologist, and counselors to oversee the screening process. In addition, a number of volunteer mothers are used to facilitate the total activities. Each youngster, with his mother, progresses from station to station. The screening activities are performed in a non-threatening, game-like atmosphere. Each child undergoes a speech screening conducted by district nurses and a perceptual-motor skills inventory conducted by members of the physical education staff. The motor skills worksheet includes a determination of balance and postural flexibility, spatial relationships, identification of body parts, rhythmic movements, locomotion, and dominance of hand, foot, and eye. The Brenner-Gestalt Kindergarten survey is administered at still another station. Eye-hand coordination and digital dexterity are measured as the child reproduces geometric figures. The last stop is a visit to the kindergarten room where the child meets the teacher and has an opportunity to explore the room and its fascinating array of materials.

Clinical Analysis of Data. Data collected in the screening process are combined with the data supplied by the parents into a summary sheet under the general categories of appearance, behavior, coordination, dominance, and self-control. The file of information is then reviewed collectively and simultaneously by the kindergarten teachers, nurse, social worker, psychologist, and other staff members who may have a contributory role in the assessment process. The outcome of the clinical analysis sessions is a comprehensive view of the child, designed to supply information to satisfy four outcomes: (1) advise parents of specific learning activities which will help to prepare their child for kindergarten, (2) alert special services personnel to the possibility of assistance for a child, (3) alert the kindergarten teacher to any particular problems a youngster may bring to kindergarten with him, and (4) to assist the teacher in selecting appropriate instructional materials.

Beginning the Program

This program was tested in one building so the staff could master the intricacies of its operation and get a quick reading on the necessity and appropriateness of certain aspects of the program. It is necessary to test this project in a building where teachers and administrators are both willing and eager to help. A careful analysis of the kinds of questions asked of parents must be made to assure the relevance of each question to the stated objectives of the project. An ambitious effort is made to enlist the support and participation of parents.

Willingness and enthusiasm are not enough to make a program succeed. Essential, too, is a rigorous training experience for all involved. It is the responsibility of the Director of Pupil Personnel Services to conduct appropriate instructional sessions for the staff and for parent volunteers.

By looking at students carefully before they enter kindergarten, necessary changes can be made in the instructional program. The extent and the number of changes we have made to meet unique needs of individual pupils indicate the value of the program.

30

Pre-kindergarten Orientation Program

Albert R. Rodick   *Principal;*
Robert D. Merriam   *Guidance Consultant;*
Mary Bird   *Kindergarten Teacher;*
Clara Mason   *Kindergarten Teacher; and*
Mary Quinn   *Teacher Aide.*
Downeast School, Bangor, Maine

Description

Although it sounds trite, the aim of education has always been the total development of each child. School education begins in the kindergarten, yet we feel that somehow our approach to individual progress in the kindergarten has been unsatisfactory. In addition, we have sensed a great lack of communication between home and school.

In our program, therefore, we attempted to develop a plan that would overcome these deficiencies. We hoped that the program would truly treat each child as an individual with his own strengths and weaknesses, and his own abilities and limitations. We wanted to help each child attain his full capacities as a learner.

The following description outlines the step-by-step development of this program by our three kindergarten teachers, a teacher aide, and the school guidance consultant.

Rationale.   We at Downeast School felt strongly that we did not know enough about our kindergarten children before they enrolled each September. We also felt that some of our children were confused by all the strange, new situations and people they encountered during the first weeks of school, and that this abrupt introduction was often detrimental to their total early school adjustment. This program, then, was aimed at satisfying both needs—the need for more information on the part of the school, and the need for better adjustment on the part of the child.

The Testing Program.   When parents registered their children in June, they were given a brief verbal description of the program and were informed that the school would set up an appointment for them to confer with the guidance consultant. During the last week of school, a letter was sent to parents suggesting an appointment time and encouraging them to reschedule it as necessary. About a week later, a second letter was sent as a reminder.

Testing began the third week in July. Each child was allotted half an hour, an amount of time later found to be inadequate for the task. About 90 percent of all registered children were screened. Then the protocols were studied carefully, and twenty-six children were invited back for re-evaluation at a second conference.

The Early Detection Inventory (Follett Educational Corp.) was used as the basic instrument for the screening process. Each item was rated on a 0-1-2 scale, so that a total score could be compiled easily. At the end of each interview, the examiner rated each child on his impression of overall readiness using the same 0-1-2 scale.

For re-evaluation purposes, the *Slosson Intelligence Test* (Slosson Educational Publications, East Aurora, N.Y.) was administered in order to obtain a mental age for each child. In cases where there were communication problems or questions of verbal ability, the *Peabody Picture Vocabulary Test* (American Guidance Service, Inc.) was used. A more in-depth conference with the parent was possible at this session, and there was additional opportunity for informal observation of the child.

Choosing the Participants. The twenty-six children who were re-evaluated after the initial screening were not necessarily those who seemed to be the least ready according to the screening device. They were children who might have the most difficulty in adjusting to the regular school program because of severe speech problems, shyness, or other social or emotional conditions. Many of them were the ones most likely to be overlooked by the teacher in the first busy weeks of school. In other words, these were the ones to whom immediate special attention should be given. Twenty-four of these children were finally invited to take part in the week-long orientation program that took place two weeks before school began.

Staff Roles. The principal originated the project. He structured the basic program, and served as the idea man and coordinator.

The guidance consultant handled most parent contacts, did all the formal testing and evaluation, recommended children for the programs, helped coordinate daily schedules, served as a male model, and grouped the children for regular class placement.

Together, the teachers developed specific classroom activities, made daily evaluations of the program and the children, and visited a day care center for a conference on children. The teacher aide helped develop activities and evaluate the children.

The teachers and teacher aide were hired for one week on Title I funds. The Guidance Consultant worked for eight weeks, four weeks under Title I funds and four weeks as part of his regular school year. The principal served in a voluntary capacity.

Planning. The staff's primary aim during the orientation week was to see that the selected group of students had as pleasant a school experience as possible. Considerable planning went into the week-long program. The entire staff helped to formulate the activity plans. Originally, the principal and guidance consultant were not to be involved in the actual teaching activities, but were to serve in a floating capacity, helping the various groups as needed. It soon became evident in our planning, however, that the male staff members were essential to the program. The children, especially the boys, needed a father model because many of them come from single-parent families with only a mother. The three teachers and the aide were each assigned five children to observe throughout the program. This arrangement gave each child more individual attention and was helpful in the final evaluation.

We decided that the orientation session should be one and one-half hours long, from 9:00 to 10:30 A.M., thus conforming closely to the schedule for the first week of kindergarten.

The areas of the kindergarten program to be included in each day's activity were outlined. On arrival, part of the staff would greet the students and visit informally with them as they put on their name tags. Then the children would go to the free play area where the rest of the staff would be ready to help them.

Some time each day was to be spent visiting parts of the physical plant of this large school. Thus the children would become acquainted with their section of the school, as well as with the areas in which their older siblings would be working.

We planned to expose the children to the various types of group activities that they would experience during the regular school year—music, art, science, storytime, group games, rest, bathroom, and washing up procedures.

The schedule would also allow time for the staff to hold a daily evaluation session immediately following dismissal of the children. Staff time in the afternoon would be spent reviewing the daily program and preparing materials for the next day. Home calls would be made in the afternoon when advisable. A party was scheduled for the final day.

We planned to divide the children into three groups that would rotate between our three learning activity stations. One teacher would handle the arts and crafts activities, one the music and rhythm activities, and the third would take charge of academic and game activities.

Orientation Week Program. On the first day, the children were welcomed by the guidance consultant and a teacher. Because they had met the guidance consultant previously, his presence provided a feeling of security. The children were directed to a large tree hung with leaves and name tags bearing the name of each child. The leaf-shaped name tag was hung around the neck of each child, and at the end of the day's session he returned it to its proper leaf on the tree. The children were sent next to two adjoining kindergarten rooms to join in large group activities. There were many things around the room arranged to attract their attention. They were encouraged to explore the areas that interested them, and good work habits were stressed.

Indoor equipment included painting materials, dolls, building blocks, pegs and pegboards, large colored beads, a library corner, and a housekeeping center. All proved to be popular with both boys and girls.

For outside activities, the children were divided into four groups. The teachers and the aide took them on tours of the building, showing them the various playgrounds, outdoor equipment, and entrances to the kindergarten rooms. We felt each child should be familiar with the principal's office, the clinic, and the intercom system.

Music included the use of rhythm instruments, and familiar nursery rhymes were sung. Musical games that included hopping, skipping, and running proved to be a most enjoyable activity. The children also heard puppet stories and made their own puppets. An American Indian motif was used throughout the program to give it some continuity.

At the end of each session, the children returned to the free play area in the kindergarten rooms for clean-up time. This ten-minute period was designed to help the children learn to put their things away and to establish good work habits.

After returning with them to the lobby to hang their name tags on the tree, each teacher took her children to the appropriate door for dismissal. She walked with them to the intersection and showed each child the correct and safe way to go home.

On the last day, we had a party. A ribbon was pinned on each child as a symbol of his participation. Awards were given to everyone—children, teachers, aide, custodians, and guidance consultant.

Evaluation

The format of the program, the small number of children involved, and the excellent rapport among the teaching team all helped make the orientation week a success even before the first day got under way.

Our pattern of welcoming and tagging was initiated in hopes that familiarity with the tags and greetings would soon put the children at ease. It worked very well. By the third day even the most reluctant youngsters were sauntering in as if they had always done so. It was satisfying to watch the withdrawn children come out of their shells as they became more comfortable with the daily routine of play period and clean-up. Interaction between the children grew, and many of the friendships formed during the week continued through the regular school term.

There seemed to be security for them in knowing a bit of what would be happening each day, as well as excitement inherent in a varied program incorporating science, art, dramatics, and concepts such as parts of the body, table manners, and color recognition. We began the practice of telling the children what they could look forward to each day, and this seemed to motivate them.

Because of the small number of pupils involved, we were able to do many individual things. We found the children enjoyed experiences such as rotating activities and tours to places of interest in and out of the building.

To these children, many from broken homes, the appearance and enthusiastic involvement of a man in the week's activities gave them something they lacked at home. We feel so strongly about this that one recommendation for next year is that we hire a male teacher aide. It is also important to note that many of the things planned for the children involved manipulative skills and required the guidance of another person besides the teacher of the activity. Our aide was invaluable here, as well as in casual communication with the children. They gravitated towards her and opened up to her easy manner.

We have great hopes for the program next year. After continuing conferences, casual get-togethers, and incidental remarks on the progress of various children, we are full of ideas. One thing generally agreed upon is that we should place greater emphasis on home visits. The connection between teacher, school, and home should be a strong one, beneficial to both the child and the staff members.

Research Activities

31

Institute for Developmental Studies

Caroline Saxe *Coordinator of Training, Institute for Developmental Studies, School of Education, New York University, New York*

Description

The Institute for Developmental Studies, under the direction of Dr. Martin Deutsch, is an interdisciplinary unit within the School of Education at New York University. The Institute's enrichment program was established in January, 1963, in an attempt to study the interplay of environment and development, and to develop an enriched and stimulating school curriculum for socially disadvantaged children. Over the years, the IDS program has evolved into a comprehensive five-year enrichment curriculum from prekindergarten through the third grade. The original demonstration schools for this program were several public schools in the central Harlem area of New York City.

The academic progress of both IDS and control children was monitored over the five-year period by administering both standardized and Institute-developed tests and observational procedures. The evidence we have supports the conclusion that, particularly in the preschool years, the IDS experience is successful. The children from disadvantaged areas can and do learn.

The IDS curriculum emphasizes those areas which have been found to be most operative in later learning. These include the cognitive areas of language, perception, and concept formation, as well as the affective area of self-concept. The program is designed to help children acquire a degree of proficiency with academic skills, as well as independence and confidence as learners.

To achieve these overall aims, several basic approaches were developed and used throughout the program. These have persisted as new grades were added and as the original curriculum was supplemented. Despite the continuous evolution of the program and the dynamic interplay of various other factors—developing curricula, personalities of individual teachers, changing needs of particular groups of children, social change in the community, uncertainties of funding—these methods were applied consistently.

One of the important aspects of the IDS program is the care that is taken to make the materials and tasks appropriate to each child's level of development. Individualized instruction pervades each step of the program. The materials, curriculum, physical setup and individualized program are all designed to meet the needs of children organized for instruction in small groups. In accordance with the philosophy of individualized instruction, no all-inclusive goals are set for each grade level. Rather, each child is allowed to proceed at his own pace, in accordance with his particular needs and abilities.

A second characteristic, common to all phases of the IDS program, is the recurrence of specific tasks throughout the classroom and throughout many of the activities of the day. The task of size discrimination, for example, recurs in materials and activities such as the three sizes of paint jars, the various sizes of blocks that have to be put back appropriately on the shelves, the discussion at circle time or lunch time, and the various games available for quiet time.

To facilitate its overall aims, a unique staffing pattern has been developed by IDS. The pattern persisted during the expansion of the program and now exists on all grade levels. The IDS team consists of teachers, assistant teachers, curriculum specialists, and supervisors whose work is coordinated by a curriculum director. Both assistants and teachers engage in classroom instruction. Assistants were trained and expected to actually teach, rather than perform custodial functions. Curriculum specialists, assistants and supervisors engage in a program of in-service training.

In addition, the IDS supervisory pattern is characterized by the small number of teachers assigned to each supervisor. For the most part, supervisors act in a supportive manner and demonstrate their suggestions by actually working with children and introducing materials into the classroom. In addition to their work with teachers, IDS supervisors periodically meet with each other to plan their activities and discuss common problems.

A fourth fundamental and persisting aspect of the IDS program is the emphasis it places on in-service training of all supervisory and teaching staff. Through a variety of activities, including workshops and conferences, the performance of teachers and pupils can be discussed. Such activities not only provide feedback on the current curriculum, but also allow for the introduction and exploration of new ideas, methods, and materials. Thus, staff and program development are built into the design of the IDS program. They help to insure the maintenance of a dynamic educational environment for the teachers and supervisors, as well as for the children.

A final aspect of the IDS program is the commitment to an active and ongoing program of parent involvement. The IDS staff continually stresses the importance of such involvement to the academic success of the children, as well as to the efficacy of the enrichment program.

In the IDS program, the child's activities are defined so that they begin with the most basic skill level, and then proceed sequentially through succeeding levels of increasing complexity. The steps leading from one level to the next are designed to provide a manageable challenge for the child. Activities are paced for each child so he can proceed step by step at the rate most comfortable and reinforcing for him.

A number of techniques and special materials are used to help students accomplish IDS goals. The Language Master is one such learning device. It is used in a number of ways to build vocabulary and enhance the understanding of basic concepts. With this recording device, a taped voice identifies an object or concept that is represented by a picture on a card. The card moves through the machine exposing that object or concept as the taped voice states its name. Finally, the child identifies the object, records his own voice, and then compares his speech pattern and sentence structure with that of the taped voice.

One of the games developed at IDS is *Language Lotto*. This game is similar to standard games of Lotto. However, it can be played at different linguistic and conceptual levels, ranging from nonverbal to verbal matching of pictures, requiring increasingly complex cognitive skills.

Teaching strategies, such as the scheduling of a Quiet Work Time within the preschool day, are also designed to meet IDS program goals. During this time, all noise-producing activities are suspended, and children work with materials such as puzzles and individual learning games. Teachers are then able to work on a one-to-one basis with children and to guide their individual and small group activities.

IDS children also work with published curricula, (the Stern and Sullivan reading programs and AAAS process approach science materials), for example, as well as with a plethora of Institute-developed learning games and individualized learning materials.

Evaluation

This description is a brief summary of the IDS curriculum and has been provided for those readers who need only an overview of curriculum methodology and orientation.

Extra-mural Training Services—Dr. Edward Ponder, Director. Requests for training in all aspects of early childhood education come to the Institute from schools in all parts of the United States. Universities and community agencies are among those who have requested information about the IDS program.

Members of the Institute's training staff conduct workshops and training programs for personnel in communities throughout the United States, providing guidance for those who wish to follow the Institute's model in establishing their own program.

From 1965 to the present, the Institute's training staff has worked with rural and urban Head Start groups, concentrating on local program and staff development. The training staff has worked also with a wide spectrum of educators (including administrators, supervisors, teachers, and paraprofessionals), lecturing and conducting workshops in many communities, as well as conducting sessions for those who come to the Institute itself.

32
Jonesboro's Discovery Method

Georgia Dunlap   *Principal of North Elementary School,*
Jonesboro Public Schools, Jonesboro, Arkansas

Description

The Jonesboro Special School District, in cooperation with Arkansas State University, has developed a model research kindergarten. This exemplary program enrolls thirty to forty children, five years old, who will be in the first grade the following year. The program is designed to incorporate the best known methods and materials for teaching children as well as for training teachers.

The general objectives of the Early Childhood Center are to serve as a demonstration and research center that can be used as a laboratory for teacher training, and at the same time serve as a model program to be visited and studied by other schools in the state.

Objectives for the Child

To maintain and develop good physical, social, and emotional health
To discover and understand his scientific world
To grow in understanding of spatial and quantitative relationships
To expand and enrich his symbolic language
To enjoy his literary, artistic, and musical heritage
To express himself aesthetically through various art media
To develop perceptual and motor skils
To develop positive attitudes toward self, other people, and learning

Curriculum.   The curriculum of the model kindergarten includes both structured and free activities. One of the purposes of the program is to make children feel good about kindergarten and school experiences and to become aware that learning is exciting and important. The underlying method used throughout the year is called *discovery*. The first phase of the program emphasizes discovering the self. It is essential that each child have a positive self-concept. Lowenfield's theory of stimulating the senses or body parts is used to develop the positive self-concept, keeping in mind that every child needs affection, acceptance, and approval, in order to achieve a major phase of development—the ability to adapt.

The second phase of the program emphasizes the discovery of cultural heritage by utilizing resource persons, films, film strips, records, reproductions of famous paintings, sculpture, design, architecture, drama, dance, and well-planned field trips. For each culture they study, the children create their own designs, songs, poems, stories, and jewelry.

An important part of both phases of the program is the development of sensory-motor operations through the use of ropes, balls, balancing boards, obstacle courses, punching bags, cooking, gardening, percept boxes, carpentry, water play, incline boards, pulleys, bean bags, and utilization of concepts from the Frostig program.

Efforts are made to identify gifted and precocious children, and the program is individualized to meet their special needs. Throughout the program, children are encouraged to develop vocabularies and sentence patterns that describe the materials they are working with and their feelings about things that affect them.

Phase One

When the five-year-olds enter the kindergarten room on the first day, they have already begun to learn through exploring, investigating, observing, and experimenting. The teacher stimulates their curiosity by offering opportunities for the children to become absorbed in activities to develop their senses.

During the first week of the program, the outline of each child's body is drawn on a large sheet of paper. Each child fills in the details on his own outline. The children, with the help of an adult, cut out their shapes and display them on the walls of the classroom. The children discover that some of the cutouts are taller than others, and the realization that some children are taller than others soon follows.

As the children become more aware of their bodies, they become interested in learning how their five senses operate. Learning becomes more real and exciting when a child's senses are involved. Keeping this in mind, we begin teaching children about their senses of perception through experiences of seeing, hearing, touching, smelling, and tasting.

The sense of sight is explored through experiences with kaleidoscopes, telescopes, microscopes, and magnifying glasses. Children are interested in learning the functions of their eyelashes, eyelids, and eyebrows. A visit to the optometrist's office is always a stimulating experience. The children express an interest in all of the equipment and listen carefully to what the doctor has to say. Back in the classroom, students make artificial eyelashes and pipe cleaner–cellophane glasses. They put these on stocking puppets, adding yarn for hair and buttons for eyes.

Awareness of the sense of smell is developed through the use of various foods and spices. A puppet named Susie-No-Nose has a number of different cardboard noses that children can put on her to discover how different noses alter the appearance of the face. From diagrams and first-hand experiences the children learn about the sense of smell.

Because learning to listen is basic to conversation, the study of hearing is extremely beneficial in the kindergarten. A field trip is often made to a hearing aid company, where each child receives a toy hearing aid. Imitating sounds, locating sounds, taping sounds, sound walks, sound boxes, and recognizing and repeating rhythmic patterns, all strengthen the children's understanding of their sense of hearing.

Through a study of the sense of touch, the children develop an understanding that they not only feel with their hands, but that their entire bodies are sense organs of touch. Clay, texture, pictures, sandpaper pictures, feel boxes, and feel games are utilized to expand this concept.

During this study of the five senses, the five-year-olds are extremely interested in diagrams of their eyes, ears, and noses. Actually, what could be of more interest to these young children than their own bodies and how they function! The next phase of the program takes advantage of this interest.

The children turn to a study of the physiological systems of their bodies and do related art projects. We begin with the skeletal, respiratory, and circulatory systems. The children make paper-straw skeletons, balloon lungs, red yarn circulatory systems, and even some hearts complete with four chambers. Various animal hearts are dissected in class. Our study of the kidneys is made meaningful through the use of a Betsy Wetsy doll. Kidney beans are used to model the shape of the kidneys in an art activity.

After studying the stomach and the digestive system, the children study the four food groups in terms of their importance to the human body. Even the youngest child knows that man needs food to live, but the teacher's job is to extend this knowledge to a deeper understanding through meaningful experiences. As the children experiment with their sense of taste, they are adding to their knowledge of the variety and importance of foods.

The children study the various roots, leaves, seeds, and stems we eat. They explore shapes and colors of fruits firsthand as they prepare them for snacks. The vegetables that grow below and above the ground become real to them as they taste them at snack time.

Next, the children visit a farm to discover food sources. They see sorghum being ground in the mill, watch a farmer milk a cow, and take a wagon ride. Back in the classroom, the children help make ice cream and butter. They have fun discovering all the different sizes of containers that milk comes in. Each child has a chance to walk a balance beam carrying half a gallon of milk. The class also takes field trips to hatcheries and poultry, egg, and fish farms.

A study of the cattle ranch is the next phase of our children's program. In this way they learn the true role of the cowboy and the part he plays in connection with our beef supply. During this part of the program, additional stress is placed on sensory-motor activities because they are easy to correlate with cowboy life. Children make stick horses to trot, gallop, ride, and race around the room. The excitement grows as the children participate in roping the cardboard cattle. They even make a large cardboard maze, similar to one ranchers use for sorting and loading cattle. Later, our classroom becomes the Big K Room Ranch and chuck wagon. Beans, stews, and various western snacks are served around a campfire in the middle of the room as the students tell stories and sing songs during Western Week.

Phase Two

As we move from the study of cowboys to the study "We Are All Americans," the second phase of our program begins. After the children discover the many races of people that make up our big country, they have fun learning about the time when there was only one race—the Indians.

Indians. The word *Indian* itself is a sufficient stimulation for a study of the Indian culture. Indian crafts, songs, activities, and games, all integral parts of the native American culture, are eagerly accepted by the five-year-olds. The children make ceremonial masks, burden baskets, archery sets, and teepees. Two Indian foods, popcorn and fish, are prepared and sampled at school. A discussion of the influences of climate and its effect on the Indians is also part of this unit.

Hawaii. For our study of Hawaii, paper palm trees and huge paper volcanoes lend a tropical atmosphere to the classroom. The children prepare for a luau by stringing macaroni, cutting flowers for leis, making a thatched house, drawing pictures with sand, and making a small paper volcano spout clouds of confetti. Crepe paper grass skirts swing to the slow tempo of the Hawaiian music. Food for the luau is baked in the ground and served on large paper leaves. Creative dances and skits add excitement to our study of the Hawaiians.

Mexico. The next stop is south of the border. The classroom becomes a Mexican market, where the children shop for candles or stop by the Leather Shop where head bands, wrist bands, purses, and belts are being made. Other children make dishes at the Pottery Shop. After spending a day at the market, the children celebrate with a fiesta. Tacos, enchiladas, and tortillas are served. To complete the celebration, they break a piñata. Discovery of simple words in the Spanish language is also exciting to five-year-olds.

Music. The world of music is next on the program of cultural enrichment. The emotional release that the children derive from expressing their feelings through music contributes immeasurably to their emotional stability and social well being. Through music, children learn to appreciate freedom of expression, grow in the ability to express themselves, and become increasingly self-confident. By learning to listen, they are developing a skill that is essential to communication.

The children enjoy exploring music through their eyes as well as their ears. Various musical instruments are brought to the room for them to see—a violin, a clarinet, a bassoon, and a trombone. After making their own musical instruments from construction paper, light bulbs, cans, and boxes, members of the classroom orchestra perform with its conductor. Jonesboro High School's band director allows the children to examine and play selected instruments in the band room, and even gives the children a chance to march with the band on the field. These two experiences are memorable ones for the children. Later, as the class watches the Arkansas State University R.O.T.C. Marching Band, the children are able to call out the names of the instruments they see.

Next, the children turn from performance to composition. They pretend they are composers and write their own music, placing notes on the lines and spaces of a staff. *The Sorceror's Apprentice* by Paul Dukain is dramatized using magic brooms and sorcerors' hats. The children listen in anticipation as the musical composition unfolds. Students take turns pretending they are the magic broom by carrying buckets filled with water up and down stairs. This exercise also helps them to develop balance and agility.

Prokofieff's *Peter and the Wolf* is easy for young children to relate to because this composer began to write music at the age of five. As the children watch the filmstrip and listen to the record of *Peter and the Wolf,* they name the instruments they hear. Paper-sack puppets dramatize the story. They practice shooting a cork gun at a target to develop eye and hand coordination.

The music composed by Gioacchino Rossini for *William Tell* becomes meaningful for the kindergartners as they make papier mâché apples, construction paper quivers, and archery sets. Circular targets are cut out and labeled with number values.

Awareness of the Swiss culture is developed as the class takes a mountain walk, practices walking on wooden skis, and makes sack tunics. Gingerbread men and houses are made of ingredients the children can measure and bake in class. When Engelbert Humperdinck was a little boy, he used to help his mother in this way. These memories formed the basis of his opera, *Hansel and Gretel,* that is played next for the class. The children gather rocks for trails in the make-believe forest and bring them to the room for painting. The fateful prick of the spinning wheel in Tchaikovsky's *Sleeping Beauty* is made real to the children by one of our local citizens who spins wool into thread as the children watch.

The ballets *Swan Lake* and *The Nutcracker* are introduced to the children as another type of musical story. The children visit a dance studio and learn the five dance positions.

Art. In the last part of our program we explore the world of art—beautiful pictures, fine statues, and splendid buildings. All of these—the works of painters, sculptors, architects, and other artists—are among the discoveries the five-year-olds make as they explore the world of art. Trips to the art department and art exhibits at Arkansas State University are scheduled. At the art show, the children note the textures of the art on display. Afterward, the children make paper palettes for mixing their own paints. For sensory-motor development, large palettes made of cardboard are put on the floor. The colored areas are used for games of bouncing balls, hopping, or jumping. The children create their own games and songs about colors.

The word *sculpture* becomes a part of the children's vocabulary as they work with stone, paper, clay, wood, and wire. They can feel the plastic qualities of the clay, the grain of the wood, and the cool, smooth texture of stone and marble. The sculpture Michaelangelo carved of David, the shepherd boy, involves a story that will always be remembered.

Drama. Like the artist and the musician, the actor tells a story to express what he knows, feels, and imagines. Make-believe stories about things they would like to do, or people they would like to be are acted out, then filmed by the kindergartners. The settings, scenery, costumes, make-up and masks, director, props, and stage designers are all integral parts of the movie. Puppets, marionettes, shadow plays, and pantomimes are also used as a means of acting out stories.

Architecture. The art of architecture introduces the creation of structures from blueprints and helps to develop the children's imagination and creativity. They excavate land, fill match boxes with concrete for the foundations, cut cardboard for beams, and raise cardboard houses.

For sensory-motor development, the children build a large 4' x 6' cardboard replica of a blueprint. In this structure that resembles a maze, children have fun hopping from room to room. Houses in different stages of construction are used to show the developmental sequence. Trips to a brick factory, architect's office, and houses under construction complete this unit.

Evaluation

Results of the evaluation indicated that our discovery method was effective. The children demonstrated increased skills in visual-motor tasks, greater fluency in vocabulary and oral communication, and had a good awareness of themselves and others. Through listening, conversation, stories, fingerplays, poetry, dramatization, puppetry, and filmstrips, the children developed skills in the language arts area. Perceptual skills and concepts were developed by the use of balls, balance boards, jumping ropes, and the Frostig Program.

The Peabody Picture Vocabulary and the Stanford Achievement pre-test and post-test were given to determine progress.

Peabody Picture Vocabulary Test

Pre-test, September, 1970		Post-test, May, 1971	
Mean M.A.	Mean I.Q.	Mean M.A.	Mean I.Q.
5.6	99	6.5	115

Stanford Early School Achievement Test, Level 1

Pre-test, September, 1970		Post-test, May, 1971	
Mean Raw Score	Mean c/o	Mean Raw Score	Mean c/o
60	37	101	53

Programs Based on the Engelmann-Becker Model

33

The Engelmann-Becker Program at Cherokee

J. Ed Sharpe *Follow Through Director, and*
Tom Hunter *E. B. Consultant, Cherokee Elementary School,*
Cherokee, North Carolina

Description

In the spring of 1970, a parent advisory committee of the Follow Through Program in Cherokee decided to adopt the Engelmann-Becker Model as the approach best likely to meet the total educational needs of Cherokee children. Presently the program involves the kindergarten, first, second, and third grades—500 students in nineteen classrooms. A quick tour of the program leaves good impressions. Children are laughing as they change classes every thirty minutes, small groups of six or seven are responding verbally and energetically to their teacher, and other children are reading stories in unison. The healthful amount of noise in each room indicates that learning is taking place, and test results confirm this impression.

Goals and Designs. The overall goal of the Engelmann-Becker Program at Cherokee is to teach Cherokee children skills at an accelerated rate in such a manner that they enjoy school and develop positive images of themselves in the classroom. Few assumptions are made about skills the children should have when they enter the program. One basic assumption made regarding the classroom, however, is the belief that whatever learning transpires does so because the children have been taught. Similarly, we assume that if the children do not learn, it is because they have not been taught. This assumption places full responsibility for learning squarely on the teacher.

The academic goals are the same for all children: mastery of the basic skills that insure success in school. Can the children read fluently and for information? Can they handle the English language logically? Are they proficient in arithmetic operations? Our goal is to be able to respond affirmatively to all those questions for every child before he leaves Follow Through. The Engelmann-Becker model is set up to assure that these goals can be accomplished.

First, the skills necessary for intelligent behavior in any area are analyzed and then subdivided into basic components. For example, what skills does it take for a child to be able to read a word like *man?* He must know that the word is read from left to right. He must be able to produce each sound in sequence and then put them together to form the word *man.* Each of these skills is taught, one at a time, beginning with the simplest and moving on to the next only when the child has mastered the first. During the first year of reading instruction, the child learns forty sounds, as well as blending, rhyming, and other skills necessary for word analysis. At the end of that year, the child can read any word in which those forty sounds appear. Words that are irregular, such as *night,* are taught as memory words. The second year, emphasis is placed on reading for information. Alphabet skills, syllabication, accenting, and dictionary skills are taught.

The value of programming instruction in this way is that children are presented with tasks in a manner that leads them to the highest level of success. They are not assigned any new work before they have mastered every necessary subskill. In addition, the teacher knows at any point in time what the children can do, and if they cannot do it, she knows the reason why. If the skills are taught properly, a child will make a mistake for one reason only, and the teacher has the information necessary to correct that deficiency.

Implementation. The program we use is published as Distar by Science Research Associates. Because one teacher cannot effectively teach twenty-five or thirty preschool children, Follow Through provides two additional aides for each classroom. The certified teacher and the teaching aides all receive intensive training for two weeks prior to the beginning of school. This training is supplied by the sponsor in the form of consultants who work with the teachers throughout the year. Teachers and aides choose or are assigned one area—reading, arithmetic, or language. When school starts, children are tested in order to facilitate initial grouping. These groupings are flexible and are made on the basis of the skills each child possesses, not on some remote measure of ability. Many children change group several times during the year. After the children have been grouped, schedules are drawn up which provide each group with thirty minutes of instruction a day in each area. Children in Cherokee move from room to room. Each room is designated as either reading, arithmetic, or language. When all children have worked in all three areas, they return to their base room for the remainder of the day for tutoring, skill expansion, spelling, or social studies.

The small group instruction period is the most intense and crucial part of the day. During each thirty-minute period, teachers and children are involved in rapid-fire question and answer activity. A great number of pupil responses, written and oral, provide immediate feedback for the teacher as she seeks to determine the extent of learning taking place. When the children respond correctly, she praises them and moves on. When the children make a mistake, she corrects them immediately before continuing.

Teacher training focuses largely on mastering the techniques required to teach Distar. Teachers work throughout the year of pacing, correction procedures, and signals. Heavy emphasis is also placed on techniques of positive reinforcement. The teacher tries to structure her presentation so that rewards are forthcoming to the children that are working hard and making gains. The children quickly learn that they will be rewarded for doing things correctly. Punishment is avoided except in unique cases.

A period in the activities room is sandwiched between the instructional periods at some time each morning. Activities vary each day. They include music, art, Cherokee language instruction, and Cherokee arts and crafts. We try to make the activity time both enjoyable and culturally enriching for the Cherokee children.

Evaluation

Testing. The Engelmann-Becker Model utilizes several means of monitoring progress. The first and probably most effective method is continuous testing. Tests are administered regularly by trained parents whose full-time job is testing the children in reading, arithmetic, and language. Each child is tested every two weeks in one of the three areas, and in any six-week period will have been tested in all three areas. The tests are based on the Distar materials. The child is tested on two to nine different skills at a level of difficulty which corresponds to what he is presently learning. He receives a different score for each skill, and his scores in addition to the scores of his classmates determine future lesson plans. Should the group score low in a particular skill, the teacher may repeat several lessons. Should the group score high in all skills, she may skip lessons, and if the group is strong in most skills but weak in a few others, the teacher will spend extra time on the problem areas.

Copies of the test results are sent to Oregon every two weeks for evaluation by the project manager. He may make assignments of a general or specific nature to the consultants or individual teachers.

Two other reports are sent to Oregon biweekly. One is a report from each teacher on the number of lessons she taught to her group during the two-week period. This gives the sponsor a short-term guide as to how quickly the teachers are reaching the goals set for each group. The other report is a day-by-day compilation of the number of errors children are making on their worksheets, based on information gained from the continuous tests.

Video.   The final method by which the sponsor is able to evaluate the teaching in Cherokee is through video-taping. All teaching personnel are filmed two to four times a year in the small group teaching situation. Before the tape is sent to Oregon, the teacher may watch it and make her own judgments about what she sees. The tape is then critiqued by the project manager, whose written comments are sent to the consultants and passed on to the teachers. The major benefit of the video-taping system is the opportunity it provides each teacher to note personal strengths and weaknesses of which she may be completely unaware.

34
Follow Through

Charles F. Ginsbach   *Follow Through Director, Rosebud Sioux Tribe, Community Action Program, Follow Through Project, Rosebud, South Dakota*

Description

Type of Program.   Federal grant through HEW

Administering agency.   Rosebud Sioux Tribe Community Action Program (CAP)

Number of students participating.   346

Grades participating.   All students from kindergarten through third grade

Date project started.   September, 1968

Staff.   One director, one parent coordinator, twelve certified teachers (in-kind contribution or maintenance of effort by local school districts), two parent workers, two data collectors, two data collector/parent workers, thirty teacher aides

Funding level.   Approximately $930 per student

Model Sponsor.   Engelmann-Becker Corporation, Eugene, Oregon

Type of Model.   Systematic use of behavioral principles that focuses strongly on academic objectives

Goals.   (1) To teach, in the most economical manner possible, the basic skills of reading, language, and arithmetic to every student and (2) to provide for maximum parental involvement in the implementation of the project

The Engelmann-Becker Instructional Model

Rosebud parents and school administrators selected the Engelmann-Becker educational model for this program because it purported to teach and measure the skills essential for reading, language, and arithmetic. In some respects, the model represents a return to the no-nonsense teaching of the three R's. As opposed to gadget-oriented remedial programs, this model places top priority on hiring and training good classroom teachers.

Reading.   A phonetic decoding approach to reading is used because it teaches the children to read in the shortest amount of time. Basic letter sounds are taught first. From these single letter and digraph sounds, the child learns to decode words that can be similarly sounded out and spoken. These are called regular words. Words which are spoken differently from

169

the way in which they are sounded out are called irregular words. The children are simply taught to recognize them as such. Diacritical marks are used to assist the child in sound identification. These marks are removed as the child progresses, so by the end of the first level he will be able to read newspaper print. Comprehension is taught as soon as the child is able to read sentences.

Language. Critical listening and logical expression are the goals of the language program. Identification and classification, verb tenses, prepositions, and polars constitute the early phases of the program. Grammar and sentence construction are introduced later.

Arithmetic. The arithmetic program is based upon the premise that all arithmetic operations are counting operations. Thus the child is not only taught to count, but he is also taught to count forwards (addition), backwards (subtraction), by multiples (multiplication) and by numbers less than one (fractions). The child also learns to solve for unknown quantities by applying the Equality Rule: "As many as you count to on one side of the equal sign, you have to count to on the other side of the equal sign."

Construction of the Program

Each of the three programs was developed and refined using four basic steps:

1. Analysis of key concepts and operations
2. Writing formats to translate the concepts into teachable forms
3. Sequencing the formats to put them in a logical order
4. Providing enough practice to insure mastery of the concepts and operations

The student and teacher material for the first two levels of each program are published under the trade name of Distar (Direct instruction for the teaching of arithmetic and reading).

Classroom Organization. Children are grouped by learning rate. Incoming students are given placement tests, while returning students pick up where they left off at the close of the previous term. Some program adjustment usually needs to be made. During the year, test results are used to regroup the students. Each day, groups of five to eight students spend thirty minutes per subject in instruction. In addition to these teacher presentation periods, the children have time to complete assignments, strengthen weak areas, or engage in other classroom activities.

Instructional and Ancillary Personnel. One certified teacher and three teacher aides constitute the usual classroom staff. The certified teacher usually teaches reading, one aide teaches language, another teaches arithmetic, and a third aide is assigned to seatwork activities. Each school assigns one aide to administer the model sponsor's continuous tests. Another aide functions as a parent worker by assisting the principal and local Parent Advisory Committee Chairman with school-parent activities.

The Continuous Testing Program. Each child is tested six times during the year in each subject. The tests are administered every two weeks on a rotating basis. Because each test covers all the various skills that have been taught up to the test day, the teacher is able to pinpoint the strengths and weaknesses of each child.

In May of each year the children are given normative tests for comparison purposes. To assess language skills, the children are given the Slossen Intelligence Test. The Wide Range Achievement Test measures reading and arithmetic skills.

Teacher Training. Because the Engelmann-Becker Follow Through model is an accelerated approach, a great deal of effort is devoted to providing in-service training for classroom personnel. This training consists for the most part of troubleshooting sessions during which video tapes of the session participants may be shown. These tapes are then critiqued by the teacher supervisor. In this way, both teaching and behavior modification techniques can be analyzed in terms of specific classroom behaviors. With or without the use of video tapes, the purpose of the training sessions is to insure that the following principal elements of criterion teaching are both understood and employed:

1. Each child must understand every portion of the presentation.
2. Each child must be provided maximum opportunity to make complete verbal responses, both alone and in groups.
3. Each child must have a clear understanding of desirable and undesirable behavior.

Clarity of intent and positive reinforcement are the major themes of criterion teaching.

In-service training is effective because the time lapse between theory and implementation is short. Personnel new to the program receive an intensive preservice workshop during which they familiarize themselves with the design and content of the program through practice teaching.

Parent Involvement. The long-range goal of the program is to perpetuate the kind of education that viably serves low-income students. Parental support is the only means of implementing the program ideals. The needs of rural Indian education have been repeatedly diagnosed, and the need for change is recognized.

In December of 1967, a delegation of parents and school officials traveled to Kansas City to review several educational models that qualified for support under the newly established National Follow Through Program. This committee reported to the local Follow Through Policy Advisory Council, that in turn decided to invite the Engelmann-Becker representatives to the area to demonstrate their program. The demonstration, held in March of 1968, was attended by more than 150 people from all over the reservation. The decision to accept the Engelmann-Becker model was unanimous because the model addressed itself to the basic weaknesses of the local educational situation, namely, weaknesses in basic math and language skills.

Subject revision and increased emphasis on the use of good teaching techniques have characterized the program since its inception in 1968. Field test results have precipitated changes in the ordering of teaching priorities, in determining the sequence of presenting a given subject and in reducing the amount of time to be spent on them.

The techniques of instruction employed do not disturb the discerning classroom observer. Development of teacher-student rapport through a sense of accomplishment on the part of each is the singular goal of the techniques. Small groups and extra teaching personnel, augmented by training and administrative and parental support, expedite the achievement of this goal.

Parents select the teacher aides for their respective schools. This highly visible mode of parent involvement obviously affects the quality of the program. Less visible but more varied social means probably do even more to implement program potential, especially when that potential is realized through a child's achievement.

35

Follow Through: A Behavioral Principles Structural Model

Willetta C. Weatherford   *Program Coordinator, Dayton Public Schools, Dayton, Ohio*

Dayton is one of several sites in the country now implementing a Follow Through progam designed by Siegfried Engelmann and Wesley C. Becker of the University of Oregon at Eugene. Based on procedures originally developed by Engelmann and Karl Bereiter, this model has been in operation in the primary grades of three Dayton public schools since the fall of 1968. Initially the program involved only the first grade. The other two levels were added in succeeding years.

The program's approach is based on the fact that disadvantaged children are usually considerably behind middle class children in learning skills when they enter school, and that if these children learn at a normal rate they will remain behind average children in school.

The Children and Their Community.   Follow Through techniques are used in the primary classes at Edison, Grace A. Greene, and Louise Troy Schools located in a Model Cities target area. More than 75 percent of the children come from families receiving welfare payments or earning less than $6500 per year. Most of the children have attended kindergarten and have participated in Head Start or similar preschool programs. About 98 percent of the children are black. Many of their parents have not completed high school.

Learning Groups and the Classroom.   Partitions along one wall of each classroom form three carrels, each with a chalkboard, where children are taught. Each class has about twenty-five children and is staffed with one teacher and two aides. Four groups of five to eight children are organized for thirty-five minute morning lessons in arithmetic, reading, and language. Each teacher takes charge of one subject, and the groups of children move from area to area in the classroom for their scheduled activities and related independent study. All classrooms are carpeted, and ceilings are acoustically treated for noise absorption.

Instructional Techniques and Materials

Distar reading, arithmetic, and language programs, published by Science Research Associates, are used for core academic instruction. The program philosophy is based on the belief that every child can achieve well in any academic area if he receives adequate instruction. Instruction must begin with the skills children bring to school and must build upon them at a rate faster than normal. The procedures used must require a far greater number of responses from the child, adjust to individual rates of progress, use programmed materials that teach essential concepts and operations required for future tasks, systematically use reinforcement principles to insure success for each child, and utilize novel programming strategies to teach general ideas rather than specifics. In this program, the child who fails is a child who has not been taught.

Students are encouraged to speak clearly. Teachers use hand or voice signals that tell children when a group response is being requested and when the teacher will continue talking. As children near the end of a task, they usually become excited and shout their answers. This behavior is encouraged. Teachers often introduce a task by saying, "I bet I can fool you with this one. This is a hard problem." When children become familiar with a task, teachers occasionally give wrong answers to problems to allow children to catch them in mistakes. At the end of each session, the teacher may shake each child's hand and congratulate him for working hard and doing a good job. Children are delighted with praise. When first-year children complete a task well, they are immediately given raisins or other edibles as reinforcements. As soon as children are mature enough to recognize and respond to reinforcement techniques, they accumulate points instead of receiving food, and are given a prize of a toy or game when they accumulate a given number of points.

As another reward, take-homes are handed out. Take-homes are worksheets requiring written responses to materials related to those presented verbally in the instructional period. Older children may receive points for correctly answering questions on take-homes.

During self-selected activities, children may work puzzles, play with educational toys, games, or housekeeping items; paint; use a tape recorder, Language Master, or record player; read, or write.

Children are placed in ability groups for each core subject area according to their pre-test scores. Those who indicate the need may receive additional tutoring. All children are tested individually in each of the three core subjects every six weeks, and the tests are staggered so that each child is tested every two weeks. Test data are charted and sent to the University of Oregon, the curriculum supervisor, and the teacher. Results show whether groups are moving at an appropriate pace, whether any tasks need to be repeated, and whether any child should be moved to a different group.

In a special entry room for children transferring from other schools, teachers instruct newcomers in the signals, skills, and response methods used in the program, so that they will be able to function in the regular classroom.

Staff. The program in Dayton is taught by forty-two certified teachers and seventy-five aides. All teachers in the program chose to participate. Although the teaching staff is racially mixed, about 98 percent of the paraprofessionals are black women, most of whom are low-income parents of children enrolled in the program. Tuition-free courses are offered to the aides at a local city college. The program provides the services of two nurses, two social workers, and three social worker aides to families of the children enrolled. Parents videotape teachers working with children, and these tapes are sent to the University of Oregon to be critiqued. Each school has a parent worker, also paraprofessional, who is responsible for contacts with the children's parents. Other paraprofessionals administer the testing program and chart data. The project has a director and four curriculum supervisors trained by the University of Oregon staff.

Teachers and aides meet for one week of preservice training to learn the structure of the program, and each receives one hour of in-service training every week. In addition, the curriculum supervisors observe the teachers each day, thus providing them with immediate feedback on their teaching and demonstrations of the proper procedures. A written critique notes such factors as the manner in which the teacher paces lessons, uses signals, and utilizes correction procedures. Copies of these forms are sent to the program sponsor and are discussed with the teachers. The supervisors record each group's progress and each child's test data so that children continue to be properly placed for instruction.

Parent Involvement. Parent participation is important in reinforcing the child's feeling of confidence in his abilities and pride in his work. Parents must also be familiar with special features of the program. In order that they may assist the child at home, parents must know, for example, that a first-year child will be learning letters by sound rather than by name. Parents also recruit other parents to work in the project.

Success of the Program

Program assessment deals with attitudes of parents and staff toward project implementation, as well as with the progress of children.

In an effort to assess the progress of Follow Through children, two studies have been made. First, reading progress of all project children has been measured by the Wide Range Achievement Test and the Stanford Reading Achievement Test. Second, changes in achievement and intelligence of those children that have completed three full years in the program have been measured by the Stanford Binet Test of Intelligence and the WRAT.

Past data on reading achievement scores of Dayton children led to the conclusion that reasonable expectancies for Dayton's Title I schools would show grade placements of 1.6 for the first year, 1.95 for the second year, and 2.3 for the third year. Table 1 shows the mean reading grade placement scores for the total second grade enrollment in each of the Follow Through schools. The scores for word recognition skills, converted to grade placement, are those made on the Wide Range Achievement Test in the spring of 1970 by classes completing second grade.

Table 1 Mean WRAT Reading Achievement Scores and Projected Reading Accountability Standards

Schools	N	Mean	S.D.	S.E.	Dayton Account- ability Standard
Grace A. Greene	51	2.89	1.40	.20	1.95
Edison	108	2.90	1.41	.14	1.95
Louise Troy	75	2.99	1.26	.10	1.95

Frequencies and percentages are presented.

Table 2 Mean Stanford Reading Achievement Scores and Projected Reading Accountability Standards

Schools	N	Mean	S.D.	S.E.	Dayton Account- ability Standard
Grace A. Greene	54	2.06	1.31	.10	1.95
Edison	84	2.14	.91	.06	1.95
Louise Troy	181	2.03	.03	.03	1.95

Table 2 records the mean grade placement scores for the same children (1970–71) in each of the three schools. These mean scores are combined scores in Word Meaning, Paragraph Meaning, and Word Study Skills subtests on the Stanford Reading Achievement Test taken in September 1970.

Several observations regarding the data recorded in the tables are significant:

1. The difference in the numbers is accounted for by changes in school enrollment and pupil absences at the time of testing. The Louise Troy group included fifty-eight children new to the program in their third year.
2. The lower mean scores indicated for fall scores on the Stanford Achievement Test may be accounted for in the following ways:
   (a) The two instruments test different kinds of reading skills.
   (b) Students tend to drop in performance over summer vacation.
   (c) When the standard error is considered, the mean scores of the two tests as well as that of the projected standard are closely related.
3. After observations (1) and (2) are taken into consideration, it is still important to note that the pupils not only reached, but in fact exceeded the established mean set for the average student in Title I schools. Significant progress is apparently being made by pupils in the Follow Through schools.

A second study of a sample of 111 children who had completed three full years in the Follow Through program indicated that the children scored a grade equivalent of 5.33 on the reading subtest of the Wide Range Achievement Test. This is approximately 1.4 grade equivalent years above what would be expected from the standardization group.

Arithmetic and spelling scores showed that Follow Through groups made somewhat less progress than expected from a standardization example.

Table 3 presents the results of the analysis of the intelligence quotients from the Stanford-Binet Intelligence Test, categorized by year of administration and sex. The Stanford-Binet intelligence quotients have a mean of 100 and a standard deviation of 16.

Administration of the Stanford Binet Intelligence Test shows a significant increase in intelligence quotient by this Follow Through sample

Table 3 Intelligence Quotients from the Stanford-Binet Intelligence Test

Sex	1968	1969	1971	Av.
Female	89.19	92.43	93.67	91.76
Male	83.43	87.05	91.14	87.21
TOTAL	86.31	89.74	92.40	89.48

over the three-year period from 1968–1971. In addition, females performed significantly better than males.

Research reports so far are difficult to interpret because, with the exception of the Stanford Binet Intelligence Test, no pre-test was administered for this group beginning the first year. In addition, no comparable control group was available. The only comparison that can be made is with the standardization group for the instruments used. However, such standardization is inadequate because socio-economic characteristics of the standardization sample are not reported, and the standardization sample for the Wide Range Achievement Test is not a nationally representative group.

Survey of Attitudes Toward Follow Through.   Another type of evaluation consisted of questionnaires answered by staff personnel and parents. On the whole, both the certified and non-certified staff of Follow Through responded favorably to questions of administration, curriculum, scheduling, and evaluation. Responses suggest that those working with the program see its potential for supporting, supplementing, and achieving both personal and academic growth of students. Teachers indicated they felt the program challenged the students, that it "spelled the end to sad memories for teachers whose students could not break the code of skills, of logical thinking, and of individual pride." One resource specialist suggested that spelling be added to the program. Several considered the testing program to be inadequate. Others thought teachers in the first and second years of the program had more opportunity to teach creatively than those in the third year.

While a minimal number of parents responded to the questionnaire, the general approval they gave to the program seems to indicate that they note measures of success, both personal and academic, in their children.

In checking program components that they thought helped their children, parents listed small group teaching, contact with several different teachers, the help of resource teachers, and special teaching methods as factors that increased the children's ability to work independently. Frequent successes, increased parent contacts, and parent cooperative activities were also listed as significant parts of the Follow Through program. Because parent participation is vital to the successful operation of Follow Through, the parent advisory council, parent coordinator, and parent workers are endeavoring to find ways to develop enthusiastic responses among more parents.

Study of the effectiveness of the program continues. Special effort is being made to observe the performance and achievement of the participants as they move from the compensatory support provided through Follow Through to the degree of independence expected of them in the elementary school when they no longer receive support of the project.

The Follow Through program in Dayton requires about three-quarters of a million dollars per school year, or about $750 per child per year, in addition to the $974 provided every child in the school district. About 65 percent of the program cost is funded by the Office of Economic Opportunity. Funds available through Title I of the Elementary and Secondary Education Act provide about 10 percent of the cost. The remainder is raised locally.

36
Grand Rapids Project Follow Through

Lola M. Davis *Project Director, Grand Rapids Board of Education, Grand Rapids, Michigan*

Description

Project Follow Through, a compensatory program for early childhood education, was adopted in Grand Rapids in 1968. Follow Through is authorized under Title II of the Economic Opportunity Act, Urban and Rural Community Action Programs. The purpose of this title can be found in Section 201 (A): to stimulate a better focus of all available local, state, private, and federal resources. The main objective is to enable low-income families and individuals to become self-sufficient. Proper motivation and acquisition of skills and knowledge is the best way this objective can be accomplished. One teaching method that considers all these elements is the model developed by Siegfried Engelmann and his associates at the University of Illinois. It is now known as the Engelmann-Becker model, sponsored by the University of Oregon. This model, selected for research and continuous development by a group of Grand Rapids parents, uses the Distar curriculum for reading, language, and arithmetic. It is published by Science Research Associates. The curriculum is a careful approach that eliminates confusion and contradictions in the child's early stages of basic skills acquisition. One of the objectives of this Follow Through model is to bridge the gap between the performance of middle class children and disadvantaged children, who have repeatedly failed in our schools. The Follow Through Program has been successful in achieving its objectives in Grand Rapids.

Parents and educators selected 250 low-income kindergarten children (Phase I) to participate in the Follow Through program. At the end of the first school year, these children moved into Phase II, and additional children were recruited for Phase I. This process continued until September, 1971, when our project reached maturity with all four phases operating, kindergarten through level three, as stipulated by the federal government. Children are assigned to forty classrooms in eight inner city schools called centers. With parental consent, eligible children are transported to centers from twenty-four elementary schools. After the 1971–1972 school year, the first group of youngsters made the transition into fourth level classrooms in various schools.

Instruction

Cognitive skills are taught from Distar materials for reading, language, and arithmetic. Three trained adults are assigned to each classroom. The adults are trained in a two-week preservice workshop during the latter part of August. One hour per week of additional in-service training is required of them during the school year. A certified teacher and two instructional aides comprise a team. Each person is held accountable for one of the three subjects. The teacher, however, is expected to supervise and coordinate all learning activities in the classroom. Three groups of children, divided by ability, are taught simultaneously. They rotate from group to group during the morning session. Because the classes are usually divided into four groups, each group of children has the opportunity to do independent seatwork or to participate in reinforcing activities that foster learning. During the afternoon sessions, Follow Through children are given instruction in all other subjects. They are afforded the same privileges as children in the regular school program.

Follow Through teachers and instructional aides are constantly monitored in one of three ways. Teacher supervisors, who are employed locally but trained by the University of Oregon, visit the classrooms daily. Each teacher and each aide is observed for a period of time. Then the supervisor gives each instructor a performance sheet, listing strong and weak points of his presentation and suggesting means of improvement. The supervising teacher returns the next day to see if the skills have been improved. Each week the supervisors meet to compile a list of problems they have discovered. These points are dealt with during in-service classes the following week.

A group of paraprofessionals is also trained to be continuous testers. They administer Distar tests designed to evaluate the children's mastery of skills in reading, language, and arithmetic. During a six-week cycle, the children are tested individually on lessons they have covered. Two weeks are used for testing reading skills, then two weeks for testing language skills, followed by two weeks for arithmetic skills. Every six weeks, the cycle begins again. Children's test results are recorded on biweekly report forms. The teacher supervisors and teachers use these results, along with their professional judgment, to regroup children as needed.

In addition, the teachers and instructional aides are monitored on video tapes. Video operators, also paraprofessionals, tape teachers and instructional aides working with groups of children. These tapes are reviewed with the instructors, so they can see how they are teaching children and identify the strong and weak points of their presentation. The tapes give them the opportunity to observe students' responses and behaviors as well.

Each teacher's biweekly report of progress and video tape is sent to the project manager at the University of Oregon, and written critiques are sent back to the school. If there are corrections that should be made, measures are taken immediately to implement them. The project manager visits the local project monthly and sends in other consultants to keep abreast of the achievement of children as well. They assist the school when there are problems.

Ancillary Services

The Grand Rapids Follow Through Project is a comprehensive one. It has all six components outlined by the federal government. All of the functional components are vital for the academic success of our low-income students.

Social and Psychological Services. Social and psychological problems are inherent in any project for low-income children and their families. A full-time school social worker, a social worker aide, a part-time psychologist, and four parent workers are responsible for providing social and psychological services to children and their families. Referrals are received from teachers, building administrators, and parent workers. These people are usually the ones who can best detect unmet social or psychological needs. The social worker coordinates social and psychological services. She enlists the support of allied social agencies and other institutions—such as child guidance clinics, family service, and community action agencies—to assist children and parents. Solutions are often a joint effort of all personnel who work with the children.

Health Services.   Medical and dental health services are provided for children in our project. Preventive as well as curative medicine is practiced. A certified nurse and a health aide coordinate the health services. The nurse is responsible for scheduling medical and dental screening in the schools and for insuring that follow-up measures are taken as necessary. The nurse identifies agencies that will provide health services to Follow Through students and their families. She also teaches health education to children and to parents.

Nutrition.   Follow Through emphasizes the importance of good nutrition for children and their parents. Children are served snacks each morning. A well-balanced hot lunch is served daily to all children in their classrooms. A paraprofessional is trained to supervise the lunch period so it can be a social and learning experience instead of merely a feeding program.

Nutrition classes for parents are held in the schools. Day and evening classes are scheduled for their convenience. The basic food groups are explained, along with basic food preparation and menu planning. Parents are given advice on how to purchase nutritious food for their families within the limits of their budgets. These classes have been very well attended by Follow Through fathers as well as mothers.

Parent Involvement.   Ideally, parents should be totally involved in the education of their children. Orienting parents to our project's objectives provides them with a means for influencing curriculum and participating in the decision-making process. When parents are involved, a closer bond is established between the school and the community. Through parent participation, children come to view their parents as being truly concerned with their academic achievement and social well-being.

Parents are involved in our project in three ways: as Policy Advisory Council members, as employees of the project, and as classroom visitors and volunteers. More than half the voting members of the Policy Advisory Council are parents. The rest of the council is composed of ex-officio members from the local Board of Education and interested community agencies. The council concerns itself with evaluating every component of the project. Parents are given priority for employment in the project. They function as parent workers, instructional aides, video operators, and continuous testers. Parent workers deal directly with parents, teaching them how to reinforce their children's learning, planning educational and social activities, organizing monthly meetings, and communicating parents' concerns to the Follow Through staff. Their efforts help prevent the alienation of parents from school and school activities.

Evaluation

In 1967 the Grand Rapids Public School System experimented with several preschool programs. One group of children was enrolled in the Berieter-Engelmann Preschool, now Engelmann-Becker, and another group was enrolled in an Enrichment Preschool program. The following year, Follow Through began using the Engelmann-Becker model at the kindergarten level. At the end of preschool, some of these children were enrolled in the Bereiter-Engelmann kindergarten (Follow Through) and others in the regular kindergarten programs. There was also a control group—children who had not had any preschool experience—enrolled in each of the two types of kindergartens. A research study was made in 1969 under the leadership of Dr. E. L. Erickson from Western Michigan University in Kalamazoo, Michigan. A program evaluation was made each year thereafter. The titles and achievement results of the studies are listed here:

1. E. L. Erickson, J. McMillan, J. Bonnell, L. Hofman, and O. Callahan. *Follow Through Studies Final Report,* Contract #OEO-4150 Experiments in Head Start and Early Education Curriculum Structures and Teacher Attitudes, November, 1969.

Three groups of children were compared at the end of kindergarten. One group of children was enrolled in Bereiter-Engelmann Preschool, another in Enrichment Preschool, and the third group, the Control Pool, did not attend any preschool. At the end of kindergarten, the children from Bereiter-Engelmann Preschool and Enrichment Preschool achieved at about the same high level in both Regular Kindergarten and Bereiter-Engelmann Kindergarten. Their achievement was a year above age level. The Bereiter-Engelmann Preschoolers had a mean I.Q. of 108.1. Those from the Enrichment Preschool had a mean I.Q. of 94.8. Those from the control pool, who were enrolled in Bereiter-Engelmann Kindergarten were able to score slightly above age level

(I.Q. 104.9). Other children from the Control Pool, when enrolled in the Regular Kindergarten, went from a mean I.Q. of 94.8 to a sample mean I.Q. of 91.5.

2. Orel D. Callahan, Edsel L. Erickson and Jane A. Bonnell. *Third-Year Results in Experiments in Early Education,* Testing and Evaluation, Grand Rapids Public Schools, Grand Rapids, Michigan, June, 1970.

The findings indicate that at the end of the first year of schooling, economically disadvantaged inner city children with three years of Bereiter-Engelmann curricular experience scored at about the same achievement levels as city-wide norms which include children from more affluent backgrounds outside of the inner city. It can also be concluded that disadvantaged pupils who are given Bereiter-Engelmann–type experiences for three years will maintain, for that period at least, their advanced intellectual levels.

3. C. Bryan, R. Horton, J. Bonnell and E. Erickson. *Fourth-Year Results in Experiments in Early Education: A Comparative Assessment of Project Follow Through, Project Read and the Basal Reading Program.* Grand Rapids Public Schools, Office of Testing and Evaluation, and Grand Rapids Public Schools, Western Michigan University Center for Educational Studies, Grand Rapids, Michigan. August, 1971.

The evidence of four years of extensive research warrants the view that the Follow Through program is meeting one of its main objectives—enhancing intellectual skills in academic areas. Children in Follow Through have maintained average or above average scores on tests which often correlate highly with school achievement. Among children of poverty and accompanying handicaps, a mean I.Q. range from 1968 to 1971 of 105 to 108.7 was maintained by Follow Through students. Conventional programs historically have produced 89 to 94 I.Q. ranges for similar groups of educational and economically disadvantaged students.

Objective evaluation led to the conclusion that Follow Through teachers held higher expectations for their children than teachers of other programs did for theirs. They felt their level of accountability was much higher than that of other teachers. The Follow Through teachers also thought they had to work harder to teach children. Nevertheless, they were satisfied with their jobs and the achievement of their children. Follow Through teachers wanted more in-service education and more parental participation.

Follow Through parents, like the teachers, held higher expectations for their children than the control group of low income parents. Expectations of Follow Through parents for their children were even higher than those of middle class parents. The Follow Through parents had more faith in the teachers and a more favorable attitude toward school than did the control group. They felt their children were achieving very well in school and were concerned that their Follow Through children were performing much better than older siblings that did not have the Follow Through experiences.

Our project undergoes continuous, informal evaluation by the staff, parents, and other educators. A questionnaire is sent periodically to administrators, teachers, paraprofessionals, and parents, to be returned to the Follow Through Office. As a result, many constructive suggestions are made and implemented to improve our project. Committees composed of a cross section of personnel are formed to resolve major problems that may occur in the Follow Through Program.

Project Follow Through has been a successful compensatory program for early childhood education. The Engelmann-Becker model is achieving its objectives in Grand Rapids, Michigan. The greatest strengths of the program lie in the teachers' high expectations for children, the parents' favorable attitudes toward and involvement in the program, and the comprehensive community services that are provided for the low income children and their families.

37

Follow Through Program Using Distar Materials

Mrs. Ted Sheffy   *Local Teacher Supervisor, South Elementary School, Dimmitt, Texas*

Description

Dimmitt South Elementary School chose to implement the Engelmann-Becker program in the belief that the majority of its students could benefit from its instructional approach. It is a what to teach and how to teach program that emphasizes positive reinforcement. The material has sequenced learning steps. A child must be taught to criterion on one step before he proceeds to the next step. The child builds on his successes, moves at his own pace, and never performs at a frustration level.

Follow Through materials are published by SRA under the title Distar—Directed Instructional System Teaching Arithmetic and Reading. The Distar Language Program prepares children to engage in discussions, think logically, and use language as a tool for thought. Language problems include not only expression or dialect problems, but conceptual problems as well.

Distar Language I is designed to teach basic language concepts. Children learn to use complete statements in identifying simple objects, and then progress to a variety of concepts such as color, shape, relative size, and class name of familiar objects. The concepts are carefully selected for their contribution to logical thought. In early lessons, words common to a child's everyday experiences are used to teach identity and action statements. When children have mastered making these statements using a simple vocabulary, they proceed slowly to words that may be new to them. Later in the program, new words are presented at a more rapid rate. Vocabulary development is emphasized in sections of the program involving statements, polars, parts, categories, and locations.

It is essential to relate what children have learned in the formal language lesson to what is being taught the rest of the school day. This language learning should be used in everyday situations throughout the day. Much supplementary information has been organized as resource material for using language skills in all subject areas. Seatwork activities, music, stories, play periods with toys, and indoor and outdoor games are devised to reinforce the skills being taught in Distar Language.

Language II teaches the children to analyze language and use it to describe qualities and relationships they observe. Children are taught opposites, synonyms, and questioning skills that focus on language itself. They are taught how to give precise descriptions, define words, make analogies, and analyze statements. Materials used in the language program include:

1. *Presentation Books.* These highly structured lessons outline what teachers will say, children's expected responses, and corrections for mistakes.
2. *Story Books.* Many questions are asked during the story in order to develop listening skills as well as vocabulary.
3. *Color Books.* Shapes as well as colors are introduced here.
4. *Take-homes.* These worksheets provide practice in skills children have learned in the lesson, and are used as reward and reinforcement.
5. *In-Program Tests.* These provide the teacher with feed-back on how well the children are doing on each skill. They also indicate the need for extra tutoring or skipping lessons in the presentation books.
6. *Skill Review.* Skills are not taught and then dropped. They are periodically reviewed in new material. A child cannot become bored by going over the same material because it is introduced in a new form each time it is presented.

Distar Reading I teaches basic code-cracking and comprehension skills. It also provides exercises in sequencing events, saying words slowly, rhyming, and blending. It provides as much drill as the child needs in each skill to assure success in future tasks. Reading I begins with verbal and sequencing operations that are required in reading words such as *mat, am,* and *me.* To read these words, the children must know that:

1. Each letter is a sound.
2. Sounds are sequenced in certain order to make a word.
3. Words that are said slowly can be said fast and identified as words.
4. Any word that can't be spoken can be spelled by holding each sound in the word.

In place of a traditional reading readiness program, the following skills are taught in the pre-skills book:

1. *Sound Identification.* All letters, vowels, and consonants are taught as sounds. No letter names are taught in Level I. The capital letter is introduced as a sound only at the time the lower-case letter is taught as a sound. Some letters are joined to represent digraphs. Long vowel sound markings are shown. Silent letters are printed in smaller type than the rest of the word.
2. *Sequencing.* The teacher performs a sequence of actions and pupils must show the correct order of performance. The action is eventually analyzed in terms of what is done first and what is done next. Sequencing is taught as a game.
3. *Say-It-Fast.* Children are taught to say words fast that are given to them slowly, thus learning a blending technique to use when sounding out words.
4. *Spell-By-Sounds.* Children sound out words orally following a guiding hand signal from the teacher.
5. *Rhyming.* Children learn the skill of rhyming by adding various roots or prefixes to a single word ending. This is a verbal task.
6. *Sound-Sliding.* Children learn how to pronounce each sound in a word slowly but without pausing between sounds, thus connecting the sounds into a word that can be said fast.

After nine sounds have been taught—m, a, s, e, f, d, r, i, th—the pupils begin to read regular words. Irregular words are introduced in Lesson 80 of Level I. These are words that are not pronounced as they are sounded, such as *said, was,* and *of.*

Children are given Reading take-homes from the very beginning of the program. At first, there will be only one or two words to work with on each take-home, and a two-day story. The take-homes have pictures that go with the story, and there are writing lessons on the backs of the papers. Take-homes are introduced during the thirty-minute teacher presentation periods. They are sent home with the pupils daily after they have mastered the requisite skills.

Workbooks in Reading I are given to the children on the thirtieth day of the program. These books teach them how to translate pictures into statements and how to sequence events.

Reading II introduces the child to more complex words, statements, and comprehension skills. The small silent letters and the diacritical marks are dropped. The children learn more about punctuation, capitals, letter names, the alphabet, and long and short vowels. By the end of the second level, they have acquired a large reading vocabulary. At this point the take-homes become more difficult and require more independent thinking skills.

Reading II takes the child into increasingly independent reading practices, using the skills taught in the first two levels. He is able to read a take-home story well now, and has learned how to answer complicated questions about the story.

Arithmetic. Distar provides for the teaching of every basic skill. Nothing is left for the child to guess, memorize, or approach intuitively. The child is taught the basic concepts of all the arithmetic skills he will need to attack a problem. The major difference between Distar and other programs is not what is taught but how it is taught. Distar teaches the child what he needs to know in order to add, subtract, and multiply. In this program, skills such as names of numerals and signs are introduced later than in a traditional program, but multiplication and fractions are presented earlier. As rapidly as possible, children are taught the skills they need to solve complex problems. Because the children have been taught every necessary component, skill mistakes can be corrected by reviewing a variation of an already mastered task. The Follow Through program does not assume that all children have the foundation for arithmetic skills, but does a thorough job of building that foundation. All Follow Through classes are based on the knowledge that complete understanding eliminates frustration and increases self-confidence. Therefore, the slow learners eventually behave like fast learners.

Planning the Program

In 1969, Dimmitt was invited to serve as a pilot site for a Follow Through program. The first grade teachers, principal, and superintendent discussed the merits of each Follow Through model. Dimmitt teachers visited several Follow Through sites, then chose the Engelmann-Becker program.

A preschool workshop, with consultants from the University of Illinois, was held to instruct teachers and aides in Distar techniques. Each classroom has twenty five to thirty pupils and is divided into four ability groups. These groups are determined by testing, teacher observation, and children's performance. Each teacher has two aides. Each of them teaches one subject—language, arithmetic, or reading—while one group of children does seatwork. Follow Through groups are taught Distar materials mainly in the mornings in thirty or thirty-five minute classes. State requirements in all other subjects are met in the afternoons.

As part of the in-service training for all teachers and aides, the sponsor teaches a psychology course, "Behavior Modification." This course is required for all teachers and aides new to the program. The course is taught by teachers chosen from the local Follow Through personnel. Through it, the staff learns techniques of applied psychology for the classroom. Dimmitt has benefited immensely from this praise-reward teaching technique.

In addition to the guidance Dimmitt receives from the program sponsors, there is a local teacher supervisor on site to work with teachers. She is trained by the sponsor. The supervisor visits classes regularly, conducts weekly in-service training programs, and teacher demonstration classes to see how well the children are progressing in each subject.

On the first day of the school year in Level I, the pupils are given a placement test. Some pupils are able to skip the preskills books in all areas. No matter how he rates, the pupil starts at his present level. The pupils in Levels II and III start as close as possible to where they were at the end of the preceding year.

The teacher presents one lesson a day, bringing all pupils to criterion on each task in the lesson. When children are familiar with the method and have the needed foundation, they are able to learn more than one lesson a day. Some, because of cultural disadvantages or a language barrier, will progress slower than others.

The goal of the Follow Through program is to have one-third of the classroom working into one-third of the next level's materials, one-third completely through the level, and one-third finishing two-thirds of that particular level.

Evaluation

Each child is tested throughout the year in all subject areas. The results of these tests give the teacher an indication of what has or has not been learned. If a child passes the test, he is able to skip some lessons. Each child moves forward at his own rate.

The program employs five testers who evaluate the children every two weeks in each subject area. Test keys are available on site, so teachers can immediately review each pupil's progress. These keys enable them to locate in their teaching manuals the skills a particular child needs to be retaught. This system is a great aid to the teachers in tutoring the children that make repeated mistakes.

Pre-tests in three subject areas are given at the beginning of school for grouping purposes. Slosson I. Q. and Wide Range Achievement Tests are given at the end of the school year. These tests are administered under the guidance of the sponsor, with local personnel doing the actual testing. Teachers are evaluated in four ways:

1. The on-site supervisor visits each class every day to evaluate methods and techniques.
2. The sponsor provides supervisors at school for eighty days of the school year.
3. The teachers are video-taped at school, then critiqued by the sponsor to insure that all facets of the program are being taught in the proper manner.
4. The teachers view the tapes of themselves and of other teachers, and then evaluate themselves.

38

The Engelmann-Becker Model of Instruction

Margaret M. Aragon   *Director, Follow Through Program, Las Vegas City Schools, Las Vegas, New Mexico*

Description

The Engelmann-Becker Model of Instruction has been used in the Las Vegas City Schools Follow Through Program for several years. Follow Through was launched initially for the purpose of building on the gains that the children had made in year-long Head Start or other preschool programs.

The program implements comprehensive program components similar to those of Head Start. Special features of the program are the parent involvement program and the instructional model approaches that serve as the research and development components of Follow Through.

The major Follow Through program components include Parent Involvement, Social Services, Instruction, Psychological Services, and Nutrition Services.

The Parent Involvement Program is based on the philosophy that parents are members of the teaching team. The goal is to involve parents in decisions affecting the education of their children and to enlist parental support in the teaching process.

These goals are met through the work of the Policy Advisory Committee, through parent education sessions, parent social activities, projects which bring the parents to school, and a home visitation program. Social services are part of the parent education program. The most important tasks of the Policy Advisory Committee are screening and recommending paraprofessionals for employment in the program, developing program proposals, developing policies for program operation, evaluating the program, planning activities for parent educators, monitoring a career development program, and participating in conferences.

The Model of Instruction used in Las Vegas is known as the Engelmann-Becker Program, and the materials used are known as Distar. Distar, published by Science Research Associates, has been developed by Siegfried Engelmann and his associate, Wesley C. Becker, at the University of Oregon at Eugene.

The program is based on the philosophy that most children can learn the skills necessary to success in school, that each child learns at his own rate, and that success in learning will develop the child's self-image.

Distar teaching techniques require a great number of responses from the child. The program utilizes novel programming strategies and systematic reinforcement principles to insure success for each child. Hand signals and correction procedures are used to increase teaching efficiency.

Distar materials are carefully programmed to teach in sequence the concepts and operations essential to future tasks. Their use can be adjusted to individual rates of learning. The materials in each subject area include both teacher presentation books and student materials that reinforce the teacher's presentation. The latter are handed out at the end of the lesson as a reward for achievement. In addition, a Library Series of storybooks is available with the reading program.

Monitoring of the program requires weekly evaluations of teacher performance by local program supervisors, and monthly evaluation by the Model Sponsor's Project Manager. Video tapes of all staff members teaching their groups are sent to the sponsors regularly.

The Level I Distar Reading Program concentrates on decoding skills—the skills that enable a child to look at a word, sound it out, and pronounce it. Initially, the program teaches alphabet sounds rather than letter names. Approximately forty sounds are taught using only lower case letters. In order to avoid confusion, some letters are joined, such as *ch, sh,* and *er.* Diacritical marks are used to discriminate long vowel sounds, and silent letters appear in smaller type. By the end of the Reading I program, children read fluently, stopping only to sound out new words.

Level II Reading is designed to teach comprehension skills. The children's vocabulary is greatly enlarged now. Letter names and capital letters are introduced, and the diacritical marks are removed. By the end of the Reading II program, all prompts have been removed and conventional orthography is used.

The children are taught to read for information in the Level III Reading program. Most of the material is based on science concepts. Traditional word study skills are taught, and comprehension is emphasized.

Distar Arithmetic, Level I, is based on counting skills that prepare the children for basic operations of addition, subtraction, and the more complex operations of solving story problems and working with algebraic unknowns.

Independence in problem solving is stressed at Level II of Distar Arithmetic. Children are taught new relationships, such as multiplication, fractions, negative numbers, and analogies. The children also learn to solve money problems.

At Level III, addition and subtraction facts are strengthened and multiplication is taught. Children learn to add, subtract, reduce fractions, and work with mixed numbers. They learn some general laws of factoring. At the end of Level III, the program provides a general review of all arithmetic skills that have been taught, including carrying in addition and multiplication, and borrowing in subtraction.

The language of instruction is the focus of the Level I Language program. Children are taught to identify objects and actions and to describe and classify objects. The program teaches the use of pronouns, prepositions, polars, and same, different, and multiple attributes. Concepts that are important for logical reasoning, such as if-then, before-after, same-only, are also taught.

The Level II Language program builds on the skills introduced in Level I and adds a new dimension, analyzing language. Language analysis is taught through opposites, synonyms, questioning skills, analogies, description, and definitions. Children are given more information about the world around them. Subject areas include classification, function, absurdity, problem solving, reasons, measurement, occupations, and locations.

Sophisticated language analysis tasks are taught in Level III of Distar Language. Children learn to discriminate among statements, questions, and commands. They learn to use verb tenses, contractions, abbreviations, and sentence analysis. Upon this foundation, they build composition skills.

Psychological Services are provided as part of the staff development program that emphasizes preventive education. A course on the use of reinforcement principles is taken by all staff members.

In order to eliminate physical obstacles to learning, Health and Nutrition Services are provided. A physical examination, including follow-up treatment, is provided. A dental examination and treatment and a vision examination and correction are provided. Nutrition services include a hot breakfast and a free or low-cost lunch.

Evaluation

There are three agencies that evaluate the Engelmann-Becker model of instruction: (1) the local school system, (2) the Model Sponsors, and (3) the U.S. Office of Education (through Stanford Research Institute).

The local evaluation is based on the Stanford Achievement Test (SAT). This test is administered to all children in the school system, including the fourteen classes in the Engelmann-Becker program. The results for 1970 and 1971 show gains as follows. In 1970 the second grade children achieved a median score of 2.3 compared with the national norm of 2.0. In 1971, second grade children achieved a median score of 2.6, and the national norm was 2.8. Third grade scores show 1970 achievement at 2.6 and 1971 achievement at 3.0; the national norm is 3.8.

An interesting sidelight on the SAT is that the third grade children in one class scored higher on the intermediate science battery than on the primary battery. Because the staff felt that the children understood many science concepts, the higher battery was administered. The class median in the primary battery was 2.3 but it rose to 3.7 on the intermediate battery. The difference in individual scores ranged from 0.4 to 2.2.

In May, 1971, the children's scores on the Model Sponsor test (Wide

Range Achievement Test) were as follows:

	Reading	Spelling	Arithmetic	National Norms
Grade 1	2.5	2.2	2.2	1.9
2	4.1	3.0	2.9	2.9
3	5.6	3.8	4.1	3.9

Another method of sponsor evaluation involves the continuous testing program. Each child is individually tested in reading, arithmetic, and language every six weeks on the continuum of skills for that area. Prescriptive feedback is given to the teacher by the program coordinators.

The national evaluation by Stanford Research Institute is based on individual and group tests of children. Parent and staff interviews are also conducted.

In general, the children are more verbal, self-confident and outgoing as a result of the program. The teachers, who have visitors, supervisors, and evaluators constantly watching them, have become more confident in their work and more open to criticism. Many actively seek help in their work with the goal of improving the performance of their children. Parents visit the schools frequently and, therefore, are more aware than ever before of what their children are learning. Parent educators act as a liaison between school and home. The feedback from parents is most encouraging. Parents are increasingly interested in their children's progress, and the children respond positively to their interest.

Teacher Preparation

39

Early Childhood Tri-state Teacher Training Project

Gloria W. Gant   *Supervisor, Early Childhood Education, Leon District Schools, Tallahassee, Florida*

Description

Tallahassee's Leon District Schools are situated in a university area that offers educational opportunities for children from kindergarten through college. We also have a Community Action Program that includes Head Start classes. Clearly, there is a need for cooperative planning for the education of young children between university school systems, public school systems, and community agencies.

For this purpose, Leon District is participating in a Tri-state (Alabama, Florida, Georgia) Early Childhood Teacher Training Project (TTT), funded by Education Professions Development Act (EPDA), and administered by the Florida Department of Education for the tri-state area.

The TTT Project has involved planning with personnel from Apalachee Elementary School, Florida A & M University School, Florida A & M University School of Education, Lively Vocational-Technical School, Leon Interfaith (Community Action Program, Head Start), and the Leon District Schools Supervisory Staff.

The TTT Program

The cooperation of these agencies has provided practical classroom experiences for students in early childhood education from Florida A & M University, in-service teachers from Apalachee Elementary School and Florida A & M University School, teacher aides from Lively Vocational-Technical child care classes, administrative and supervisory personnel from Leon District and Florida A & M University, and parents. These persons have taken the team approach in implementing an early childhood education program in both open and self-contained classrooms.

Objectives of the TTT Project are as follows:

1. To develop an essential and related early childhood education program between the University, public school, and special agencies
2. To provide for needs of each school system in relation to the needs of the others
3. To provide leadership for meeting the needs of each agency
4. To provide essential in-service training for professionals, college students, teacher aides, and parents
5. To provide field experiences so that professionals, college students, teacher aides, and parents can plan and work together
6. To further develop and participate in an early childhood education program with open classrooms
7. To provide in-service education to help facilitate the open classroom plan
8. To disseminate information about promising practices to district and tri-state participants
9. To focus upon school, university, and community resources for children and their families

Training Activities. Participants are involved in the following training activities:

1. Seminars for the purpose of updating specific skills and competencies
2. Mini courses: *Teaching the Kindergarten Child with Minimal Language Experiences; Organizing the Kindergarten for Independent Learning* and *Small Group Instruction*
3. Workshops for administrators, teachers, teacher aides, participating students, and parents include the following:
   (*a*) Human relations
   (*b*) Team teaching
   (*c*) Construction of teaching aids
   (*d*) Parent involvement
4. Tri-state visitations
5. Tri-state in-service education

6. Practical classroom experiences—Teaming of teachers, university students, aides, parents
7. Visits to early childhood learning centers
8. Use of the available services of community agencies

Practical classroom experience involves early childhood students from the University, child care teacher aides from the Vocational-Technical School, classroom teachers, and parents. This group works in the classroom with the children on specific needs, as diagnosed by the classroom teacher. They work together in three-hour blocks at least two days per week.

School, district, and university personnel work as a team to coordinate the early childhood program. University students and teacher aides are encouraged to develop specific skills as they work with children and other adults. Teachers acquire skills as they work with children and other adults. Teachers acquire skills in working as team members, diagnosing children's needs and delegating responsibility. Parents learn how to work with children other than their own.

Evaluation

Evaluation of this project is based upon accomplishment of the stated objectives as assessed by the project participants. The following example is taken from the evaluation form:

Participant Evaluation of Early Childhood
Education In-service Component

You have participated in the Early Childhood Tri-State Teacher-Training Project. We are asking that you, as a participant, evaluate the component in terms of its objectives.

Please evaluate each objective as to one of the four levels of achievement. In order to ascertain a concensus of achievement, each objective is weighted 0 to 3.

First Objective: To develop an essential and related Early Childhood Program between the University, the public school, and special agencies.

( ) 3 Objective achieved
( ) 2 Substantial progress made
( ) 1 Some progress made
( ) 0 No progress made

40

Primary Training Unit

Marion Hazelton *Primary Project Leader, Cedar Rapids Community Schools, Cedar Rapids, Iowa*

Description

The Cedar Rapids Community School District is committed to a comprehensive program of staff development through in-service opportunities. This in-service program is headed by a director-level administrator and is carried out by a staff of sixteen coordinators and project leaders along with an ever-increasing number of Unit Leaders. One of the high-priority objectives of the Cedar Rapids Schools is to provide in-service training for new teachers. This program, which we call the Primary Training Unit, is one of the strategies agreed upon to reach this goal.

The Primary Training Unit program requires the services of one superior primary teacher, who serves as a Unit Leader for from four to eight new teachers of the same grade level. The Unit meets daily during the preschool workshop and monthly during the school year. In addition, members of each Unit make periodic half-day visits to the Unit Leader's room, and these visits are returned by the Unit Leader. Unit Leaders meet with the

	Monday	Tuesday	Wednesday	Thurdsay	Friday
1st Week				Unit Leader training	Unit Leader training
2nd Week	Unit Leaders arrange rooms; orientation of new teachers	Introduction; Primary training units	In-service training in unit leaders' classrooms	New teachers assigned buildings; Unit Leader visitation	Media workshop
3rd Week	Evaluation day and superintendent's luncheon	Building meetings	Work in own building	Workshops, conferences with co-ordinators	Work in assigned building; Unit Leader visitation

District's primary project leader to receive training to coordinate their programs.

A brief description and schedule of the current in-service program will demonstrate how the Unit Leader Plan functions as one element of the overall staff development plan in Cedar Rapids.

Ten days of the 190 contract days are designated as in-service days. No classes are held on these days; instead, staff development programs are scheduled. Four of the days are spent at the annual pre-school workshop in August, and six are on Fridays throughout the year. In addition, new teachers have extended assignment time for six half-days before the pre-school workshop.

The schedule on p. 198 outlines a typical pre-school workshop for the primary level.

Training Programs

In August two training programs are scheduled—a comprehensive two-day workshop for the Unit Leaders and an in-service training program for new teachers.

Unit Leader Workshop. On the first day, the Unit Leaders met in general session to discuss the purpose and background of the program and the proposed year-long schedule. Next, the teachers met according to grade level.

The kindergarten group discussed the following subjects: Cedar Rapids Kindergarten Syllabus, Kindergarten Units, the Iowa Handbook, Metropolitan Tests, report cards, parent conference reports, colored slides of kindergarten activities, available kindergarten materials. The group decided on topics to discuss with new teachers and they made a list of suggestions for preparing the classroom for the first day of school. They also made a list of suggested activities for the first week of school, giving special attention to the schedule for the first day. Names and building assignments of new teachers were distributed. Finally, the Unit Leaders discussed techniques for adapting the program to meet the needs of children in the various economic areas represented by the assignments.

New Teacher In-service Training Program: Preschool Workshop. An optional six half-day pre-school workshop was offered for new teachers before the regular pre-school workshop. Then, after meeting with their principals on the first day of the required workshop, all new teachers met at the local high school where the pre-school workshop was held. School officials explained school policies and distributed various forms. The morning session closed with a luncheon at which the superintendent welcomed the new teachers. Other administrators were also present at the luncheon where the new teachers could speak to them and ask questions informally.

The next morning, after being briefed on the Unit Leader Plan and meeting the Unit Leaders, the new teachers adjourned to their Leaders' classrooms, which were already set up for the first week of school. Each Leader had bulletin boards and materials ready for the training session. The small training group toured the classroom, becoming familiar with the guides, materials, and supplies she would find in her own building. The Unit Leader gave suggestions for arranging a primary classroom. New teachers who needed letter patterns, bulletin board ideas, or special help had the opportunity to copy, trace, sketch, and take notes. Much attention was focused on activities that precede the opening of school and on schedules for the first week. The groups discussed suggested daily schedules and each new teacher, under the guidance of the Unit Leader, made up a schedule for her first week and listed possible follow-up activities for the first month.

After spending two days in the Unit Leaders' classroom, each new teacher worked in her own room for a day. The Unit Leader visited each teacher and helped her locate supplies. She also met with the principal and kept him informed of their progress. The next day, all new teachers returned to the high school to learn about community activities and to attend a Media Workshop.

On the sixth day, principals and new teachers evaluated all aspects of the pre-school workshop. Primary Training Units were ranked high by both principals and teachers. The returning teachers then joined the new teachers in a four-day series of building and district-level meetings and workshops, with time set aside to work in rooms. On the last day the Unit Leaders visited each new teacher's room to review a last-minute checklist, answer last-minute questions, and give words of reassurance.

New Teacher In-service Training Program. During that first week, the Unit Leaders received many calls from new teachers asking for ideas and for advice on how to handle specific situations. During the third week of school, the first in-service training meeting was held.

The group shared their experiences of the first weeks and offered suggestions for solving each other's problems. They made plans for observing in the Unit Leader's room during October and November. Mainly the new teachers wanted to see how a veteran teacher handled discipline, how she arranged her daily schedule, and how she handled routine incidents. Additional visitations were made throughout the year whenever they were requested by the new teacher or her principal.

Unit Leaders also visited each new teacher's room for a half-day session. The Leaders stayed after class to discuss their observations and offer reassurance and suggestions for improving problem areas. At all times the Unit Leader reassured the new teacher that she was there to help, not to evaluate. The idea of helping was stressed from the beginning. Each teacher is part of the team, they were told, and every member of the team had the same goal—to provide the best education possible for every student.

These visitations were supplemented by regular staff meetings. Activities for these monthly meetings and in-service day workshops were planned to coincide with coming events on the school calendar. "How to Conduct a Parent Conference" came early in October before report cards were sent home. When it came time to plan holiday activities, each Unit Leader and new teacher shared her ideas with the group. In this manner, everyone was provided with a variety of suggestions for holiday activities. Toward the end of the school year, time was allotted for discussing the Metropolitan Test and for deciding on the best way to organize classroom activities for the final weeks.

Evaluation

In the spring a detailed evaluation of the Primary Unit Program was made by the entire staff—principals, coordinators, administrators, new teachers, and Unit Leaders. Even though the teachers were overwhelmingly in favor of continuing the in-service program, they had many suggestions for improving it. Two main changes in the 1971–72 program were made as a direct result of these suggestions. First, we have now set up training teams, a system in which a second-year teacher is teamed with a master teacher. This arrangement gives the younger teacher an opportunity to receive further in-service training under a leader who was herself a new teacher the previous year. Second, we now make allowance for experience. Under this new plan, teachers who have had previous classroom experience are grouped together and meet according to their needs. This plan enables Unit Leaders to spend more time training the first-year teachers.

The Unit Leader program provides a personalized in-service program for new and returning teachers. It provides guidance for the new teacher and enables the Unit Leader to make an in-depth review of the areas of her responsibility. Each time the program is evaluated, alterations will be made to provide a well-balanced in-service program suited to the District's needs.

Preparing for the First Day of School

I. Consult with the principal regarding:
   A. Anticipated enrollment
   B. Assignment of children to sessions
   C. Letter or method of informing parents about
      1. Session child will attend
      2. Opening and closing time
      3. Length of first-day session
      4. Supplies children bring from home (labeled shirt, rug 18″ x 36″, box of tissues)
      5. Greeting to each child from you
II. Prepare classroom:
   A. Make bulletin boards colorful and interesting
   B. Label lockers and cubicles using an identifying picture
   C. Make name tags
      1. Yarn so they can be worn
      2. Accurate manuscript writing
      3. Extras for unexpected children
      4. Picture-symbols on each card for identification
   D. Room arrangement
      1. Allow for quiet and noisy areas
      2. Allow for small and big group activities
   E. Room atmosphere
      1. Attractive plants, pictures, and so on
      2. Careful selection of toys and books
      3. Uncluttered but attractive feeling
III. Lesson plans:
   A. Make them flexible
   B. Overplan—better too much than too little
   C. Daily and weekly plans ready
IV. Class lists:
   A. Have names for both sessions handy
   B. Review names so they become familiar
V. Registration arrangements:
   A. Outside the actual classroom, in hall or office
   B. Special helpers available to answer questions and assist with registration

VI. Yourself:
    A. Dress comfortably but attractively
    B. Be rested and self-assured

First Day Schedule

The first day should provide the child with a pleasant taste of things to come. First impressions are important. The first day of kindergarten may affect the child's early adjustment to kindergarten and to primary years.

1. Get acquainted: with each other and with the room
2. Free play period
3. Roll call
4. Music experiences
5. Rest period
6. Story hour
7. Game time
8. Outdoor play
9. Dismissal

Helpful Hints for that First Week

Be sure that this training week is also fun!
Be prepared.
Don't hold them too long at one activity.
Have plenty of short stories, finger plays, and songs available.
Have simple games and puzzles on game table.
Stress care of materials, but don't make students afraid to use them.
Outdoor play is a *must* when weather permits.
Avoid hurrying children from one activity to another.
Above all else—HAVE FUN!

Resources Section

1

Early Childhood Education—
An Overview

Berlie J. Fallon

There are many names for early childhood education—nursery school, kindergarten, day care centers, Head Start, developmental programs. All involve the education of three-, four-, and five-year-old children. All provide early developmental experiences that prepare these youngsters to capitalize better on later educational experiences, although early childhood education is definitely education in its own right. Early childhood education is not meant to minimize the importance of the child's education at home, but rather to augment and enrich the entire constellation of his early learning experiences. A working partnership between home and school is essential. Ideally, it should involve mutual effort and concern.

Why Early Childhood Education?   Psychologists have hypothesized that because the child develops about 50 percent of his intelligence by the age of four years, 30 percent between the ages of four and eight, and 20 percent between the ages of eight and seventeen, the very early years are the ideal time to begin organized learning experiences. The child's intelligence grows as much during the first four years as it will grow in the next thirteen years.

Early childhood education seems to be the most promising method of attacking educational deficiencies among the poor. Disadvantaged children usually lag from one to three years behind more advantaged children in the public school setting. It has been shown that a child's environment can account for as much as forty I.Q. points, as evidenced by formal testing. How well and how rapidly children develop their mental model of the world depends largely on their environment. The more the child has seen and heard, the greater is his desire to see and to hear. The greater the variety of things he has learned to cope with, the greater his capacity to cope. Much that traditionally has been taught to older children can and should be taught in the early years.

When Should Education Begin? Preschools are beneficial for most children but are considered essential for disadvantaged children because of their experiential lag. Most educators and child development specialists tend to agree that few three-, four-, and five-year-olds gain the essential background for optimal development from the home environment alone. If a child has developed half of his intelligence by the time he begins the fourth year of his life, it seems imperative to expose him before then to as many learning experiences as possible that are conducive to his conceptual development.

Potential Scope of Early Childhood Education in the United States. In 1970 children under the age of five accounted for approximately 13 percent of the total population of the United States. By 1970 there were 25 million children under five years of age. Half this amount, or 12.5 million, were between the ages of three and five years, ranging from well-to-do to deprived in socio-economic status. Four million children were enrolled in some type of early schooling in 1968, and by 1975 it has been estimated that an additional 5 million children will join them.

If every three- to five-year-old child in the United States were enrolled in some form of preschool program, an additional 800,000 school personnel would be required in order to maintain a ratio of one adult to every ten children. In 1968 only 3,200 teachers were graduated from colleges and universities in the United States with specialized preparation in early childhood education.

Some Influences in Early Childhood Education

Since the mid-nineteenth century, various educators have pointed out the need for developmental programs for young children. The contributions of a few leaders in the early childhood education movement will be mentioned here.

Fredrich Froebel. In 1840, Froebel, a German educator, recognized the value of play schools for young children. He gave these institutions the name of *kindergarten,* meaning "child's garden." Froebel recommended that the children have time for individual activity, group activity, creativity, and motor expression. Individual development was the aim of his kindergarten, motor expression its method, and social cooperation its means.

Because of his belief that young children could profit by learning through a series of organized experiences, Froebel developed a set of educational methods and materials known as the "Froebelian Gifts and Occupations." The gifts, to be used in a precise order and manner, included balls, cubes, blocks, and cylinders.

Some experts have criticized the Froebelian school as excessively teacher-dominated and directed. Some have stated that Froebel's concept of creative independent activity should undergo careful assessment. Still others have felt that the European philosophy and program for the kindergarten were transplanted to the United States with little regard for the uniqueness of the American way of life. Nonetheless, Froebel's influence on the development of the early childhood education movement cannot be denied.

Maria Montessori. One of the foremost influences on early childhood education was Maria Montessori, the first Italian woman to earn the M.D. degree. She became a specialist in the training of mentally defective children and later turned to experimentation and theory in education. Dr. Montessori believed that education should be based on the child's desire to master certain skills. Her materials for teaching were designed so that when used in the proper sequence, they led the children to an understanding of abstract ideas. After the teacher introduced the materials to the child, one by one, she was to retire into the background while the child taught himself. The program in its entirety involved three parts and was usually designed to begin with children at the age of three. Part I involved exercises in daily living, such as cleaning, sweeping, polishing, and pouring. Part II involved sensory discrimination, such as the use of rods for visual perception of length. Part III involved visual and auditory discrimination and taught reading, mathematics, and writing.

Dr. Montessori's principal contribution was her emphasis on learning and the importance of the environment in the learning process. Her methods and accompanying materials are used in many schools today precisely as she prescribed their use in the early 1900's. The materials were designed to encourage self-motivation of very young children in a structured environment of cognitive materials developed for specific stages of growth. The Montessori plan was first introduced in the United States in 1912 and then reintroduced in 1953. In the present surge of interest in early childhood education, there is likely to be renewed study and implementation of Montessori's theories.

Jean Piaget. Piaget, a well-known Swiss developmental psychologist, emphasizes the growth of intelligence in terms of both environment and heredity. Basic to his theories is the assumption that enriched experiences in early childhood are important to later intellectual development. Two principal components comprise Piaget's theory. His *stage-independent theory* is concerned with the framework of concepts and terms. He views intelligence as the pyramiding of experience upon experience, thus forming schemas of progressively increasing complexity. According to Piaget, experience, maturation, social transmission, and equilibration are the four principal factors influencing intellectual growth. His *stage-dependent theory* depicts the actual stages of intellectual growth from birth to maturity. The four main stages of growth he defined included:

1. *The sensory-motor stage, birth–two years.* The child learns through use of the muscles and senses, and develops certain habits for dealing with external objects and events. Language and symbolization begin to develop.

2. *The pre-operational or representational stage, two–six years.* Organized language, greater growth and outside world representation occur in the child and magical experiences make sense to him.

3. *The concrete stage, seven–eleven years.* As the child acquires finer motor skills, he can move things around, fit things together into patterns, and organize and solve problems.

4. *The stage of formal operations, twelve–fifteen years.* Controlled experimentation occurs now, as does the development of hypothetical reasoning based upon logic of all possible combinations.

As a result of Piaget's work, new emphasis is now placed upon the cognitive development of the young child, and new curricula are being developed.

J. McVicker Hunt. Hunt, an American psychologist, has centered his research around the role of early experiences in the development of intelligence and maturation. He has discredited the theory of fixed intelligence, and has shown that children's I.Q.'s increase after enriching experiences. To him, early experiences are analogous to programming by computer. Feedback—sensory input with motor output—is the function of the nervous system. His experiments have demonstrated the importance of early perceptual and cognitive experiences. Hunt's studies show that children's I.Q.'s increase when parental discipline consists of responsive and realistic explanations. According to him, infants are motivated by new interests. Curbing their locomotor and manipulative development may result in negative effects that can be long-lasting.

Jerome S. Bruner. Bruner, a Harvard social psychologist, is studying children from four months to three years of age in his research on the cognitive process and motor control. He agrees basically with Piaget's concepts. According to Bruner, any method of instruction should aim at leading the child to discover for himself. His themes for teaching and learning include: (1) importance of structure, (2) readiness for learning, (3) intuitive and analytical thinking, and (4) motives for learning. Bruner's much-quoted hypothesis that any subject can be taught effectively, in some intellectually honest form, to any child at any stage of development has added validity to the notion that at least some elements of the fundamental disciplines can be taught in any early childhood education program.

James L. Hymes, Jr. Hymes, one of America's foremost authorities on childhood education, writes for parents as well as for educators. He states a wide range of goals for the kindergarten program. The common aim of all early childhood education, he says, is to help children learn in such a way that the youngsters spend their preschool years in the richest, most satisfying, most constructive manner possible. Hymes further believes that young children are ready to learn if educators but have the wisdom and the sensitivity to adjust their methods to suit the children. These young children should be taught to live the early years of life with joy and meaning, with more purpose and satisfaction. Hymes' method for judging kindergarten lies in assessing the joy and fulfillment that school brings to the child's life.

Trends in Early Childhood Education

Although additional trends may emerge in the near future, a number are discernible at present. Relatively generous funding for innovative programs may be expected—indeed, the impetus behind early childhood education may be one of the most extensive and exciting recent developments in education.

Influence of the British Infant Schools.   Established during the latter part of the eighteenth century as a result of the Industrial Revolution, the British infant school was a dream of Robert Owen. Owen saw early childhood education as a means of improving conditions for working people that lacked the time and materials necessary for the training of their children. Owen first established a playground and then an infants' school that taught good habits to children who were too young for formal instruction. The British infant school today is a division of the public elementary system that provides education for children from the ages of three to eight. The purpose of the infant school is to help boys and girls reach their full development as individuals, to help shape their character, develop their intelligence, and prepare them for life. Among its major goals are health, good habits of speech, and mastery of the three R's.

The British infant school maintains no rigid daily schedule. How the time is spent is left entirely to the individual teacher. There are no classrooms, either. Each child chooses his own learning experiences from a wide array of materials and activities. The teacher is always present—observing, stimulating, assisting the child, and keeping detailed records of his progress. Several activities such as painting, music, and reading may go on simultaneously. Teachers in open classrooms emphasize learning rather than teaching. The open, flexible space is divided into functional areas. The environment includes ample concrete materials, books, and other media. It is difficult to define what is being learned at any particular time, because many learning options exist for the individual child. Among the ideas adopted from the British infant school, the open school concept has been by far the most popular.

Montessori Schools.   Montessori schools are based on the belief that the child possesses a sensitivity and a mental capacity for absorbing and learning from his environment that is quite different from those of adults. Using self-teaching materials, the Montessori child works in a non-graded class. He is free to pursue whatever interests him as long as he does not disturb other children or abuse the equipment. The teacher acts as his guide. She introduces new materials and experiences when the child is ready. She prepares the environment, but the child learns through the exercise of inner discipline. A Montessori classroom requires about $800 worth of special equipment, designed for use at the preschool level. The teachers, in order to be effective, must have received special training in the methods of Montessori.

Engelmann-Bereiter Program.   The academically oriented preschool, designed for disadvantaged children by Carl Bereiter and Siegfried Engelmann, has been referred to as an intellectual pressure-cooker. In this daily, two-hour program, children have three teachers for language, reading, and arithmetic. The children move from center to center for twenty-five minute sessions of intensive instruction that are balanced by relaxed activities such as singing, art, and listening. The program resembles an athletic drill session, in that language instruction involves patterned drills and the reading program emphasizes phonics. As many as 500 responses may be required of a child during one twenty-minute session. Test scores indicate that students can make striking gains in a school year. Some have jumped ahead as much as two years in a period of six months.

Three highly trained teachers work intensively with fifteen children at a time. The program requires no special equipment. The designers say that their evidence does not suggest that early exposure to academic instruction develops negative attitudes toward schooling. Instead, it builds positive attitudes toward school that should provide a basis for better adjustment to school in later years.

Head Start.   "The Kiddie Corps," as Head Start was originally named, was implemented in the summer of 1965 when children from a few disadvantaged neighborhoods were first given eight weeks of preschool experience. The Head Start Program attempts to reach children between the ages of three and five through a preschool program. The program provides language opportunities, both speaking and listening, as well as a wide variety of experiences and behavior models for the children. Also included are medical and dental examinations and corrections. A definite attempt is made to involve parents in all aspects of the program. The basic objective is to break the poverty cycle at an early age, in response to evidence indicating that the early years of childhood are the most crucial ones in educational development.

Television.   Statisticians predict that preschool children spend 4,000 hours watching television before they begin their formal education. TV is coming into its own as a tool of education with such programs as "Sesame Street," "The Electric Company," and similar series. The intent is to entertain young children and to teach them skills at the same time. It is anticipated that the time will come when television programs will be used flexibly, so children can replay a favorite program just as they now do a favorite record.

Group Size.   Groups of children tend to become smaller as age levels are mixed in early childhood education programs. In some classrooms, three- and four-year-old children are mixed, and the group is limited to about fifteen. Class size is relative. It depends on the goals of the teacher for the children, the methods of teaching, and the ages of the children. Some experts suggest that a good class ratio is two teachers for twelve three-year-old children, two teachers for sixteen four-year-olds, and two teachers for twenty five-year-olds. Compensatory education requires smaller groups with added adult supervision.

Use of Aides.   The trend to using aides in early childhood education programs is growing. Some experts maintain that every classroom of very young children should be served by an aide. Aides must be oriented to the jobs they do and to the children with whom they work. Teachers must provide most of the direct orientation for aides, although school districts must take the responsibility for any broad-based program of in-service training and orientation. Aides may be paid paraprofessionals, volunteers, or parents. The important thing is that the aides be dependable and cooperative.

Schedule.   The average program in early childhood education lasts from two hours to four hours, depending on the needs of the children and the schedule of the school. Some schools find it necessary to provide double sessions—one in the morning and one in the afternoon—to accommodate all the children who wish to enroll. For the very young child, it seems advisable to limit the time spent in stimulating experiences to a very short, daily period.

The shorter the time these children spend in school, the longer the time available to the teachers for planning. Much time is needed to plan the preschool program, as well as to visit with the children in their homes. More frequent home visits are necessary during the preschool years than during the years spent in the primary grades.

Parent Involvement.   Nationwide, a concentrated effort is being made to reach parents and to involve them in the early learning experiences of their children. Telephoning and making home visits are important ways teachers can establish good lines of communication. Group meetings and participation as aides or helpers are other excellent methods of getting parents involved. At no other level of education has parent involvement been more enthusiastic and effective than in early childhood education.

School Organization and Subject Matter. Innovation in the broad field of primary education can begin easily and naturally in the early childhood years. The School of Inquiry, located in a slum area in Rochester, New York, features multi-age grouping coupled with interest centers strategically located throughout the school. At the University Elementary School at the University of California at Los Angeles, multi-age groupings and team teaching focus on individual diagnosis and prescription for young children.

Currently, experimentation and change are highly evident in preschool programs. This experimentation involves mathematics, reading, science, and social studies. The emphasis is on principles rather than facts, on learning through problem solving rather than by precept, and on individual differences of children.

A well-balanced program in early childhood education ordinarily includes opportunities for many child-selected experiences, time for quiet as well as active experiences, opportunities for self-directed individualized experiences as well as group experiences, and sufficient flexibility in scheduling to permit children to spend time with activities that interest them. Classrooms must be arranged around interest centers, such as arts and crafts, dramatic play, block building, manipulative materials, library, music, display, and other areas that will attract the interest of young children and provide highly active learning experiences for them.

2
Title I Kindergarten Program, Albuquerque Public Schools

Albuquerque Schools, Albuquerque, New Mexico

Philosophy of the Kindergarten Program

The philosophy on which the Kindergarten Program is based consists of a number of components. They are as follows:

I. *Principles of Child Development.* Consideration of the characteristics of a five-year-old: What is a child like at this age? How does he act? What can he do or be expected to do?

Consideration of the child's entire life space and all its elements—home, neighborhood, school, and community.

Consideration of the nature of each child as a unique human being—with all the many facets of individual personality, including its cognitive, emotional, and physical aspects.

II. *Jean Piaget's Cognitive Psychology.* The five-year-old is at the pre-operational stage of development. Concrete, manipulative experiences are necessary at this stage of a child's conceptual development. He must have real experiences with objects and activities before he can symbolize or abstract concepts.

Classroom activity is focused on skill development and is directed at teaching the child to use all his senses to perceive experiences more precisely, to improve his ability to classify and organize these experiences into concepts, and to improve his language ability so that he can express what he has experienced.

III. *Self-Actualization Theory.* This theory, developed by Carl Rogers, A. Maslow, and others, stresses encouraging the child to feel good about himself and helping him to feel that he can respond and react positively and productively to his environment.

The child should be encouraged to talk, to investigate, to try, to be aware of and talk out his feelings, and to develop self-participation in relation to others.

216

IV. *Language Experience.* Because language is internal, it is tied to the child's total life style. It grows as his life experience increases. Growth—in terms of enlarging vocabulary, spontaneous expression, listening skills, processing ideas—has to be accomplished on an oral level before the reading of symbols comes about.

The classroom offers children many opportunities to talk freely about a lot of different kinds of activities. Many common experiences are provided so that children can communicate and share ideas with each other.

V. *The Discovery Method.* The environment should be enriched with a variety of materials and equipment that entice exploration.

Adults are not expected to supply all of the answers, but rather to encourage intellectual curiosity and investigations with objects and situations close at hand, so that children themselves can find answers.

Opportunities for planning, decision-making and problem-solving are provided. Opportunities for classroom management can be provided so that independence, responsibility, and self-confidence in tasks can be developed.

VI. *Parent Participation.* Parents are encouraged to come to the classrooms at any time, so that they can see their child in the school setting. In this way, parents can often learn ways of helping the child in learning situations at home, and understand why the child may be having certain experiences at school.

VII. *Community Relations.* Because the child brings to school all his life experiences, the teacher is encouraged to be aware of community influences that may have meaning to the child.

VIII. *In-service Training for Teachers.* Because there is continuous research and discovery in the field of early childhood education, it is felt that there is a need for on-going, in-service training to acquaint teachers with the latest findings in child growth and development and learning theory.

3
A Typical Table of Contents for a Curriculum Guide in Early Childhood Education

Newark Schools, Newark, New Jersey

Foreword
Preface
Acknowledgments
Introduction
Goals of the Early Childhood Curriculum Guide
The Five-Year-Old's Growth and Development
The Suggested Learning Environment
    The Physical Learning Environment
    Planning the Daily Program
Self-Image: Developing an Awareness of Self in the Child
Suggested Methods of Evaluation and Record Keeping
Language Arts
Mathematics
Science
Social Living
Arts and Crafts
Music
Health and Safety
Motor Coordination
Auxiliary Personnel
Parent Involvement
Multi-Media Tips
Bibliography

4

Objectives of the Early Childhood Education Program

Panama Schools, Panama, New York

The objectives of the program were derived from the project proposal and the style of the consultant, Dr. Louis Raths. As an authority on value teaching and instructional processes which enhance ego development, decision making, and value clarification, Dr. Raths was concerned about the quality of classroom interaction as well as the specific teaching objectives of the following program proposal:

1. Teachers, aides, and parents will better understand the methods and techniques involved in early childhood education.
2. The focus is on each child and his active role in learning.
   (*a*) The general health of these children will gradually show improvement.
       (1) Each child will have a physical examination, and the general health of each child will show some improvement.
       (2) Each child will have dental and eye care provided by an outside agency if necessary.
   (*b*) The general nutrition of these children and their families will improve.
       (1) Each child will be able to select a balanced meal at the school cafeteria.
       (2) For the children who carry their lunches to school, the mothers will prepare nutritionally balanced meals.
   (*c*) The self-image of each child will improve as follows:
       (1) Each child will develop social confidence by establishing a friendship with at least one other child in the preschool program.
       (2) Each child will have the opportunity for successful experiences through acceptance of his work in the program's creative activities.
       (3) The physical coordination of each child will improve through organized physical activities.
       (4) Each child will be able to differentiate between acceptable and non-acceptable classroom behavior.
   (*d*) The children will be better able to adjust to their environment.
       (1) Each child will know his bus route to school.
       (2) Each child will be familiar with the school plant—its offices, classrooms, and other facilities.
       (3) Each child will adjust more quickly to school life through orientation to scheduled activities.

(*e*) The children will become more actively involved in creative activities.
    (1) Each child will have the opportunity to become actively involved in creative activities.
    (2) Each child will choose to become deeply involved in at least one creative activity.

(*f*) The children will develop the ability to listen and to enjoy new cultural experiences.
    (1) Each child will develop the ability to listen to stories within a group.
    (2) Each child will learn to enjoy at least one new social experience, such as picnics, or the zoo.

(*g*) The parents will develop new perceptions of their children and the school through volunteer services and planned activities.

(*h*) The children will be able to understand and create ideas congruent with their emotional development. Each child, as he grows emotionally, will develop new concepts of learning and playing. This growth will be measured through goals established for each child based on his need.

The wide range of specific program objectives listed here has been reorganized by the evaluators for reporting purposes. These specific objectives were immeasurably influenced by the personality and ideas of Dr. Louis Raths. His program can perhaps best be described in terms of five broader objectives:

1. To demonstrate care for the health and safety of every child
2. To persistently share the child's meaning (frame of reference) in the communication process
3. To create alternatives that facilitate children's decision making
4. To use clarifying responses in order to stimulate the children's thinking about their goals and actions (valuing processes)
5. To provide an individualized instructional program in which each child's behavior is consistent with his goals.

5
Growth and Development of the Five-year-old Child

Albuquerque Schools, Albuquerque, New Mexico

By age five, most children have entered a period of slower growth. Though the boys are usually larger, most girls are ahead of the boys in skeletal and muscular development. The five-year-old's growth is uneven. The heart is growing rapidly, but the lungs are still relatively small. Hence, vigorous exercise should be alternated with quiet activities or rest periods. His large muscles are much more developed than the small muscles which control his hands and fingers. He needs to exercise and to strengthen the large muscles of his arms, legs, and trunk before trying to write. Many five-year-old children may not be ready for the exacting control required to hold a pencil and try to form small letters, but will profit by using a large brush and painting on a large surface. The child's handedness is usually determined by this age. However, his eye-hand coordination may still be unsure. He is likely to misjudge distance and to spill or knock things over. The five-year-old is usually quite independent and delights in the power he has gained to control and manipulate his environment.

I Can Do It Myself!

At this age, the child gains confidence by knowing he can touch home base when necessary, and therefore welcomes the adventure of learning through discovery, and the challenge of problem solving in new situations. During this period, the child relishes his growing awareness of sensory experiences. Tasting a lemon, feeling a warm chicken egg, smelling freshly popped corn, listening to a bird chirp—all awaken his sensory perception. His memory at this stage is highly developed, so he has the capacity to absorb and relate new learnings to past experiences.

Although the five-year-old is usually eager for interaction with his peers, he often needs assistance with social skills that will help him develop meaningful and positive relationships. A common complaint might be: "They won't let me play with them. Nobody wants to play with me. I can't

221

play anywhere!" This child is usually responsive to sympathetic adults. He will participate in small group activities for short periods of time.

Listening to stories and poems about familiar experiences, singing, chanting, viewing short films, and planning projects are usually enjoyed by most kindergarten children in small groups.

The child of this age is refreshingly imaginative. He expresses his imagination in all areas of the kindergarten program.

- See that J on the mountain. The Indians made that two thousand years ago. It means Jesus.
- This song sounds like elephants taking a bath.
- My painting isn't a face. It's a gumball machine filled with red and black balls.
- I am a fairy and I can turn you into a yellow frog or a fiery flying horse.
- This is another world and the people here don't need any legs.
- That's not a pumpkin. It's an orange sun.

He derives satisfaction from seeing his imaginative products displayed. The child of this age group is sensitive, impressionable, and capable of deep affective experiences. He is extremely vulnerable. Significant attitudes toward self and others can be profoundly affected by his experiences in the kindergarten. He is also unpredictable and volatile. At one moment he can kick or bite the teacher, and seconds later he can hug and console her.

Physical Development

The importance of body image for accurate perception of outside objects is emphasized by Bender, Frostig, Schilder, Kephart, and other authorities. Increasingly, evidence from research studies seems to indicate that learning is an integrative, cyclical process involving the total organism; therefore, physical education is actually a part of reading. Motor activities are not completely independent of intellectual activities, as was once thought. Learnings acquired in an appropriate physical education program at the kindergarten level must now be considered essential to future intellectual development.

Physical education is not limited to outdoor activities. Elements of this program will overlap with many indoor activities. Physical skills are developed daily through rhythms, music, art, and block play. Health education, too, is an essential part of the physical education program. The kindergarten child needs to learn how to care for his body.

Rationale. Children's awareness of their own body parts and their relationship to each other provides a base from which they develop the perceptual skills necessary for them to function successfully in all areas of the academic program. The teacher can select and invent many activities and games which will help the children become more aware of their bodies.

Braley, Konicki, and Leedy have developed a program entitled *Daily Sensorimotor Training Activities* that emphasizes physical development in the following areas: body awareness, space and direction, balance, basic body movement, hearing discrimination, symmetrical activities, eye-hand coordination, eye-foot coordination, form perception, rhythm, large muscle activities, and fine muscle development.

Indoor Equipment	Uses
Boxes, all sizes	Paint boxes of various sizes. Use to set up obstacle courses. Use for sorting PE equipment: balls, ropes, buckets, and trowels.
Inner tubes	Use for obstacle course.
Walking board	Use to develop balance.
Masking tape	Use to define game areas.
Small blocks	Build a bowling alley and use them as pins.
Any spherical object	Use for a ball. Let the children discover materials to adapt for use in games.
Standard room furniture and equipment	Children can gain perception of weight, space, shape, and distance, as well as discover their own physical abilities, by manipulating objects in the room.
Equipment for sand and water play	Tubs, buckets, measuring cups, spoons, funnels, egg beaters, plastic bottles, containers with lids. Use in sand box and for water play. Children develop large and small muscle coordination and eye-hand coordination.
Bean bags of various shapes and weights	Develop coordination, judgment of distance, size, and weight.
Art equipment Clean-up equipment	Sponges, brooms, mops, paper towels, cleanser, soap. Strength and dexterity as well as eye-hand coordination can be gained from squeezing a sponge or mop, sweeping dirt onto a dust pan, or cleaning equipment with a towel.

Outdoor Equipment	*Uses*
Jungle gym	Climbing, chinning, moving through and between bars. Children enjoy pretending it is an animal cage. They can invent other games.
Swings	Develops many muscles.
Parallel bars	Chinning, climbing, swinging.
Climbing tower	Helps to develop ability in climbing, balance, and judging distance.
Slides	Helps develop balance, sense of body in space.
Jump ropes	Develops balance, rhythm, coordination, strength.
Wagons	Hauling and loading wagons involves coordination, judgment of space, size, and weight.
Balls	Helps to develop strength, coordination, sense of direction.

Games and Activities. Follow the Leader, Simon Says, the Farmer in the Dell, Ring Around the Rosy, Drop the Handkerchief, Duck, Duck, Goose, Bounce the Ball or Dodge Ball, Red Rover, Monkey See, Monkey Do, relay races, broad and high jump over blocks, and holiday chase game, a variation of Drop the Handkerchief; children improvise chants about holidays or pets, after teacher gives examples.

Examples

Choo Choo

The choo-choo train is coming,
Choo! Choo! Choo!
The engineer stops it
Right behind who?
Not here. Not here.
HERE!
(Child who is "it" drops the
handkerchief behind a friend.)

The Witch

The Witch is on her broomstick
Where is she?
We will find her.

Wait and see!
She's not here.
She's not here.
Here she is!
Whee!

6

Activities Environments

The Suggested Learning Environment
Newark Schools, Newark, New Jersey

The Physical Learning Environment

In setting up the physical facilities for an early childhood program, the apparatus must be carefully chosen. The room and the arrangement of equipment should meet the needs of the young child.

1. Furniture should be movable and should fit small children.
2. Toilets should be low and easy to reach.
3. Drinking fountains should be low and easy to reach.
4. Playground equipment should not be too small.

The room should be divided into several centers of interest:

The Housekeeping Center

1. What is a Housekeeping Center?
   A place where children can imitate, play and dramatize home relationships: father, mother, baby, older siblings, grandparents
2. What goes into a Housekeeping Center?
   Screens to create the appearance of a small room, dolls, doll beds, carriages, kitchen toys, stove, refrigerator, sink, cupboards, dishes, pots and pans, table with tablecloth, chair, mirror, and chest of dress-up clothes, community helpers, hats

Little guidance is needed in this area. Children are encouraged to clean up when finished. Each item should have a proper place.

The Block Center

1. What is a Block Center?
   A place where children build with blocks to create stores, churches, firehouses, or their houses
2. What goes into the Block Center?
   Shelves low enough for children to reach; blocks neatly arranged by sizes and shapes; large hollow blocks; wooden people—ethnic groups and family groups; plastic soldiers, Indians, and cowboys; transportation toys such as cars, planes, boats, and trains

Guidance and Comments.   Building is one of the most satisfying activities for all types of children. It requires little guidance. Shy children sometimes begin building if a teacher or a parent offers them several shapes of blocks or places a "lumber pile" of blocks in a secluded place for them. Aggressive children sometimes need to knock down their own buildings, and they build for that purpose. No dramatic issue should be made about knocking down buildings, either accidentally or on purpose. Comments can include encouragement about careful construction, successful balance, or an interesting layout. Cooperative effort can be developed by suggesting that the class make city street markings or traffic lights. Occasionally, a well-constructed building that is precious to the child may be sketched by an adult before it is taken down. This picture is a most satisfying keepsake for the child and is often shown at home with great pride.

The Library Center

1. What is a Library Center?
   A place where a child can go to look at books alone, or where a group of children and the teacher can listen to a story together
2. What goes into the Library Center?
   Table and chairs, bookcases or improvised shelves, books
   > Stories of general interest of varied difficulty
   > Stories related to social studies
   > Science books
   > Children's magazines
   > Picture file—pictures collected from magazines and travel folders are mounted and filed under various classifications
   A bulletin board for displaying reading slogans, such as "Read for Fun," or "Come and Read"
   > Appropriate pictures and bookjackets
   > Newspaper book reviews of children's books
   > Illustrated short book reviews by the children
   > A variety of dictionaries of varying levels of difficulty: *Pixie Dictionary, Animal Dictionary, Words I Like to Read and Write*

A variety of reference books on topics relevant to the immediate environment and children's interests

The Science Center

1. What is a Science Center?
   A place where materials are available for science experiences; where children can go to explore independently the how, what and why of things; where children can carry out group experiences related to or arising from anything the curriculum stimulates
2. What goes into the Science Center?
   An Odds and Ends box containing a variety of simple science equipment, such as magnets and iron filings; toys that involve scientific principles, such as magnetic games, wind-up toys, and whistles
   Science phenomena such as pictures of
      Rain and clouds
      A river frozen over to show change of liquids to solids
      Smoke to show that hot air rises
   Simple science displays such as
      A fish bowl with fish
      An aquarium
      A cage with an animal
      A rock or shell collection
      A collection of different types of leaves
      A growing plant
   Books or other printed material for children to consult

The Arts and Crafts Center

1. What is an Arts and Crafts Center?
   A place where children have the opportunity to use a variety of creative materials. This Center should be placed near water.
2. What goes into the Arts and Crafts Center?
   Easels
   Equipment for painting and drawing
      Tempera paint and drawing paper
      Brushes
      Finger paint and finger painting paper
      Sponges and water
      Crayons
      Charcoal
      Large newsprint and drawing paper
      Smocks or aprons
      Large wooden clothes rack or clothes line for drying paintings
   Equipment for modeling
      Clay kept in airtight crock or can
      Clayboards for a work surface

A What Not box for children to use freely as a source of art materials. It might contain small pieces of

fabrics	furs	tape	toothpicks
yarn	feathers	beads	sandpaper
leather	sequins	cotton	cellophane

The Writing Center

1. What is a Writing Center?
   A place where children dictate stories to be written down by adults; a place where children have the opportunity to do their own writing. Formal writing should not be emphasized at this level.
2. What goes into the Writing Center?
   Tables and chairs; a wide variety of paper textures, shapes and spacings; lined and unlined papers, including newsprint in column width; unruled paper, colored papers, $1''$, $\frac{3}{4}''$, and $\frac{1}{2}''$ ruled paper; a wide variety of writing tools, including felt colored marking pens, and crayons; name cards, A, B, C cards, word cards, labels, picture dictionaries, a primary typewriter

The Music Center

1. What is a Music Center?
   A place where children can experiment with various types of musical instruments
2. What goes into the Music Center?

autoharp	bells
tonebells	shakers
record player	sticks
tape recorder	drums
tambourines	triangles

The Math Center

1. What is a Math Center?
   A place where children can manipulate concrete materials related to topics they are studying; a place where a child can go to explore independently the how, what, and why of numbers
2. What goes into the Math Center?
   A flannelboard with objects to put on it
   Containers for liquid measure: quarts, pints, cups
   Materials for linear measurement: rulers, yardsticks
   Objects for counting

toy money	ice cream sticks
cardboard circles	an abacus
buttons	number cards
a cardboard clock	simple number games
beads	plastic numbers
pegs	sandpaper numbers

Charts related to whatever the children are currently studying
Books about numbers

The Woodworking Center

1. What is a Woodworking Center?
   A place where children can create things out of wood
2. What goes into the Woodworking Center?
   A hammer, a saw, sandpaper, a saw horse with a vise, some pieces of wood gathered on a trip to the lumber yard, and suggested layouts of projects for various levels of skill
3. Just Hammering
   Materials: hammer; plasterboard; nails with big heads; pieces of 2″ x 4″s sawed into lengths of about 12″
   Presentation: Start a row of nails in each 2″ x 4″. If the children want to start the nails, make holes in the 2″ x 4″s with a gimlet, or let the children make them under supervision. Then they can insert the nails and hit them without smashing their fingers.
4. Just Sawing (not advised for irresponsible children)
   Materials: soft wood (pine) not more than $\frac{3}{4}$ ″ thick and about $1\frac{1}{2}$ ″ wide; a good, well-set crosscut saw (about 12″ is best); a clamp or vise
   Presentation: Fasten the wood into vise or clamp with an appropriate amount projecting. The children can do this with help. Make a groove to start the saw for the children, or encourage them to saw easily and rhythmically, without pressing or bending the saw. Give them a hand now and then if they need it, so they can have the satisfaction of sawing off a piece. Sawing is hard work. Choose very soft wood.
5. Simple Constructions
   Materials: hammer, lathe nails, odd shaped bits of soft wood, and ends of boards (pine) in a basket or box. Odd pieces of lumber may be picked up from the firewood pile or at any lumber yard.
   Presentation: children four and five years old sometimes want to make a boat or a truck, and they can be helped to saw selected shapes. Children at this age can work on a project for several days, and even paint it when they finish.

The Rug Center

1. What is a Rug Center?
   A place where children come for group activities. It may be near the piano, if there is one in the room. Mats or rugs may be used on the floor.
2. What goes on in the Rug Center?
   Group planning, singing, discussions, listening to stories told or read by teacher or a child, listening to records, dances, rhythms, and body movement

The Play Area

1. What is a Play Area?
   A place where children are provided space and equipment for both structured

and free play activity. If possible, all young children should have access to an outdoor playground designed especially for the young child. A large indoor room should be provided for use in bad weather.

2. What goes into the Play Area?

jungle gym	toys with wheels	horizontal ladder
swings	buckets, cans	spades and spoons
sandbox	rocking boats	ropes of various lengths
balls	pools for splashing	bean bags
walking boards	see-saws	tricycles
merry-go-round	punching bags	tires of all sizes
slide	tunnel	innertubes
spring-type rocking horse	ladder box	

The Learning Environment
Albuquerque Schools, Albuquerque, New Mexico

Room Arrangement. Carefully planned activity areas are essential to a productive kindergarten program. Listed below are some areas the teacher may want to consider when setting up her room:

housekeeping area	science area
block area	pet center
art center	library
manipulative toys	listening center
work bench	large group area
music center	

These areas can be alternated and supplemented throughout the year as the children develop new interests. Some of the areas will overlap. For example, the manipulative toys, library, and listening center might be combined into one area for quiet, individual work. Science materials could be placed throughout the room. Some music materials might be placed in the listening center, and others could be near the rug in the large group area.

Careful consideration in the placement of these areas is necessary because their arrangement affects the total mood of the learning environment. Poor arrangement may result in chaos and lead to increased discipline problems.

Art supplies—paste, crayons, paper, scissors—should be placed near the art tables. Easels, drying racks, and painting supplies should be placed near the water supply. Clean-up materials should be accessible to the children. Various types of stimulation equipment—trucks, wheel toys, small flexible dolls—should be kept in the block area to encourage a variety of building experiences.

Traffic patterns should allow free movement from one area to another without causing a disruption. The teacher should be able to scan the entire room from nearly any given point. Both children and teachers need to have a large amount of space in which to move about. Children will also become more involved in dramatic play and housekeeping activities if a sense of separateness can be created by careful arrangement of large furniture.

Each child should have a place for his personal belongings. For example, the teacher could use cubby holes or small boxes marked with his name. It should be available to him at all times. Other children and the teacher should not have access to it without his permission.

Each child should have an area in the room marked with his name where he can display his work. He should soon learn how and where to put those items he wishes to display.

Supplies and Materials. The teacher must be constantly aware of the changing interests of her students. Supplies and materials must change to provide an ever stimulating environment. *Don't put everything out initially* is a good precaution. Otherwise, the children will be overwhelmed. Some material should be saved to surprise the children later in the year. Besides, some of the materials will be too advanced for the children at first.

Books, records, manipulative toys, puzzles, housekeeping supplies, dress-up clothes, block-building materials, and interest centers should be changed constantly. The slightest change can create new enthusiasm for a forgotten area.

Encourage parents and children to bring things of interest into the room to share or display. The children will soon realize that the school room is *their* room, and they will develop a sense of responsibility for items in the rooms. A kindergarten teacher becomes a pack rat, saving anything and everything for her classroom. She soon has friends and neighbors collecting useful items for her class, too. Items the teacher and class can bring to enrich the environment include:

Rug or rug samples
Dress-up clothes (remember the boys, too): jewelry, shoes, hats, ties, vests, purses, gloves, belts, dresses, aprons, scarves, costumes, robes, eye glasses

Store items: empty boxes, cans, bottles, containers, jars
Art and collage items: bits of wrapping paper and foil, buttons, ribbon, yarn,
   string, egg cartons, meat trays, tubes, bottle caps, magazines, material scraps,
   cotton balls

Listed below are standard materials that might be found in any
kindergarten classroom.

Housekeeping Area

stove	doll carriage
refrigerator	dolls, ethnic and white
sink	set of cooking pans
rocking chair	luncheon set
folding tables and chairs	house cleaning set
child-size doll bed	telephones
ironing board and iron	set of baking pans
full-length mirror	silver set
doll bedding and clothes	

Block Area

Set of hardwood blocks, variety of shapes
Small wood trucks, cars, trains
Set of rubber farm animals
Set of flexible rubber black family dolls
Set of flexible rubber white family dolls
Large metal and plastic trucks, fire engines, airplanes, boats
Set of flexible community helpers

Science and Math Areas

tripod magnifier	magnifying glasses
magnets	prisms
color paddles	pan balance scale
educational thermometer	spring scale
aquarium	incubator
electric supplies for experiments	matchmates
large dominoes	peg numbers
geometric shapes, steel and wooden	sequence counter
number sorter	fruit plate (fractions)
counting frames	liquid measuring set
plastic trays, funnels, buckets,	calipers
pans, cups	animal cage

Manipulative Area

wood puzzles	table games
peg boards	beads (stringing)
color cones	lacing shoe
lotto matching games	table top construction sets

Audiovisual Materials

books	science story
pictures	flannelboard
animals	globe
family	puppets
Mother Goose	filmstrip projector
nursery rhymes	listening center earphones

Music Area

phonograph	large rubber tom-tom
rhythm band set	autoharp
records	

7
Teaching Tips

Newark Schools, Newark, New Jersey

1. Encourage experimentation.
2. Allow the child to do his own work.
3. Display all the children's work, but not all at the same time.
4. Provide varied experiences.
5. Encourage the use of various media.
6. Discourage the use of patterns.
7. Praise the child for his honest efforts. Respect his ideas.
8. Encourage a pleasant atmosphere.
9. Guide his understanding by asking him questions.
10. Encourage safety habits.
11. Encourage health habits.

12. Encourage total participation.
13. Encourage creativity.
14. Use a neighborhood walk to stimulate discussion periods.
15. Encourage children to be prompt by having a good beginning activity such as:
    Playing a special record
    Opening the mystery box
    Cooking pancakes for a morning treat
    Sharing a new library book
16. Encourage the use of the five senses.
17. Introduce one science concept at a time.
18. Have materials available before activity begins.
19. Plan simple experiences at first to insure success.
20. Encourage the children to plan and to participate in the activity.
21. Encourage the children to taste the finished product the same day.
22. Encourage the children to talk about their activities.
23. Encourage parent involvement by sending recipes home with the children.
24. Try the experience first yourself before introducing it to the children.
25. Vary your activities from day to day and from week to week.
26. Establish the rule: No one at the workbench unless he is working.
27. Permit sawing or nailing only at the workbench.
28. Teach the children to hold the saw and hammer safely.
29. Always supervise woodworking.
30. Have children fasten their work in the vise when sawing.
31. Get wood scraps from your nearest lumber company.
32. Make a table easel from a cardboard box.
33. Visit print shops for surplus scrap paper, cardboard tickets, and letter sheets. They make good collage materials.
34. Visit tile stores that may have broken patterns of mosaic tiles to give or sell. They are good for math projects.
35. Use empty telephone cable spools for tables.
36. Make books illustrating experiences the children have had.
37. Label pictures.
38. Keep a monthly calendar to correlate math, science, and social living.
39. Make graphs and classify objects such as foods, modes of travel, shapes, shells, and animals.
40. Make number booklets, charts, and clocks.
41. Use varied teaching techniques.
42. Change the activity when the children become restless.
43. To move children in a more orderly manner from one activity to another, call them in groups by category, such as those wearing certain colors, shoelaces, or buckles.
44. Have all materials available before the lesson begins.
45. Know where you are going and how to get there.
46. Plan according to the children's needs.
47. Aim for total involvement in different activities.
48. Give the children a chance to discover a concept, an experience, an object themselves.

8
The Kindergarten English Curriculum

Bakersfield Schools, Bakersfield, California

In kindergarten, the English curriculum includes listening, speaking, and readiness for writing, spelling, and reading. English is an integral part of the total kindergarten program. The kindergarten environment provides experiences which promote auditory and visual discrimination, oral expression, motor skill, and improved emotional and social adjustment.

The total reading program from kindergarten through sixth grade has been divided into seventeen developmental levels. These levels are assigned to different grades. The chart illustrates how these levels overlap. This cur-

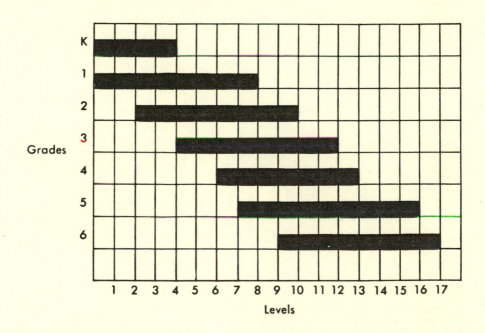

riculum provides a wide range of opportunities to meet the needs of all children. Individuals with special needs may have to go below or above these established limits.

The developmental levels for kindergarten are described in the following outline.

English Developmental Levels

Objective	Grade

Level 1

1. To develop an awareness of self through physical, emotional, and   **K, 1**
   social experiences
2. To listen courteously during a listening experience
   ignore distractions
   show response
3. To explore the environment by observing and manipulating objects
   react with show of interest
   ask questions
4. To handle books with a sense of
   exploration
   curiosity
   satisfaction
5. To speak to be understood
   speak clearly
   begin a transition from a dialect or foreign language to standard
       English
   modulate the voice to fit the occasion
   improve speech problems

Level 2

6. To listen to a single direction and be able to give a   **K, 1, 2**
   simple body response
   body-motor object response
   vocal-motor response
7. To classify objects by
   color
   size
   shape
   function
8. To listen when others talk about a given subject and be able to answer or ask questions of the speaker
9. For the child to realize that he has a store of useful information, interesting experiences and worthwhile feelings; to grow in his ability to convey this knowledge clearly
10. To listen to or observe literature, music, and art and to react   **K, 1, 2**
    creatively
    with voice

Objective	*Grade*

with symbols
with action

11. To listen to literature or to another child's own story to determine whether it is fact or fancy
12. To accept and give constructive criticism
13. To listen to specific sounds and to identify them
    with voice
    with symbols
    with actions

Level 3

14. To listen to a sequence of specific directions and to respond correctly   K, 1, 2
15. To listen to stories, songs, poems, or incidents and recall them sequentially
    with voice
    with symbols
    with action
16. To listen to specific sounds and compare them to
    sounds around us
    musical sounds
17. To experiment with shapes, signs, and symbols using a variety of materials
18. To perceive that writing is "talk written down"
19. To listen to words, verses, and stories and to discover rhyming words

Level 4

20. To listen to, and discriminate between, beginning sounds of words   K, 1, 2, 3
21. To write one's own name and identify it orally and visually
22. To know that the set of letters used in English is called the alphabet and to discover that each letter in the alphabet has its own place in an ordered sequence
23. To understand the concept of "letter" and to discover that words are made up of letters

Each kindergarten teacher is given a Kindergarten Curriculum Guide listing suggested learning experiences for each objective. Our present Curriculum committees are writing the guides in terms of Performance Objectives, including pre- and post-test items for each objective, as well as suggested learning experiences. When the present English section is revised it, too, will be stated in those terms. We believe that the present English section is extremely valuable to teachers.

9

Concept and Value Development

Coexistence and Man's Nature
Caddo Parish Schools, Shreveport, Louisiana

Major Concept: Man Strives to Improve Total Coexistence

Contributing Concept: There are varying degrees of individual and group interdependence

Behavioral Objective

Names family needs that are usually met by expenditure of money

Activities

Discuss where money for the family is secured, and how it is spent.
The following questions might be used:

Where does your family get money?
What does the family do with the money it receives?
How does money help to provide for food? What kinds of food are usually bought?
  Where do our clothes come from? Does your mother ever make your clothes?
  Where does she get the material, thread, buttons, zippers?
  Does money help to provide shelter? In what way? Is the money ever spent to
  make your home a nicer place to live? How is it spent?

Discuss the role of work in meeting family needs.

1. Discuss the role of the mother within the home in meeting the family needs for food and clean clothing.
2. Draw pictures of mother working in the home.
3. Discuss the role of the father within the home in meeting the family needs and helping to care for things.
4. Draw pictures of father working in the home.
5. Discuss jobs that mothers may have outside the home, what is done with the money earned, and how this money helps to provide needs of the family.
6. Draw pictures of mother working at her job outside the home.
7. Discuss jobs that fathers may have outside the home, what is done with the money earned, and how this money helps to provide for the needs of the family. (Buys clothing and food, pays for the home in different ways, ownership or rent.) Questions to stimulate discussion may include:

238

Why do fathers work?
Are there many kinds of work that fathers do?
Would it be a good thing for all fathers to do the same kind of work? Why?
How does your father's job help you?

Major Concept: All Men are Alike in Some Ways: All Men Are Different in Some Ways

Contributing Concept: The acculturation of an individual is affected by the community he lives in

Behavioral Objective

Determines differences in family composition

Activities

1. Lead children into a discussion of their families and homes by asking questions such as:
   How many of you have younger brothers and sisters at home?
   What things can you do that these younger brothers and sisters cannot do?
   How many of you have older brothers and sisters at home?
   What kinds of things can they do that you cannot do?
   Can you do things to help your younger brothers and sisters? What kinds of things?
   Do your older brothers and sisters help you? In what ways?
   How many of you have relatives or people other than your family living with you at home? Who are they?
   How many of you live with grandparents or aunts and uncles?
   What kinds of things does your mother (grandmother, aunt) do to help you?
   What does your father (grandfather, uncle) do to help you?
   Could you do all these things for yourself?
   In what ways can you help your mother (grandmother, aunt) and father (grandfather, uncle) at home?
2. Collect pictures of families and family members.
3. Select pictures of persons composing their family at home from a large variety of pictures. The Dennison family group cutouts offer a possible source of pictures.
4. Draw family pictures. The children might discuss their drawings. The teacher might label the pictures with the names of the individual family members.
5. Make family portraits using the lid of a shoe box for a frame. Rick-rack, sequins, and ribbon can be used to dress up the picture.
6. Read the story *The Three Bears* to the children.
7. Dramatize the story *The Three Bears.*
8. Finger Plays:

Our Family

Five in our family sitting by the door (*Holds up five fingers*)
Father goes to work, then there are four. (*Holds up four fingers*)
Four in our family, happy as can be,
Mother goes to wash some clothes, then there were three. (*Three fingers*)
Brother goes with father, then there are two. (*Two fingers*)
Two in our family, sitting in the sun,
Sister goes to school, then there is one. (*One finger*)
One in our family, nothing can be done,
Baby goes to take a nap, then there is none. (*Closes hand*)

"The Family"

This is the father, full of good cheer. (*Holds up thumb*)
This is the mother, kind and dear. (*Holds up index finger*)
This is the brother, strong and tall. (*Holds up middle finger*)
This is the sister, who plays with her doll. (*Holds up ring finger*)
This is the baby, the pet of all. (*Holds up little finger*)
This is the family, great and small. (*Holds up all fingers*)

9. Songs
   "How Many People Live at Your House," *Singing Fun,* p. 49.
   "The Family," *Music for Young Americans,* p. 11
   "Mother," *Merrily We Sing,* p. 11
   "A Song to Mother," *American Singer,* Bk. 1, p. 11
10. Filmstrips
    "Family Fun," (Encyclopedia Britannica)
    "Helping Mother and Father," (Encyclopedia Britannica)
    "Brothers and Sisters," (Encyclopedia Britannica)
    "The Family at Home," (Tom Hardy)
    "Your Family," (Coronet)

Panama Preschool
Panama Schools, Panama, New York

The following open-ended, clarifying responses are designed to lead children to components of valuing. Check YES or NO according to your use of the particular response with a child or children during preschool. Also, please write between responses any variations of the questions you may have used during the past ten weeks.

	YES	NO

1. Is this something that you prize? — —
   Are you proud of that? — —
   Is that something that is important to you? — —
2. Are you glad about that? — —
3. How did you feel when that happened? — —
4. Did you consider any alternatives? — —
5. Have you felt this way for a long time? — —
   When did you first begin to believe in that idea? — —
   How have your ideas changed since you first considered the matter? — —
6. Was that something that you yourself chose? — —
7. Did you have to choose that, or was it a free choice? — —
8. Do you do anything about the idea? — —
   How does that idea affect your daily life? — —
9. Can you give me some examples of that idea? — —
10. What do you mean by _____? — —
11. Where would that idea lead? — —
    How would that work out in practice? — —
12. Would you really do that or are you just talking? — —
13. Are you saying that . . . ? (*Repeat*) — —
14. Did you say that . . . ? (*Repeat in distorted way to see if child attempts to correct the distortion*) — —
15. Have you thought much about that idea (or behavior)? — —
16. What are some good things about that notion? — —
17. What do we have to know for things to work out that way? — —
18. Is that what you said earlier about . . . ? (*Note something else the child said or did that may point to an inconsistency*) — —
19. What other ways are there? — —
20. Is that a personal preference or do you think most people should believe that? — —
    Is this idea so good that everyone should go along with it? — —
21. What seems to be the difficulty? — —
    Where are you stuck? — —
    What is holding you up? — —
22. Is there a purpose behind this activity? — —
23. Is that very important to you? — —
24. Do you do this often? — —
25. Would you like to tell others about your idea? — —
26. Do you have any reasons for (saying or doing) that? — —
27. Would you do the same thing over again? — —
28. How do you know it's right? — —
29. Do you value that? — —
    Is that something that you value? — —
30. Do you think people will always believe that? — —
    Did people long ago believe that? — —
31. Have you heard the term "clarifying responses" before reading this paper? — —

Social Science
Albuquerque Schools, Albuquerque, New Mexico

Rationale. The young child brings to school with him perceptions and attitudes regarding his role in the family, the relationship of his family to the neighborhood, and the relationship of his neighborhood to the larger community.

Opportunities for helping the child understand social science concepts occur daily throughout the activities of the kindergarten program. The kindergarten social studies program should help the child gain specific information regarding various community institutions, the functions of community workers, and the ways they affect his own life. It is the teacher's responsibility to help the pupil understand the interdependence of people and to build his respect for the contributions of all workers by helping him discover the ways they serve him.

The social studies curriculum includes the following categories: the community, community workers, and environmental awareness.

The Community

Goals

1. The child identifies his family as a social unit in the community.
2. The child explores his neighborhood.
3. The child can explain the relationship of his neighborhood to the larger community.

Suggested Activities

Have each child make pictures and write stories about his family.
Have each child assume various family roles in dramatic play.
Use art media to illustrate family activities.
Show films about family life.
Read books, stories, and sing songs about the family.
Take walking trips through the neighborhood.
Draw maps of the neighborhood.
Build a relief map of the neighborhood using boxes, sponges, or blocks.
Mold adobe blocks and build a structure.
Observe the neighborhood from a high building or a hillside.
Take field trips to other parts of the city.
Display airplane views of the city.
Discuss city transportation systems that connect the neighborhood to other parts of the city.
Make a mural of the community.

Community Workers

Goals

1. The child can name various community workers.
2. The child can explain the contributions of various community workers.

Suggested Activities

See films, read stories about community workers.
Learn poems about community workers.
Use art media to illustrate community workers.
Dramatize community workers.
Have a Community Helper Day. Every child dresses like a community helper.
Take field trips.
Invite various community workers to visit your class.
Have a Hat Day. The children make hats representing various workers, wear them, and show them to other rooms in the school.
Make pipe cleaner people and dress them like community workers.

Environmental Awareness

Goals

1. The child can recognize the natural and man-made elements in his environment.
2. The child can determine factors that improve or detract from the beauty of his neighborhood.
3. The child can identify the polluting factors in his neighborhood.

Suggested Activities

Take a Nature Walk in your neighborhood. Discover various kinds of plant life.
Collect leaves of various kinds in your neighborhood.
Collect various kinds of soil in your neighborhood and examine them under the magnifying glass.
Take a House Walk in your neighborhood. Discover the various kinds of houses in the community, such as adobe houses, brick houses, trailer houses, frame houses, two-story houses.
Visit playgrounds and parks in your neighborhood.
Draw a simple outline of a house on the chalkboard. Ask children to landscape the house with grass, trees, and flowers.
Have art materials available to use for landscaping in the block area.
Make a Litter Tree in the room. Encourage children to pick up litter they find and tape it to the tree.
Decorate a box as Lobo, the Litter Monster. Feed any litter the children find to Lobo.
Visit a garbage disposal area. Discuss why refuse must be picked up and where it goes.
Present a burning experiment to show them how smoke pollutes the air.

10
Prekindergarten and Kindergarten Schedules

Newark Schools, Newark, N.J.

A Prekindergarten Schedule for the A.M. Group

8:35–9:30   Informal greeting and conversation
Health inspection
Free choice of activities such as puzzles, tables games, books, blocks, houskeeping corner
Clean-up
Opening exercises—flag salute and a song
Informal and formal planning for the day's learning activities by the teacher, teacher aide, and children
9:30–10:30   Opportunities and experiences, guided by the teacher and teacher aide, in art, science, language, social living, and music
10:30–11:15 Clean-up, toilet, snack, and rest
11:15–11:30 Wash for lunch
11:30   Dismissal to lunch room or home.

A Suggested Prekindergarten Schedule for the P.M. Group

12:35–1:15   Informal greeting and conversation
Health inspection
Free choice of activities such as puzzles, table games, books, blocks, housekeeping corner
Opening exercises—flag salute and a song
Informal and formal planning for the day's learning activities by the teacher, teacher aide, and children
1:15–2:00   Opportunities for experiences, guided by the teacher and teacher aid, in art, science, language, social living, and music
2:00–2:30   Clean-up, toilet, snack, and rest

2:30–3:05	Stories
	Visual Aids
	Rhythms and dramatization
3:05–3:15	Prepare for dismissal
3:15	Dismissal

A Kindergarten Schedule for the A.M. Group

8:35–9:00	Arrival
	Opening exercises
	Library period—Children select books from the classroom library
9:00–9:30	Musical, audio-visual, language, or number activities
	Planning for the day's activities
9:30–10:15	Activity period—small groups work in the centers with pegs, beads, number and language games, art, housekeeping, and blocks. The teacher works with five children; the teacher aide works with another five. The rest of the children work at selected tasks, such as language development, numbers, or reading.
10:15–10:55	Clean-up
10:55–11:15	Rhythms
	Story, poetry, dramatic play
	Evaluation of the day's work
11:15–11:30	Prepare for dismissal.
11:30	Dismissal

A Suggested Kindergarten Schedule for the P.M. Group

12:30–12:45	Arrival
	Children select books, puzzles, or blocks.
12:45–1:15	Music—songs or records.
	Language or number introduction or discussion
	Planning for the day's work
1:15–1:45	Activity Period—small groups work in the centers with pegs, beads, puzzles, number games, language games, art, housekeeping, or blocks. The teacher works with five children, the teacher aide with another five. The rest of the children work at selected tasks, such as language development.
1:45–2:40	Clean-up, toilet, snack, rest

2:40–3:00   Rhythms, story, or dramatic play
3:00–3:15   Prepare for dismissal
3:15   Dismissal

11

Evaluation Procedures

Panama Central School
Prekindergarten Child Development Center
Panama Schools, Panama, New York

Parent Evaluation Sheet #1

1. Does your child enjoy the program?   __ Yes __ No
2. What phase of the program does he enjoy most: outdoor play, stories, painting, music, workbench and tools, housekeeping corners, or other? _____

_____

3. Is there any part of the program he objects to seriously?   __ Yes __ No
   If so, explain _____

_____

4. Does he enjoy snack time?   __ Yes __ No
   If not, explain _____

_____

5. Is the transportation arrangement to and from school satisfactory?   __ Yes __ No
6. Do you feel your child is benefiting from this program?   __ Yes __ No
   If so, in what respect? _____

_____

7. Have you visited the program?   __ Yes __ No
8. Do you plan to visit the program?   __ Yes __ No

9. Please give us your suggestions for improving the program.

_____

_____

_____

_____

_____

Behavioral Objectives
Newark Schools, Newark, New Jersey

The following items are some behavioral objectives for the prekindergartner and kindergarten child. Please check only those items in which the child has demonstrated proficiency.

Prekindergarten

Social Development

1. Knows legal first and last name —
2. Knows age in years —
3. Knows and uses names of adults in classroom —
4. Knows home address —
5. Knows names of adults in his home —
6. Identifies self as boy or girl —
7. Likes school —
8. Attends school regularly —
9. Makes friends in school —
10. Exercises reasonable self-control —
11. Demonstrates self-confidence —
12. Uses "please" or "thank you" —
13. Follows school routine —
14. Speaks freely to peers and familiar adults in school —

Intellectual Development

1. Enjoys stories, pictures, books —
2. Holds picture book right side up —

3. Expresses curiosity   —
4. Listens and responds to music   —
5. Builds creatively with blocks   —
6. Participates in dramatic play   —
7. Speaks in sentences   —
8. Uses equipment and material for constructive purposes   —
9. Recognizes and names objects in classroom   —
10. Thinks critically   —
11. Likes to draw, paint, paste   —

Physical Development

1. Is toilet trained   —
2. Has motor coordination   —
3. Handles classroom materials with ease (scissors, manipulative toys)   —
4. Uses two feet alternately in going up and down stairs   —
5. Fastens own shoes   —
6. Feeds self   —
7. Has good posture   —

Kindergarten

Social Development

1. Knows names of other children in the class   —
2. Plays constructively alone   —
3. Plays constructively with other children   —
4. Is aware of the rights of other children   —
5. Shares materials with classmates   —
6. Recognizes community helpers   —
7. Adapts to changes in room and in curriculum   —

Intellectual Development

1. Names and groups things that go together   —
2. Sees likenesses and differences in sizes, shapes, and colors   —
3. Has developed certain concepts: up-down, large-small   —
4. Identifies common sounds   —
5. Relates ideas in sequence; retells stories   —
6. Pronounces sounds distinctly   —
7. Shows ability to pay attention   —
8. Narrates own experiences   —
9. Memorizes and sings simple songs   —
10. Uses descriptive adjectives   —
11. Begins to develop a sight vocabulary: recognizes own name on crayon
    box and cubby, helpers' chart, weather chart, safety signs, color names,
    number names   —

12. Recognizes numerals as distinguished from letters of the alphabet   —
13. Follows simple verbal directions   —
14. Displays curiosity in experimentation   —
15. Asks questions of adults   —
16. Recognizes nine colors: red, orange, yellow, green, blue, violet, black, white, brown   —
17. Recognizes numerals from one to ten   —

Health and Safety Habits

1. Knows correct way to cross street   —
2. Knows what to do if lost   —
3. Recognizes community helpers   —
4. Washes hands without a reminder before eating and after using the toilet   —

Teacher's Comments—Special Talents or Needs

_____
_____
_____
_____

Parent's Comments

_____
_____
_____
_____

12
Working With Parents

School for the Fives
Nebo School District, Spanish Fork, Utah

Dear _____ :

Your five-year-old will begin his school life next September. This is a very important event for him. Together, his parents and teachers must make this experience of leaving home and coming to school a happy one that will help him develop new powers of independence as well as new skills in living well with others.

This booklet will tell you some of the things you may want to know about the school's program, and about your part in helping your child grow well while he is five. It will give you some answers to these questions:

1. What will your child learn at kindergarten?
2. What will your child do in kindergarten?
3. How can you help prepare your child for kindergarten?
4. How can you help your child get along well in kindergarten?

Be sure to read the last page. It gives *Information and Instructions for Registration* and other items.

Sincerely yours,

NEBO SCHOOL DISTRICT

What Will Your Child Learn In Kindergarten?

Learning is a continuous experience, and each child learns at his own rate. A good school experience for your child will offer him many opportunities to continue growing. When he arrives at kindergarten, he will already have learned many behaviors. While he is in kindergarten he will learn new ways of behaving. The school hopes that during the kindergarten year, your child will make consistent progress in his individual pattern of development. He will have many experiences which will contribute to the following kinds of learning:

Learning to feel all right about leaving home
Learning to do many more things to help himself
Learning to get along well with other children
Learning to take care of his daily health habits
Learning to work and play safely
Learning physical controls and coordinations that will contribute to writing and to other hand skills at a later time
Learning to use and care for materials
Learning new interests in the world around him; this interest is basic to later reading ability
Learning to speak fluently and well. This skill also is basic in learning to read
Learning to listen well when necessary
Learning what numbers mean, as well as learning to recite them
Learning to recognize his name as a written symbol
Learning to enjoy stories, poems, and books
Learning to accept responsibility for his own behavior and decisions
Learning when it is important to conform and when it is important to be different
Learning the difference between what is real and what is make-believe in his world of things and ideas
Learning that school is a good place to be, and that he is an important member of the school group

What Will Your Child Do In Kindergarten?

He will get personally acquainted with the teacher.
He will explore many activities such as painting, constructing, manipulating, building, and observing.
He will talk with others his age. He will plan with them and share stories or experiences with them.
He will take care of all his health chores such as going to the bathroom, washing his hands, and drinking from the fountain.
He will have juice or milk regularly with an unsweetened cookie.
He will rest on his mat after playing outside.
He will play outdoors during a directed period.
He will use the playground apparatus.
He will dramatize his own interpretations of the policeman's role, the life of a soldier, or a mother's role.
He will work quietly and alone at times on some activity he enjoys. This may be putting a puzzle together, arranging pictures in sequence, or matching like objects.
He will work with clay, sand, wood, paper to make something of his own.
He will listen to music and will sing many songs.
He will interpret rhythmic patterns through bodily movements.

He will observe animal and plant life as well as weather changes to help him understand his world.

He will experiment to find out how simple scientific principles work to help people. Such things as a magnet or a wheel may invite experimentation.

He will take short trips to find out what is going on in the neighborhood.

He will practice bodily skills such as catching, throwing, jumping, skipping, balancing, and climbing.

How Can You Help Prepare Your Child for Kindergarten?

Give your child plenty of love and security through infancy and early childhood.

Show affection through closeness and gentleness.

Avoid scheduling body processes too rigidly

Provide opportunities for learning to do things, but do not force learnings too soon

Give approval more often than correction.

Avoid comparing your child with others who learn at a different time and rate.

Help your child anticipate pleasant experiences at school.

Speak about the teacher as being "kind" and "nice," not as a threat to the disobedient. Talk about school being a place where a child may do things, not as a place where he "mustn't."

Don't worry your child about what he will have to know and do at school.

Let him get acquainted with the kindergarten room and teacher before school begins.

Make certain that you child's health and safety come first.

Schedule a physical examination for him before school begins.

Provide for necessary physical corrections before he starts school.

See that he gets the recommended immunizations.

Establish good health habits in relation to meals, bathroom, and rest.

Keep your child home if he has a cold or is not feeling well.

Teach your child his name, address, and telephone number.

Teach him how to walk safely to and from school, or how to wait for the school bus, board and get off it safely.

Teach him to obey traffic rules and signals.

Dress your child in clothing that allows for active participation in the program.

Select clothing that is easy to wash and iron.

Label each article with your child's name—cap, mittens, galoshes, coat, and sweater.

Provide clothing suitable to weather changes. A light sweater or coat for the in-between seasons is advisable.

Choose fasteners easy for your child to manage by himself.

Select clothing that is comfortable and not too tight in the crotch, arms, legs, or waist.

How Can You Help Your Child Get Along Well in Kindergarten?

Help your child to attend kindergarten regularly.

Help him to be on time.

Attend group meetings that will be called in the interest of the program.

Confer often with the teacher about your child. Feel free to make the appointment yourself.

Welcome your child's voluntary talk about school, but do not insist that he report on all his learnings.

Expect the same types of growth that the school expects. Do not urge skills that are beyond the maturity level of your child. Consult with the teacher regarding how kindergarten will contribute to reading, writing, and number skills.

Information and Instructions for Parents of Kindergartners

West Haven Schools, West Haven, Connecticut

1. Register your child at the time scheduled by the school. The appointment for your child's registration is at ____ o'clock on _____. Please come on time and bring your child so he can get acquainted with the kindergarten teacher and the room. If your child is transferred later to another school, the situation here will probably be comparable to the one there.
2. Fill out the *Permanent Record Form* at registration time.
3. Secure forms for a Health Examination from the principal at the time of registration. Make certain that the child receives the examination before he begins school in September. Return the form that will be filled out by the examining physician when the child comes to school. The parent will be responsible for securing this form from the doctor.
4. Present a birth certificate at the time of registration to verify the child's age. He must be five years old on or before October 31 of this year.
5. School will begin on _____.
6. The normal school day lasts two-and-one-half hours. There will be two sessions, a morning session beginning at nine o'clock and an afternoon session beginning at one o'clock. Your child will be assigned to one of these.
7. Parents will assume responsibility for the transportation of all bus children one way.

The first week the child will come for only one hour a day.

| Group I | 9:00–10:00 | Group III | 1:00–2:00 |
| Group II | 10:30–11:30 | Group IV | 2:30–3:30 |

The second week

| Group I | 9:00–10:20 | Group III | 1:00–2:20 |
| Group II | 10:40–12:00 | Group IV | 2:40–4:00 |

The third week

Group I & II together 9:00–11:00

Group III & IV together 1:00–3:00

The fourth week

The child will come for two and a half hours, or the full time. Your child's schedule will be announced in August.

Fill out the *Cooperative Home Report* and return it to the school. This form will be given to you at the beginning of the school year.

The child will need a small rug and a light blanket for resting time. Send these items with the child the first week of school. Both items must be labeled at home with the child's name.

The five-year-old should not be given spending money to take to school. He is not mature enough to take care of it, and it poses a problem for the child who does not bring money,

Please read this booklet and refer to it often. Other pages will be added to it as the pupil-parent-teacher relationships develop and suggest new topics of common concern.

Parent Education Program

It is a myth that the skill of raising children comes naturally. For some it is easier than others, but for all parents there are difficulties and concerns that could be made easier with some outside help. Personnel of the West Haven School System, together with mental health workers from the West Haven Field Station, a branch of the Connecticut Mental Health Center, are planning a series of discussions around the subject of raising children from the ages of three to ten. The purpose of holding these small group discussions would be to provide:

1. Information
2. An examination of various approaches to child rearing
3. A better understanding of the parent-child relationship

We would like you to complete the following survey in order to help us plan this program.

Name_____ Address_____
Telephone_____ Name of School_____
Would you and/or your spouse be interested in the Parent Education Program described above?
Very much_____ Somewhat_____ Not at all_____
Who would be able to attend? Mother_____ Father_____ Both _____
Which time of the day would be most convenient? Morning _____
Afternoon_____ Evening_____
What are the ages of your children (in years?)__ __ __ __ __ __ __ __ __
Is this your first child entering kindergarten? Yes__ No__
Below are listed a number of topics that are often of concern to parents in raising their children. Mark (X) the 3 topics that you and your spouse would be most interested in discussing and learning about in a parent education program. If there are topics you feel are more important, but are not listed, write them in at the bottom of the page.

__ Ways to discipline children at home and school

__ Normal sexual development in children

__ A child's relationships with other people—mother and father, sisters and brothers, friends and playmates

__ How to help a child become independent

__ How to stimulate a child's thinking and intellectual growth in preparation for school activities such as reading and solving problems

__ Physical growth—eating and sleeping patterns, nutrition, and medical care

__ The importance of play and a child's use of free time—TV viewing, toys, play equipment

__ How to help a child express and deal with his feelings of anger, love, hate, frustration, and affection

__ Preparation and adjustment to school

__ _____

__ _____

Parent Involvement

Newark Schools, Newark, New Jersey

P   is for People and Participation
Parents are people interested in the growth and development of children. Through worthwhile participation, they will learn improved methods of rearing children.

A   is for Appreciation and Acceptance
Parents appreciate the many ways the school aids in extending children's environment. In turn, they will help in providing extracurricular activities for children because, as parents, they are accepted as individuals interested in the learning process.

R   is for Responsibilities
Parents are interested in discovering new ways of helping children. They visit homes, participate in discussions, and willingly add that extra inspirational ingredient wherever and whenever possible.

E   is for Experiences
Parents enjoy the varied experiences the school offers.

N   is for Need
Parents realize that they as individuals can make contributions to the school community for the benefit of children. They work for improved conditions in the school community.

T   is for Teamwork
Because parents are individuals, they recognize the value of togetherness. Excellent teamwork at home, at school, and in the community are positive reinforcements that help children mature.

I   is for Initiative
Parents utilize this ingredient to improve their leadership abilities.

N   is for New and Improved Skills
Parents have many talents and skills that can be beneficial in school organization. In working closely with other parents and school personnel, they extend individual talents and learn new ways of solving problems.

V   is for Volunteers
Parents as volunteers or classroom aides bridge the gap between home and school. After discovering how children learn, parents can apply their new knowledge to routine home activities

O   is for Opportunities
Many and varied opportunities are provided for parents to utilize organizational and creative abilities.

L   is for Leadership and Love
Parents understand that the success of any program depends upon the ability of the leader to be open minded. Love for children and the desire to help individuals are attributes of parent involvement.

V   is for Values
The success of the parent-teacher-child relationship will be visible in the home. Parents will practice activities at home similar to those that children have experienced in school.

E   is for Enrichment
Enrichment enables a parent to build a better self-image through interaction with other individuals.

M   is for mothers and fathers
Both these individuals are essential to successful parent programs. They interact with the school in the role of resource personnel.

E   is for Experimentation
Parents initiate various ideas for fund raising projects. They continue sensory learnings in the home with the use of available materials.

N   is for Nutrition
Parents are interested in balanced diets. Through health workshops, they discover how good eating habits can help their children grow socially, mentally, and physically.

T   is for Trust
Trust is a basic ingredient of parent involvement. Trust and confidence in individuals at school and at home mean security for children.

Parent Involvement
Albuquerque Schools, Albuquerque, New Mexico

Rationale. Effective communication between parent and teacher is essential for optimum growth of the kindergarten child. The teacher must know about feelings and attitudes prevalent in the home, and the parent must be aware of the educational goals the teacher has set for his child.

It is the teacher's responsibility to take the initiative to develop meaningful relationships in the following three areas: teacher-parent, parent-pupil, and parent-parent.

Ways to Develop Teacher-Parent Relationships

Home Visits

Get-acquainted home visits should be made before the child comes to school. They give the child the opportunity to meet the teacher in the security of his own home and let the parent know that the teacher is concerned about the child and his home. These visits should be brief and can be made with or without an appointment, depending on the community and the teacher.

Home visits are an effective way to continue communications throughout the year, especially when parents are unable to come to school.

Home visits are particularly appreciated when the child has been absent for an extended length of time, when the child deserves special recognition, when a new baby is born in the family, and when a problem arises and the parents are unable to come to school.

Parent-teacher conferences. Parent-teacher conferences give the teacher an opportunity to listen to and learn about the feelings, attitudes, problems, and expectations in the home, as well as to discuss the child's adjustment and progress in school. Appointments may or may not be necessary, depending on the schedule of both parties involved. The teacher should make every effort to be available when parents desire a conference.

Teacher-written Notes. The teacher can write notes to communicate with parents. BE SURE THAT THE PARENTS OR SOMEONE IN THE FAMILY CAN READ ENGLISH. Notes to parents are most effective when they are brief and positive. For example, the teacher might say, "I am happy to inform you that Conchita gave up her turn to paint in order to help Debby fix her broken clay cat today. She is learning to be a helpful friend."

Notes should not describe undesirable behavior, but rather inform the parent that a conference is desired. During the conference, the teacher and parent can work together to solve the problem.

Parent Visitations to Schools. Teachers must work constantly to make parents feel welcome in the school room. Learn to recognize all parents and greet them by name when they bring their children to school. Encourage children to invite their parents to see something they have made or built in the room. A good time to encourage parents to come to the room is when they bring the child or pick him up. If they seem hesitant to enter the room, you might say

> "Anthony built an airport during the block play today. We saved it for you to see."

or

> "Come in and see our new rabbit. The children have been painting a cage for him."

Have Parents Chaperone Field Trips. Field trips provide parents the opportunity to participate as co-learners with their children in real-life situations. Parents readily volunteer to assist in field trip activities.

Use Parents as Resource People. Women can enrich the program by working with the children in areas such as cooking, sewing, and crafts. Men might demonstrate skills of their profession or vocation—policeman, fireman, carpenter, baker.

Encourage Parents to Visit and Participate in Classroom Activities. The teacher must take the responsibility to encourage parents to participate in daily classroom activities. Parents will feel most comfortable when they are given a specific task. For example, have a parent come to help the day you will be decorating a Christmas tree or baking cookies for a party. Parents can also work with a small group of children on an assigned task. Many parents are eager to help and need only your encouragement.

Organize a Kindergarten Parents' Group

Meetings should be arranged to involve fathers as well as mothers.
Invite guest speakers to discuss topics of interest.
The parents' group might choose to sponsor activities similar to those listed below:
    Set up or build playground equipment
    Paint or repair room furniture or equipment
    Make audio-visual aides for the classroom
    Raise money to buy new equipment for the room or to pay for field trips
    Organize a clothing bank
Show films on topics of current interest.

Organize Small Parent Interest Groups or Discussions. Find topics that small groups of parents would like to discuss. Some areas to consider might be a new baby in the family, sibling rivalry, and understanding children's developmental stages.

Help parents become acquainted so that they can work together to provide social activities for their children.

13

A Prekindergarten Home School and Neighborhood School Design

Provo Schools, Provo, Utah

Rationale

The national interest in prekindergarten education was given official recognition when the U.S. Office of Education established an Office of Child Development. A more recent indication was contained in President Nixon's address to Congress on March 3, 1970. The President recommended establishing a network of experimental centers to "... discover what works best in early childhood education." He further emphasized the need to work formally with children at earlier ages, stating that "... child's play is serious business."

Stressing the importance the federal government is attaching to preschool programs, Gudridge notes:

> Another clue to Administration interest in the infants and toddlers is the fact that the prestigious Presidential Science Advisory Committee, through its research and developmental panel, has been charged with the task of coming up with strategies that "will work" in educating the 1- to 3-year-olds and the 3- to 5-year-olds.
>
> The Administration's hunch that supporting early childhood education may be the most promising way to attack educational deficiencies among the poor is based on much recent research by cognitive psychologists like J. McVicker Hunt of the University of Illinois, who maintains that the child's intellectual stimulation will never reach the heights of which [he] might be capable.
>
> One study reported by the National Institutes of Mental Health has shown that, when children are very young, regardless of social or racial origin, one group will perform much the same as another on developmental tests. Beginning somewhere between 18 months and two years, however, the curve representing the performance of children from the lowest socioeconomic level begins to drop, and from then on, these children as a group score significantly lower than other children on measures of ability and achievement.
>
> Such intellectual handicaps, say NIMH researchers, can be prevented or corrected if, at a very early age, the poor youngster is provided with stimulation he does not receive at home—being caressed and loved and talked to and read to; having interesting things to look at, grab, explore, and play with.

If administration planners are interested in findings like these, which tend to show that the best years of a child's learning life occur well before the ripe old school-entering age of six, big business is enthralled by them. Some entrepreneurs are already predicting that preschool education will become a flourishing new industry.*

Provo School District became interested in early childhood education as a result of an E.S.E.A. Title III grant awarded three years ago. We have used the funds to more nearly meet the needs of our children in the primary grades. Fine programs have been designed, and much knowledge acquired about children of kindergarten age.

Procedure. In cooperation with Brigham Young University College of Family Living, Provo District has proposed a project to determine better ways of designing learning experiences for prekindergarten children. The control group in the study will be a group of children selected at random from those enrolled in the University's regular nursery program. These children are selected by application and come from homes in the metropolitan area. An experimental group will be established at the Edgemont Elementary School for four-year-old children who live within the school boundaries and volunteer to attend the class. Two classes will be held at each school. A traditional nursery curriculum will be taught in one session, and a more academically oriented approach in the other. Results of the two methods will be compared so that any differences can be examined.

Another facet of the program will include a parent-home instructional plan for mothers with four-year-old children. A curriculum guide and an instructional plan will be designed for the parents, and books and materials for teaching the children at home will be supplied. Workshops will be held with the parents on a weekly basis to assist them in presenting the materials properly to their child. Because social interaction is such a vital part of the child's growth and development, opportunities will be provided for the children to associate with one another in formal social settings. Plans have been made for groups of four or five children to meet together in one home for instruction and social activities under the direction of the parent and an aide from the University. Supervisory assistance will be available for the home program, as well as for the two school programs.

In addition to growth differences between the Edgemont school children and the University control group, the program will determine how the parent-home program compares with the experimental and control groups.

*Beatrice M. Gudridge, "And Now, Center Stage for the Pre-schooler," *Education Summary,* (March 1, 1970), p. 5.

Personnel. Personnel for the program will be provided by Brigham Young University, Provo School District, and funds made available in the grant. Four nursery school teachers will be provided by Brigham Young University to teach at the University and Edgemont Schools. Student teachers will be assigned by the University to assist in the classroom and to reduce the pupil-teacher ratio to six. Additional student teachers will be available to assist with the parent-home program.

Supervisory assistance will be provided by the public school district and University. Released time will be made available to a consultant at the University for spending one-fourth time on the project for the purpose of selecting and developing materials for program, curriculum, and workshop activities. A part-time supervisor will be hired to give supervisory assistance to parents in the home and to supervise the student teachers assigned to the home project. Psychological services will be made available by the district.

Facilities. Classroom facilities will be donated by the University and Provo School District. In addition, individual homes will be utilized for the parent-home project. Space will be made available at the Edgemont School for workshop activities.

Evaluation. One of the difficulties in evaluating a program of this nature is the lack of measuring devices available to properly assess student growth. At the conclusion of the program, a study will be made to determine the instruments most likely to be useful. If necessary, others will be constructed to measure the program's objectives. An innovative program such as this has potential national significance.

14

Format of a Proposal for Federal Funds—Budget

Provo Schools, Provo, Utah　　.

Expenditure Account No. 100

Expense Class	Name & Title, Purpose, or Item	Project Time Part	Full	Quantity	Salary, Rental or Unit Cost	Budgeted Amount
Local Contribution						
	Consultant Services	x				$ 2,500.00
	Mailing & printing					250.00
	Supervision	x				850.00
	Classroom					1,800.00
	Custodial care					
	Fixed charges					250.00
					Total	$ 5,650.00
Funds Sought						
	Administration	x		1/10		$ 1,200.00
	Secretarial	x		1/10		350.00
	Materials & supplies					250.00
	Consultant Services					900.00
	Travel					250.00
					Total	$ 2,950.00
				TOTAL BUDGETED AMOUNT		$ 8,600.00

Expenditure Account No. 200

Expense Class	Name & Title, Purpose or Item	Project Time Part	Project Time Full	Quantity	Salary, Rental or Unit Cost	Budgeted Amount
Local Contribution			x			
	Teachers (B.Y.U.)			4		$16,000.00
	Teacher Aides			8		9,500.00
	Psychological services					450.00
					Total	$25,950.00
Funds Sought						
	Supervision for home program	x				$ 1,800.00
	Materials & supplies (developed & purchased for home use)					1,100.00
	Workshop consultants				20 weekly sessions @ $30.00.	600.00
	Travel	x				120.00
	Teacher aide					900.00
	Test materials					450.00
					Total	$ 4,970.00
					TOTAL BUDGETED AMOUNT	$30,920.00

Table of Descriptor Terms

Descriptor Terms	Program Innovation No.*
ABC Dandy Dog's Early Reading Program	9
ability to adapt	32
Academic Achievement Project	1
accelerated instruction	33
accountability, teachers	36
activities, art	12
activities, learning center	28
activities, nature of	6
activity as a key to teaching	8
activity, free	12
aides	5, 9, 10, 12, 20, 21, 22, 26, 28
aides, bilingual	3
aides, choosing of	21
aides, tuition-free courses	35
aides, use of	21
all-day program	24
anecdotal records	7, 9
application form, aides	21
aquarium	9
art as reading	12
art for growth	12
association of ideas	1
associative vocabulary	3

*Note that these numbers refer to the programs in Section I, not to the Resource Section.

Descriptor Terms	Program Innovation No. *
audiology screening	1
awareness, other cultures	32
balanced kindergarten program	7
balancing activity and rest	2
basic behavioral components	33
Becker	36, 37, 38
Behavior Analysis Approach	22
behavior observation study	6
behavioral principles	34
behaviorally stated goals	1
Bereiter	35
bicultural children	13
bilingual approach defined	13
bilingual children	10, 13, 14, 33, 38
block fun	7
bodily awareness	32
body movement as communication	8
book center	5
Bremmer-Davis Phonics Program	13
British Infant Schools	9
Caldwell Preschool Inventory	4
carrels as teaching spaces	35
centers of interest	5
checklist	9
child care center	3
child-centered furnishings	4
children's reactions to program	26
class grouping	4
classroom climate	18
classroom design and educational goals	20
classroom, home away from home	18
classroom intervisitation	1
clay modeling	12
clinical analysis, child data	29
cluster arrangement, classrooms	16
code-cracking	37

Descriptor Terms	Program Innovation No.*
in-service training	20, 24, 31, 40
Institute for Developmental Studies	31
instructional staffing	34
instructional support teams	20
instructional teams	36
I.Q. gains	3
interest centers	9
Kindergarten Task Force	1
laboratory students	20
language arts	2
language development program	5
Language Lotto	31
Language Master	10, 30, 31
language symbols	5
large muscle equipment	1
lead teachers	40
learning materials specialists	20
learning theory, movement education	8
learning through doing	2
letters from parents	26
linguistic skills	3
listening stations	7, 9, 17
low achievers	25
Macmillan's *Bank Street Early Childhood Education*	9
male college volunteers	20
manipulative experience	1
manipulative games	17
manipulative materials	9
mathematics concepts	7
McGraw-Hill materials	11
medical and dental procedures	6
Metropolitan Applied Research Center, Inc.	1
Metropolitan Readiness Test, Form A	1
Michigan Oral Language Series	13
migrant children	14
Model School Preschool	1

Descriptor Terms	Program Innovation No.*
Wee Winkie Bear flannel board materials	4
Wide Range Achievement Test (WRAT)	35
Winter Haven learning kit	9
work habits	7
work-play period	1, 7

Sources of Information in Early Childhood Education

American Association of Elementary-Kindergarten-Nursery Educators, 1201 Sixteenth St., N.W., Washington, D.C. 20036

Appalachia Educational Laboratory, Charleston, W. Va.

Association for Childhood Education International, 3615 Wisconsin Ave. N.W., Washington, D.C. 20016

Association of Classroom Teachers, 1201 Sixteenth St. N.W., Washington, D.C. 20036

Association for Supervision and Curriculum Development, 1201 Sixteenth St. N.W., Washington, D.C. 20036

Bank Street College of Education, 610 West 112th St., New York, N.Y. 10025

Bureau of Elementary and Secondary Education, U.S. Office of Education, FOB 6, 400 Maryland Ave. S.W., Washington, D.C. 20202

Center for Research and Demonstration in Early Education of Handicapped Children, University of Oregon, Eugene, Oreg.

Child Study Association of America, 9 East 89th St., New York, N.Y. 10028

Day Care and Child Development Council of America, Inc., 1426 H St. N.W., Washington, D.C. 20005

Early Childhood Education ERIC Clearinghouse, University of Illinois, 805 West Pennsylvania Avenue, Urbana, Ill. 61801

Early Education Research Center, University of Chicago, Chicago, Ill.

Far West Laboratory for Educational Research and Development, Berkeley, Calif.

Kansas Center for Early Childhood Education, University of Kansas, Lawrence, Kans.

Mental Health Materials Center, 419 Park Avenue South, New York, N.Y. 10016

National Association for Mental Health, 10 Columbus Circle, New York, N.Y. 10019

National Association for the Education of Young Children, 1834 Connecticut Ave. N.W., Washington, D.C. 20009

National Association of Elementary School Principals, 1201 Sixteenth St. N.W., Washington, D.C. 20036

National Association of Independent Schools, Inc., 4 Liberty Square, Boston, Mass. 02109

National Education Association, 1201 16th St. N.W., Washington, D.C. 20036

National Institutes of Health, Bethesda, Md.

Office of Child Development, U.S. Department of Health, Education, and Welfare, P.O. Box 1182, Washington, D.C. 20013

Office of Economic Opportunity, 1200 Nineteenth St. N.W., Washington, D.C. 20505

Pittsburgh Learning Research and Development Center, University of Pittsburgh, Pittsburgh, Pa.

Public Affairs Committee, 381 Park Avenue South, New York, N.Y. 10016

Research and Development Center in Early Childhood Education, University of Arizona, Tucson, Ariz.

Research and Development Center in Early Childhood Education, Syracuse University, Syracuse, N.Y.

Research Program in Early Childhood Education, Cornell University, Ithaca, N.Y.

Science Research Associates, 57 West Grand Ave., Chicago, Illinois

Southwest Educational Development Laboratory, Austin, Texas

Southwest Regional Laboratory, Inglewood, Calif.

Teachers College Press, 525 West 120th St., New York, N.Y. 10027

Wisconsin Research and Development Center for Cognitive Learning, University of Wisconsin, Milwaukee, Wis.

Eleven Preschool Success Stories

. These stories were cited in *Preschool Breakthrough,* 1970, published by the National School Public Relations Association, 1201 16th St. N.W., Washington, D.C. 20036.

Infant Education Project, Washington, D.C.
Academic Preschool, Champaign, Ill.
Ameliorative Preschool Program, Champaign, Ill.
Early Education Project, New York, N.Y.
Preschool Program, Fresno, Calif.
Diagnostically Based Curriculum, Bloomington, Ind.
Project Early Push, Buffalo, N.Y.
Preschool Program, Oakland, Calif.
Language Stimulation Program, Auburn, Ala.
Perry Preschool Project, Ypsilanti, Mich.
Learning to Learn Program, Jacksonville, Fla.

Selected Bibliography

Books

Almy, Millie, *Young Children's Thinking* (New York: Columbia University Press, 1966).

American Association of Elementary-Kindergarten-Nursery Educators, *Current Approaches to Teaching Reading* (Washington, D.C.: NEA Center, 1965).

Association for Childhood Education International, *Early Childhood Crucial Years for Learning.*
Reprints from *Childhood Education,* Washington, D.C., 1966.

Association for Childhood Education International, Margaret Rasmussen, ed., *Feelings and Learning* (Washington, D.C.: ACEI, 1965).

Association for Childhood Education International, *Readings from Childhood Education—Articles of Lasting Value* (Washington, D.C.: ACEI, 1966).

Association for Supervision and Curriculum Development, 1970 Yearbook Committee, *To Nurture Humanness: Commitment for the 70's* (Washington, D.C.: Association for Supervision and Curriculum Development, 1970).

Baker, Katherine R., and Xenia Fane, *Understanding and Guiding Young Children* (Englewood Cliffs, N.J.: Prentice-Hall, 1967).

Bangs, Tina E, *Language and Learning Disorders of the Pre-academic Child: With Curriculum Guide* (New York: Appleton-Century-Crofts, 1968).

Beadle, Muriel, *A Child's Mind: How Children Learn During the Critical Years from Birth to Age Five* (New York: Doubleday, 1970).

Bereiter, Carl, and Siegfried Englemann, *Teaching Disadvantaged Children in the Pre-school* (New York: Prentice-Hall, 1966).

Bernhardt, Karl S., *Being a Parent: Unchanging Values in a Changing World* (Toronto: University of Toronto Press, 1970).

Berson, Minnie Perrin, *Kindergarten: Your Child's Big Step* (New York: E. P. Dutton, 1959).

Bettelheim, Bruno, *Children of the Dream* (New York: Macmillan, 1969).

Beyer, Evelyn, *Teaching Young Children* (New York: Pegasus-Western, 1968).

Blackie, John, *Inside the Primary School* (New York: Her Majesty's Stationery Office, 1967).

Burton, Blatt, and Frank Garfunkel, *The Education of Intelligence* (Washington, D.C.: The Council for Exceptional Children, 1969).

Bloom, B.S., *et al.,* eds., *Taxonomy of Educational Objectives: Handbook I: Cognitive Domain* (New York: David McKay, 1956).

Brackbill, Yvonne, and G.G. Thompson, eds., *Behavior in Infancy and Early Childhood: A Book of Readings* (New York: Free Press, 1967).

Bradley, Helen and others, *Pre-school Teachers' Kit* (Elgin, Ill.: Cook, 1967).

Brown, Mary, and Norman Precious, *The Integrated Day in the Primary School* (New York: Agathon Press, 1969).

Christianson, H. M. Rogers, and D. Ludlum, *The Nursery School: Adventures in Living and Learning* (Boston: Houghton Mifflin, 1961).

Chukovsky, Kornei, *From Two to Five* (Berkeley: University of California Press, 1963).

Copeland, Richard W., *How Children Learn Mathematics: Teaching Implications of Piaget's Research* (London: Collier-Macmillan, 1970).

Dawson, Mildred A., *Language Teaching in Kindergarten and the Early Primary Grades* (New York: Harcourt, 1966).

Deutsch, Martin, *The Disadvantaged Child* (New York: Basic Books, 1967).

Education Commission of the States, *Early Childhood Development, Alternatives for Program Development in the States* (Denver, Colo.: The Commission, 1971).

Emlen, Arthur C., *Realistic Planning for the Day Care Consumer* (Washington, D.C.: ERIC, 1970) 29 pp.

Englemann, Siegfried, and T. Englemann, *Give Your Child a Superior Mind: A Program for the Pre-School Child* (New York: Simon and Schuster, 1966).

Fantini, Mario D., and Gerald Weinstein, eds., *Toward a Contact Curriculum* (Washington, D.C.: NEA, Dept. of Elementary-Kindergarten-Nursery Education, 1970).

Foster, Josephine, and Neith Headley, *Education in the Kindergarten,* 4th ed. (New York: American Book, 1966).

Fox, Robert, *et al., Diagnosing Classroom Learning Environments* (Chicago: Science Research Associates, 1966).

Fraiberg, S. H., *The Magic Years* (New York: Scribner's, 1959).

Frazier, Alexander, *et al. Early Childhood Education Today* (Washington, D.C.: Association for Curriculum Development, NEA, 1968).

Froebel, Fredrich, *Pedagogics of the Kindergarten,* William T. Harris, ed. (New York: D. Appleton and Co., 1896).

Frost, Joe L., *Early Childhood Education Rediscovered—Readings* (New York: Holt, Rinehart and Winston, 1968).

Fuller, Elizabeth M., *Values in Early Childhood Education* (Washington, D.C.: Dept. of Kindergarten-Primary Education, NEA, 1960).

Furth, Hans G., *Piaget for Teachers* (Englewood Cliffs, N.J.: Prentice-Hall, 1970).

Gardner, D. Bruce, *Development in Early Childhood: The Preschool Years* (New York: Harper & Row, 1964).

Gardner, Dorothy E. M., and J. E. Cass, *Role of the Teacher in the Infant and Nursery School* (Elmsford, N.Y.: Pergamon Press, 1965).

Gesell, Arnold and Frances L. Ilg, *The Child From Five to Ten* (New York: Harper and Brothers, 1946) pp. 388–89.

Goodman, Mary E., *Race Awareness in Young Children: A Cultural Anthropologist's Study of How Racial Attitudes Begin Among Four-Year-Olds,* rev. ed. (New York: Collier, 1964).

Gray, Susan W., and Rupert A. Klaus, *Before First Grade* (New York: Teachers College Press, 1966).

Hamlin, Ruth, Rose Mukerji, and Margaret Yonemura, *Schools for Young Disadvantaged Children* (New York: Teachers College Press, 1967).

Hartup, W. W., and N. L. Smothergill, eds., *The Young Child: Reviews of Research* (Washington, D.C.: National Association for the Education of Young Children, 1967).

Headley, Neith, *The Kindergarten: Its Place in the Program of Education* (New York: The Center for Applied Research in Education, 1965).

Hechinger, Fred M., *Pre-school Education Today* (New York: Doubleday, 1966).

Hymes, James L., Jr., *Teaching the Child Under Six* (Columbus, Ohio: Charles E. Merrill Publishing Company, 1968).

Hymes, J. L. *The Child Under Six* (Englewood Cliffs, N.J.: Prentice-Hall, 1963).

Ilg, Frances L., and Louise Bates Ames, *School Readiness* (New York: Harper & Row, 1965).

Isaacs, Susan, *Intellectual Growth in Young Children* (New York: Schocken Books, 1966).

Jones, Molly Mason, *Guiding Your Child From 2–5* (New York: Harcourt, Brace and World, 1968).

King, Edith W., and August Kerber, *Sociology of Early Childhood Education* (New York: American Book, 1968).

Landreth, Catherine, *Early Childhood Behavior and Learning* (New York: Knopf, 1967).

Leeper, Sarah Hammon, Ruth J. Dales, Dora Sikes Skipper, and Ralph L. Witherspoon, *Good Schools for Young Children: A Guide for Working with Three- Four-, and Five-year-old Children,* 2nd ed. (New York: Macmillan, 1968).

LeShan, Eda J., *The Conspiracy Against Childhood* (New York: Atheneum, 1967).

Logan, Lillian M., *Teaching the Young Child* (Boston: Houghton Mifflin, 1960).

Matterson, E. M., *Play and Playthings for the Pre-school Child,* rev. ed. Edited by Evelyn Beyer (Baltimore: Penguin Books, 1967).

Montessori, Maria, *The Montessori Method* (New York: Fredrick A. Stokes, 1912).

Moore, Eleonora H., *Fives at School* (New York: Putnam's, 1959).

National Assocation for the Education of Young Children, *Montessori in Perspective* (Washington, D.C.: NAEYC, 1966).

National School Public Relations Association, *Preschool Breakthrough: What .Works in Early Childhood Education* (Washington, D.C.: NSPRA, 1968).

National School Public Relations Association, *The First Big Step: A Handbook for Parents Whose Child Will Soon Enter School* (Washington, D.C.: Dept. of Classroom Teachers and National Congress of Parents and Teachers, 1966).

Piaget, Jean, *The Origins of Intelligence in Children* (New York: International University Press, 1952).

Pitcher, Evelyn Goodenough, and Louise Bates Ames, *The Guidance Nursery School* (New York: Harper & Row, 1964), pp. 44–51.

Rambush, Nancy, *Learning to Learn: An American Approach to Montessori* (Baltimore: Helicon Press, 1962).

Read, Katherine, *The Nursery School: A Human Relations Laboratory,* rev. ed. (Philadelphia: Saunders, 1966).

Robison, Helen F., and Bernard Spodek, *New Directions in the Kindergarten* (New York: Teachers College Press, 1965).

Rulolph, Marguerita, and D. Cohen, *Kindergarten—A Year of Learning* (New York: Appleton-Century-Crofts, 1964).

Ryan, Bernard, Jr., *Your Child and the First Year of School* (Cleveland: World, 1969).

Schulman, Anne Shaaker, *Absorbed in Living—Children Learn* (Washington, D.C.: National Association for the Education of Young Children, 1967).

Scott, Leland H., *Child Development: An Individual Longitudinal Approach* (New York: Holt, Rinehart and Winston, 1957).

Stolz, Lois Meek, *Influences on Parent Behavior* (Stanford, Calif.: Stanford University Press, 1967).

Taylor, Katherine W., *Parents and Children Learn Together* (New York: Teachers College Press, 1967).

Texas Education Agency, *Preschool Instructional Program for Non-English Speaking Children* (Austin, Texas: The Agency, 1964).

Todd, Vivian E., and Helen Heffernan, *The Years Before School: Guiding Pre-school Children,* 2nd ed. (New York: Macmillan, 1970).

Torrance, E. Paul, and R. L. Myers, *Creative Learning and Teaching* (New York: Dodd, Mead, 1970).

Wallach, Michael A., and Nathan Kogar, *Modes of Thinking in Young Children* (New York: Holt, Rinehart and Winston, 1965).

Weber, Evelyn, *Early Childhood Education: Perspectives on Change* (Belmont, Calif.: Wadsworth, 1970).

Weber, Evelyn, *The Kindergarten: Its Encounter with Educational Thought in America* (New York: Teachers College Press, 1969).

Widmer, Emmy Louise, *The Critical Years: Early Childhood Education at the Crossroads* (Scranton, Pa.: International Textbook 1970).

Wills, Clarice, and Lucille Lindberg, *Kindergarten for Today's Children* (Chicago: Follett, 1967).

Winn, Marie and M. A. Porcher, *The Playgroup Book* (New York: Macmillan, 1967).

Wylie, Joanne, ed., *Creative Guide for Preschool Teachers* (Western Publishing, 1965).

Periodicals

Bradburn, Elizabeth. "Britian's First Nursery-Infant School." *The Elementary School Journal* (November 1966), pp. 57–62.

Butler, Annie L. "Areas of Recent Research in Early Childhood Education." *Childhood Education* vol. 48, no. 3 (December 1971).

Carter, Lowell Burney. "The Effect of Early School Entrance on the Scholastic Achievement of Elementary School Children in the Austin Public Schools." *Journal of Educational Research* (October 1956), pp. 91–103.

Costin, Lela B. "New Directions in the Licensing of Child Care Facilities." *Child Welfare,* vol. 49, no. 2 (February 1970), pp. 64–71.

Developmental Day Care Services for Children. 1970 White House Conference on Children, Report of Forum 17, working copy (ERIC, 1970), 33 pp.

Douglas, Virginia. *Community Coordinated Child Care: A Federal Partnership in Behalf of Children, Final Report* (ERIC, December 31, 1970), 516 pp.

Educational Day Care: An Installation Manual. South Central Regional Education Lab. Corp., Little Rock, Arkansas (ERIC, 1969), 105 pp.

Educational Policies Commission, American Association of School Administrators, *Universal Opportunity for Early Childhood Education* (Washington, D.C., 1966), pp. 8–10, 12.

Emlen, Arthur C. *Neighborhood Family Day Care as a Child-rearing Environment* (ERIC, November 1970), 18 pp.

Gordon, Ira. "The Young Child: A New Look." *Early Childhood Education Rediscovered.* Edited by Joe L. Frost. (New York: Holt, Rinehart and Winston: 1968), pp. 11, 13.

Gritzka, Karen *et al.* "An Interdisciplinary Approach in Day Treatment of Emotionally Disturbed Children." *Child Welfare,* vol. 49, no. 8 (October 1970), pp. 468–472.

Hunt, J. McVicker. "The Psychological Basis for Using Pre-school Enrichment as an Antidote for Cultural Deprivation." *Merrill Palmer Quarterly of Behavior and Development.* vol. 10, no. 3 (1964), pp. 209–248.

Hymes, James L. Jr., "Why Programs for Young Children?" *Today's Education,* vol. 59, no. 4 (April 1970), pp. 34–36

Karens, M.B., J.A. Taska, and A. S. Hodgins. "The Effects of Four Programs of Classroom Intervention on the Intellectual and Language Development of Four-year-old Disadvantaged Children." *American Journal of Orthopsychiatry* (1970), pp. 40, 58–76.

Levenstein, Phyllis. "Learning Through (and from) Mothers." *Childhood Education* (December 1971), pp. 130–34.

Lindberg, Lucile. "The Function of Play in Early Childhood Education." *The National Elementary School Principal,* vol. 50, no. 1 (Department of Elementary School Principals, NEA, September 1970).

Messick, Samuel. *A Statement on the Comprehensive Preschool Education and Child Day-care Act of 1969 before the Select Subcommittee on Education of the House Committee on Education and Labor, March 3, 1970* (ERIC, March 1970), 10 pp.

Mills, William H. and Garry L. McDaniels. "Montessori—Yesterday and Today," in *Montessori in Perspective* (Washington D.C.: National Association for the Education of Young Children, 1966), p. 63.

Mitchell, Mabel M. "Universal Education for Four-Year-Olds?" *Early Childhood Education Rediscovered*. Edited by Joe L. Frost. (New York: Holt, Rinehart and Winston, 1968), pp. 9, 10.

Morgan, Gwen G., "State Action to Improve Child Services." *Compact,* vol. 3, no. 6 (December 1969), pp. 24–25.

Overton, Willis F. "Piaget's Theory of Intellectual Development and Progressive Education." in *Yearbook of the Association for Supervision and Curriculum Development, 1972*. Washington, D.C., pp. 95–103.

Piaget, Jean in "Foreword," Almy, Millie, Edward Chittendon and Paula Miller. *Young Children's Thinking*. (New York: Teachers College Press, Columbia University, 1966), p. iv.

Programs for Infants and Young Children, Part III: Health. Appalachian Regional Commission (Washington, D.C.: ERIC, October 1970), 169 pp.

Riles, Wilson. "The Early Childhood Education Program Proposal." Dept. of Education, State of California, Sacramento (1972), p. 7.

Sale, June. *Programs for Infants and Young Children. Part IV; Facilities and Equipment*. Appalachian Regional Commission (Washington, D.C.: ERIC, October 1970), 72 pp.

Schaefer, Earl S. "Toward a Revolution in Education: A Perspective from Child Development Research," *The National Elementary Principal,* vol. 51, no. 1 (September 1971), p. 18.

Shane, Harold G. "The 'Domino Effect' of Early Childhood Education on the Elementary School." *The National Elementary School Principal*. Dept. of Elementary School Principals. NEA, vol. 50, no. 1 (September 1970), pp. 31–35.

Smith, Nila B. "Early Reading: Viewpoints," in *Early Childhood Crucial Years for Learning*. Edited by Margaret Rasmussen. (Washington, D.C.: Association for Childhood Education International, 1966), pp. 61–62.

Spaulding, Jean. "Universal Education for Four-Year-Olds?" *Early Childhood Education Rediscovered*. Edited by Joe L. Frost. (New York: Holt, Rinehart and Winston, 1968), p. 10.

"Getting Smarter Sooner." *Time*. 26 July 1971, p. 38.

Weikart, David P. "Learning Through Parents: Lessons for Teachers." *Childhood Education,* vol. 48, no. 3 (December 1971), pp. 135–137.

Westinghouse and Ohio University. "The Impact of Head Start: An Evaluation of the Effects of Head Start on Children's Cognitive and Affective Development," in *The Disadvantaged Child*. Edited by Joe L. Frost and Glenn R. Hawkes. (Boston: Houghton Mifflin, 1970), pp. 197–201.

White House Conference on Children and Youth, 1970, *Report to the President*. (Washington, D.C.: U.S. Government Printing Office, 1970), pp. 97–98.

White, Sheldon H. "Some General Outlines of the Matrix of Developmental Changes Between Five and Seven Years." *Bulletin of the Orton Society,* vol. 20 (1970), pp. 41–57.

Widmer, E.L. "In Kindergarten." *The Elementary School Journal,* vol. 67, no. 4 (January 1967), pp. 185–191.

Yarrow, L.J. "Separation from Parents During Early Childhood." Edited by Martin and Lois Hoffman. *Child Development Research I*. (New York: Russell Sage Foundation, 1964), p. 127.